About the author

Chuck Spezzano, Ph.D. is a world-renowned counsellor, trainer, author, lecturer and visionary leader. He holds a Doctorate in Psychology. From 28 years of counselling experience and 24 years of psychological research and seminar leadership, Dr Spezzano and his wife, Lency, created the breakthrough therapeutic healing model Psychology of Vision. The impact of this model has brought deep spiritual, emotional and material change to thousands of participants from around the world.

IF IT HURTS, IT ISN'T LOVE

Secrets of Successful Relationships

Chuck Spezzano, Ph.D.

Hodder & Stoughton

First published in Great Britain in 1991 by The Psychology of Vision
Published in 1999 by Hodder and Stoughton
A division of Hodder Headline PLC

10 9 8 7 6 5 4 3 2

British Library Cataloguing in Publication Data
A CIP catalogue record for this book
is available from the British Library

ISBN 0 340 75195 9

Typeset by Hewer Text Ltd, Edinburgh
Printed and bound in Great Britain by
Caledonian International Book Manufacturing Ltd.

Hodder and Stoughton
A division of Hodder Headline PLC
338 Euston Road
London NW1 3BH

I would like to dedicate this book to my daughter, J'aime.
She inspired us with her name before she was born,
and ever after with her living of it.

'The whole reason for my work is to make psychology available to everybody at every level in society. I want to put it into everyday language with everyday principles so people will know they have the power and the tools to transform themselves in every situation in every relationship.'

Chuck Spezzano, Ph.D.

ACKNOWLEDGEMENTS

I would like to acknowledge the many clients and participants of my workshops who taught me so much and continue to teach me how little I actually know.

I would like to acknowledge Sam Hazo, poet and mentor for lesson title #35 and for the continuing gift of his presence in my life and the world.

I would like to acknowledge Roxi Lewis for her typing and devotion to this book.

I would like to acknowledge Betty Sue Flower, Ph.D. Her generosity, vision, friendship, and editing skill were the midwifery gifts necessary to birth this book. Without her obvious help I would still be pregnant.

I would like to acknowledge Marcia Crosby for her final editing and concise preparation of the revised edition for publication from the previous version of this book.

I would also like to thank Jane Corcoran and Susan How for their computer skills in rendering the previous version into its present rendition.

I would like to acknowledge Donna Francis and Bonnie Close for their excellent editorial contribution to this second edition.

I would like to acknowledge my wife, Lency, who has inspired me with love to learn what it means to love. These days a book is really a team effort. I would like to again acknowledge my wife and my children, Christopher and J'aime, for their time donation to this book. Also to my friends and readers who helped improve this book with their attention and suggestions.

Finally, I would like to acknowledge *A Course in Miracles* for its profound effect in my life, the healing and its gift to me, my clients and this book. Many of the principles in this book I first learned from *A Course in Miracles* and many were corroborated by what I had already learned.

FOREWORD

Calling all angels, calling all heroes.
Calling all lovers, calling all healers.
Listen. Listen to the call.

Calling all souls, calling all minds.
Calling all hearts, calling all bodies.
Listen. Listen to your call.

Time is now, opportunity is here.
We are destined, you and I,
to choose love over fear, to choose
love over fear.

In this small world of big and little personal dramas, each
individual soul elects to live a life where they finally, eventually, choose love over fear. Love is, after all, the whole point
of everything. Love is essence. Love is the ultimate goal, the
only real goal. Other goals – lesser goals – such as happiness,
security, success, safety, power and wealth, lose all value and
meaning without love. What would it profit you to gain the
whole world and lose love? We live for love.

Life works when you love; it falls apart when you don't.
Love is attractive. You attract great things when you choose to
love. Love is heaven, and yet many of us go through hell to
get there. In our quest for love we have stumbled and fallen
many times. Tired, defended and battle-weary, we traipse on,
alone. Night falls; light fades. We sleep. Our dreams are dark
and fearful. We dream that 'love hurts', 'love fails' and 'love
dies'. We dream 'love is cruel'. We dream we 'fall in love' and
'lose in love'. We even dream we will never love again.

Wake up. Confuse not love with fear. Chuck Spezzano's message is clear: love can only love. Love cannot hurt. If it hurts, it is not love. Only the fear of not being loved hurts. Only our resistance to love hurts. Only our lack of faith in love hurts. Chuck Spezzano's ground-breaking work helps us to heal our relationship to love. He helps us heal our mis-perceptions of love and our fears of love. He inspires us to believe in love once again.

If It Hurts, It Isn't Love is like a great big road-sign on your spiritual path. Indeed, there are 366 road-signs – one for every day of the year (including a leap year). Each road-sign is different and the same all at once. The essential message is, if you are in pain, you must have chosen something other than love. Therefore, choose love. When in pain, feel it, but choose love. When afraid, be honest, but choose love. When unhappy, be truthful, but choose love. When you choose love, you are choosing heaven.

Chuck Spezzano is the Carl Jung of our times. His book is a masterpiece. It is a beautiful rendition of love. I honestly believe your life is about to change for the better. Why? Because you want it too. And because you hold this book in your hands. Choose to read this book. Choose to live the message of this book. Choose love.

Robert Holden
author of *Happiness Now!*

INTRODUCTION

This book is a collection of principles that heal. They are based on what has worked for me personally and as a therapist since 1971, with over 11 of these years spent as a marriage counsellor.

Some of these lessons may seem simplistic, but they actually have the simplicity of principles. I know these principles work as used. They are some of the principles at the heart of the *Psychology of Vision*® that I have been developing since my doctoral dissertation. I have witnessed innumerable transformational and miracle-like experiences in therapeutic situations. I reach to live these principles continually in my daily life and especially at the times when it unfolds in problematic ways.

You will notice many of these principles go beyond common wisdom; they are meant to do so. I learned many of them in mind-blowing, jaw-dropping experiences. They represent, in part, my exploration of the subconscious mind. Although there is much more to the mind than this book attempts to cover, it is a good start.

This work is unabashedly spiritual. Spirituality is what I have found to be an essential part of the human mind and experience by whatever name it is called.

Whether you believe this book or not, whether you like this book or not, it can still be helpful if you practise it.

Finally, this book is meant to be a gift – a guide to looking at the world in a way that heals pain. I have seen a great deal of emotional pain in my life. Now, I understand that most, if not all, pain is absolutely unnecessary. This is my gift to you – a sincere desire that your life has the love and happiness you deserve.

In many ways this book is a gift of inspiration to me from all the teachers, therapists, and people of wisdom and heart who helped me learn and unlearn along the way. This book is a form of heartfelt thanks to them.

HOW TO USE THIS BOOK

Welcome to the adventure of relationships. *If It Hurts, It Isn't Love* is an exploration of the living principles that make relationships work. Congratulations on this investment in yourself. Your willingness and commitment to discover that which will help you understand and be more successful in your relationships is to be highly commended. Using these principles will resolve any relationship problems and help you to enjoy, learn, and grow from your relationships. In truth, relationships provide the greatest opportunity for love, joy and delight. Although without the awareness of these healing principles, relationships can be your hell on earth. The intent of this book is to help you have your relationship be Heaven on earth. Your relationship will then be an inspiration for others and a highly accelerated vehicle for healing and transformation. Viewed properly, a relationship provides the fastest path for growth, and this book is meant to be a guide along the way.

This book can be used in a number of ways and it is up to you to discover what works best for you. The book has been intentionally set up to fit a synchronistic pattern. This means that if you opened the book to a certain page at random, or intuitively selected a certain number between one and 366, you would find the lesson that is most important for you now. It is uncanny how the key lesson, what we need to know and understand the most, is always selected. This method is particularly good for specific problems, but it can also be used for understanding and awareness in all your relationships. Another way is to read a lesson a day starting with lesson one, for a whole year. There are 366 lessons; one for each day of a leap year. Remind yourself of the theme of the lesson throughout the day and practise the exercise whenever possible. To have this book be transformative rather than just informative, I highly recommend that you complete the exercises each day, as best you can.

There is no problem that is not a relationship problem, and with this book you now have the ability to change your life for the better. You now have the tools to begin to look at yourself, your relationship, and the world with new eyes. May love and the spirit of aloha fill your life.

1. INTIMACY CAN HEAL ANYTHING

Whatever assails us in a relationship, whatever brings questions, doubt, or pain, whatever the problem is, the answer will come when we truly move toward our partner. In fact, joining with our partner and recognising a new level of *connectedness* will heal anything. It can heal all of the deadness, doubt, boredom, fear, sense of unworthiness, and emptiness that, sometimes, come into a relationship. Moving toward our partner does not mean giving up our own position or our own values; it simply means moving toward our partner, in love.

Exercise

Today, take some time and imagine the problem between you and your partner. Now, imagine moving toward them, feeling that you are getting closer and closer. At the point of joining, you have moved past the problems, deadness, doubt, and fear; you have reached your partner.

If you are having a conflict with or feel distant from anyone, move toward them. You can actually do this physically or you can give them a call or write a letter. Share the truth of your own feelings, not to try and change your partner, but to say, 'I won't let this come between us. I want to join with you. I value this movement forward, and I value you more than this problem.'

Do not let yourself be stopped by anything. Love is the thing that matters the most. Do not cheat yourself. Let joining give you the benefit of having this person as your ally, your partner, your friend, your loved one, and finally, the one who saves you.

2. ANY BEHAVIOUR THAT IS NOT LOVE
IS A CALL FOR LOVE

Be aware of all of the different behaviours that the people around you are acting out. Which ones are loving? Which are not? The behaviours that are not loving are really a call for love. If there is an attack on us specifically, it is a call for *our* love. Our willingness to respond to that behaviour, not by defending ourself, but by moving toward the attacker and giving to them, will win an ally. This person who was attacking will be very loyal to us in the future, both in good and hard times. Right now, however, they need our love.

Some people are caught in deadness, and others are caught in attack. We are being asked to remember what it's like to be in need and the cries we have made for help when we could not even speak the words. In the same way, those who are attacking us are also crying for help, asking for our love. If we look around we will see to whom we are called to respond, who we are called to move toward, and who we are called to help.

Exercise

Today, think of the person who is attacking you the most in your life. Imagine them here with you and that you are moving toward them responsively, realising that their attack is the call for your specific help. What is the help that they need from you? How is it that you can assist them? See how you are inspired to respond to them. Are you inspired to call them? To write to them? To give something to them? To talk to them?

In assisting them, you will find that these are the very people who have answers for you, if not now, in the future. If it is not in some direct way, it will be as a reflection of the part of your mind they represent, so that in helping them, you help yourself.

3. FORGIVENESS CHANGES PERCEPTION

The beauty of forgiveness is that it releases us from patterns where we are caught. It releases us from being a victim and being caught in situations we do not like. Forgiveness changes our perception. When we see situations differently, things actually are different for us. Basically, all healing has to do with changing our perception and seeing things in a new light. Forgiveness allows us to live in a way that raises us above the situation, thus the situation changes.

Some people are afraid that forgiveness will lock them into a situation of sacrifice where they will continue to be abused. This is not the truth because forgiveness actually shifts the relationship pattern, changing us and the other person. Any area where we feel stuck, or any place where a person is bothering us is a place that calls for forgiveness. Every problem, temptation, distraction, and all *busyness* that is avoidance occurs because we are afraid to change. Guilt hides the place where we are afraid, and because we get stuck in it, and the bad feeling, we do not recognise the healing and change that forgiveness brings. It is forgiveness that moves us through both the guilt and the fear.

Exercise

Today, take a look at your life. Look at the scarcity in which you live and at the places where you are in conflict; these are where you are stuck and afraid to move forward. Look at any illness or injury you have because it hides a situation where you chose not to forgive someone. Now, take a moment to dwell on what the illness is. Remember, all problems are relationship problems, so every situation that seems to be about something else always comes back to an interpersonal level.

Every hour today, practise forgiveness in a specific area, either relating to a person or situation. Say to yourself, 'In this situation, I forgive you (naming the person), so that I am free. In this situation (naming it), I forgive (the situation), so that I am free.' With one moment of utter sincerity, saying these words can free you. You are worth this investment of time.

4. FORGIVENESS IS NOT SOMETHING I DO, IT'S SOMETHING THAT'S DONE THROUGH ME

Forgiveness is a choice, an asking on our part to free ourself, to free the situation, and to free those around us. It is not something that we do. It is a choice that allows the grace to move through us to transform the situation.

In situations that seem completely beyond us, where we are completely stuck, or in utter pain and despair, asking our Higher Power to bring about forgiveness will help move us through our unwillingness and fear, thereby allowing our Higher Power to do all the work for us.

Exercise

Today, once each in the morning, afternoon, and evening, sit back and choose a situation that seems chronic to you, that seems utterly beyond your power to change. Take five minutes to think of this situation, and ask your Higher Power for the help and forgiveness to move through you to transform the situation.

This is the day of your release. Allow the blessing of forgiveness to come through you. This blessing frees you and helps you to know that anything can be done through the grace of your Higher Power.

5. COMMITMENT AND FREEDOM
ARE THE SAME THING

Our commitment is the extent to which we give ourself in any situation. Many people are afraid of commitment because they think that it is a form of slavery, a loss of freedom. Their fear is a reaction to a lack of freedom they felt as a child, or to relationships in which they gave up being themselves for others' approval. This is a place of fusion, of counterfeit commitment, that everyone has to face and heal in relationships. It keeps us in slavery and sacrifice.

Commitment is neither slavery, nor sacrifice; commitment is freedom. There are two types of freedom. One is an independent form of freedom *from* things, a freedom where we get away from this that bothers us. The other is true freedom that comes from within, a freedom *toward* things, a freedom we feel in any situation because of our level of commitment, our level of giving. For example, if we are in jobs where we feel bound, in sacrifice, because it is something we have to do, all of the fun and capacity to receive is gone. We feel that we have lost our choice. However, we always have the power of choice. We can choose to be there, committed, giving ourself fully. Our choice allows us to transcend our job description or role, and to feel the freedom of commitment.

The answer to the question, 'Is there life after commitment?' is '*Yes*,' because what we give creates our freedom. This freedom gives us space to breathe and receive in a way in which we have not received before. We get to feel more at peace, and we do not have to avoid or run away. Commitment helps us focus on what is important; it helps build our life.

7

Exercise

Today, you are being asked to commit yourself to someone or to something. If it is someone, you are being asked to make a choice for them because it is your choice that will make them better. The extent to which their life gets better is the extent to which you will also feel freed. So who is it? Your ability to receive comes from your giving. If it is something that you are being asked to give more of yourself to, what is it? Your commitment to whomever or whatever it is, is your freedom.

6. THE OTHER PERSON IN THE RELATIONSHIP IS ON MY TEAM

Our recognition that others are on our team allows us to receive from them. They can be the ones to save the day and help us. Other people have something to give to us, just as we have something to give to them.

Exercise

Today, ask yourself if you act as if the people in relationship to you, especially those closest to you, are on your team? Do you realise that they are part of your movement forward in life, that they increase your ability to win? Have you recognised that as they succeed, so will you? Have you been treating them like strangers? Have you been acting as if they've been the enemy? Have you been fighting over who's going to get their needs met first? If they are losing or failing in some way, it isn't by accident. You have been competing with them as if they were on the other team to show them and the world that you are better.

Begin in the morning by choosing someone who is close to you, either in your family or at work, and whom you have considered to be on the other team. For the rest of the day, act toward them as if they are on your team, starting with your thinking, then with your feeling, and then with your behaviour.

This evening choose somebody that you truly love, your partner or someone who is dear to you, and think of them as on your team, too. Their winning is your winning; their success is your success. Give them your support. Let your creativity emerge as you think of ways to support the persons dearest to you.

7. MY PARTNER IS NOT HERE TO MEET MY NEEDS

Many times, we experience a glow at the beginning of a relationship. We think that the relationship was made in Heaven, that we've found the person who is going to meet all our needs! Of course, when they don't, we decide this is a relationship from hell.

One of the greatest mistakes we make is to think that our partner is here to take care of us, to be our sugar-daddy, our sweet mama. Expecting our partner to meet our needs actually holds back the relationship because, whether they meet our needs or not, any time we have a bad feeling we will blame them. Any time a need is not met, we think they must go into sacrifice to take care of us. There is no way for our partner to win. This is not the purpose of a relationship.

Happiness is the purpose of a relationship, and it does not come from our partner meeting *our* needs. Happiness comes from *our* ability to make contact, to give and receive, and to bridge the differences to form an integration for a new level of confidence in our relationship.

Exercise

Today, if you feel that you are not happy, take a look at your attitude toward your partner. If you feel they have been put here to meet your needs, be willing to change your attitude. Be willing to move past this mistake. Be willing to make another choice. Be willing to see that your partner is here to co-create with you, to make contact, to communicate, to move forward together, arm in arm, and heal with you until you become fully happy.

8. THE MORE I CONTROL MY PARTNER, THE DULLER THEY GET

When we first start a relationship, we are greatly attracted to our partner. They thrill and excite us. As we move further along in the relationship, things that excited us become the very things that threaten us. We try to control them to shut down that area of attractiveness because we want them to share it only with us and not with anybody else. Of course, doing this does not work. When we shut down attractiveness in any area, it begins to shut down in every area. Controlling our partner to make them safe also makes them dull. We create our own boredom.

Our willingness to give up our control and let our partner be attractive will stir up the fear we have inside, that little area where we feel threatened. Willingness to experience this brings back the excitement. If it gets too fearful, rather than try to shut down our partner, we can communicate about the fear, which creates healing. Our partner's attractiveness is a gift to everyone, just as ours is.

Exercise

Today, begin to lift the controls that you've had on your partner. It may be time to communicate about your fear that you might lose them because of this area where you have been frightened of the gift that they have. Communicate with your partner about how much you value them and how much you appreciate their gift. Take off the control. Take off this form of blackmail. Just let them be who they are, and fully enjoy them.

11

9. I CAN ONLY FEEL REJECTED
WHEN I AM TRYING TO TAKE SOMETHING

We can only feel hurt, rejected, or heartbroken when we surreptitiously take from our partner under the guise of giving. If we feel rejected, we are being asked to take a look at where in the situation we are giving to take. We can only feel rejected when we get our hand slapped as it sneaks toward the biscuit jar.

Wholeness makes no demands. No one can reject us when there is nothing that we need. In moving forward, fully giving, and asking nothing, we cannot be pushed away, because we are irresistible. It does not matter what the other person's behaviour is because we are not trying to have them do it our way to meet our needs. Even if they pushed us away, we would only feel ourself loving them, because we are not trying to get something from them.

Nobody can stop our love, nobody can stop our giving, and this is what we really want, just to give to them. We can give to them even from thousands of miles away. Only when we are giving to take can we feel hurt at all.

Exercise

Today, let go of what you have been trying to take, and give fully. Give your support without asking that anything be returned to you. Giving is not a form of manipulation or a sacrifice to get something back from someone. When you truly give, it will move you forward, open, enlarge, and enhance you. Through it, you will truly receive and enjoy the fruits of your own giving – love itself.

10. TO RECOGNISE BONDING IS TO HAVE LOVE, FORGIVENESS, AND BLISS

Bonding is the natural state of things. We do not recreate it, we recognise that it is already there. In realising this, we move through the illusion of separation, and experience a sense of connection where we feel energised and supported; we feel the Source within.

By holding on to the misperception of separation, we lose an opportunity for healing, thereby creating a place of even greater pain and seeming separation.

One form of healing is simply to go back to the beginning of the perception of pain and reconnect with everyone. As full understanding takes place around the mistake of separation, it is replaced with the awareness of the bonding and we experience love, giving forth which is forgiveness, and bliss.

Exercise

Today, look at where you have seen distance, and choose to see the real connections. You may have been looking only at the places of separation. Now, look beyond that for the things you share with people, look for places where you are connected with people and where you feel as one. As soon as you recognise one place where you feel connected, you will begin to see others.

Where there is a problem in a situation, think about what you share with others because in that way you can begin to realise the connection, healing, love, and bliss. You can begin to enjoy the abundance.

11. A BROKEN HEART IS ALWAYS AN ATTEMPT TO CONTROL SOMEONE THROUGH GUILT

A broken heart means that we are on the losing end of a power struggle. Basically, our broken heart is an attempt to make others feel guilty so that they will meet our needs or do things our way; it's a form of emotional blackmail. The attempt to control will neither bring happiness, nor will it get our needs met; it will just create a bigger power struggle.

Exercise

Today, be willing to move toward instead of away from your partner. Be willing to not use your feelings as a bludgeon to get your partner to do what you want them to do. Rather than fighting with your partner and using different forms of manipulation, give them a gift. This can be a physical gift or an emotional gift, as long as it is something you freely and fully give to them.

Be aware, though, that if someone has broken up with you, an external gift may be a form of manipulation, and refused as such. If this has happened to you, give them an internal gift, such as forgiveness, letting go, gratitude, or sending them love without attachment. The extent of the gift that you give will be the extent of your release.

12. UNDER EVERY DEFENCE
IS A PLACE OF OLD PAIN

Every place where we are defensive, and every place where someone else is defensive, is a place of old pain. Our defence is against this old pain. The problem is that although the defence does not always block this pain, it does always block the good things.

Exercise

Today, it is now time to be willing to experience the pain under the defence, to have courage about this feeling, and to recognise that it is an illusion. Look for a place where you are or someone else is defensive. Where they are defensive, there is pain and need. If you ask yourself what they need, and respond to it, you will find them willing to let go of their defensiveness to move toward you.

Find the feelings that you are hiding within yourself by looking for places where you run away or attack. These are the two favourite forms of defence. Now, take some courage and be willing to feel your feelings. Be willing to move through your old pain until it is over. Remember, no feeling is bigger than you are. Continue moving through your feelings until you get to a place of peace. Once this is done, you will be freed of having to carry around all this extra armour. The energy from the defence, as well as the energy from the feelings that have been hidden beneath your defences, are given to you to use for your life. You are now back in the flow, and you can, once again, receive.

13. I CONTROL BECAUSE
I CANNOT STAND IT BEING SO GOOD

All of our control operates as a means of self-protection. However, control only protects and perfects our fear of getting hurt. This covers up the fear that if we let go of control, things would get really great and we would be overwhelmed. It would be so good that we would just go into *meltdown* and be totally lost, so good that all purpose would be gone and we would die. But guess what? This is only our ego scaring us with death. If we gave up control, we would not die; only our ego would. Then we would feel like we have died and gone to Heaven.

Exercise

Today, take a look at your life. What is the control situation staring you in the face? Do not forget that you are capable of using others by having them control you. This is so bottom-line, yet unrecognised. It is how you arrange things to prevent feeling so overwhelmingly good because you think you could not stand it. Give up control, and a giant reward will come to you. This is a day for you to receive in a big way.

14.   TO HAVE WHAT I WANT IN A RELATIONSHIP, I KEEP SEEING AND FEELING WHAT I WANT

Our ability to imagine, see, feel, and even to hear what we want in a relationship creates the fact. Our mind is a great creator. Often, in relationships when healing is taking place, we experience side effects that we do not wish, and things seem to get worse. When this is happening, if we keep in mind the healing we want, and allow ourself to feel and see it, we can help realise more quickly and easily what we want. By doing this, we remember what our goal and the truth is; if it does not contain true greatness, it's not the truth.

Exercise

Today, your goal is to feel what it is that you want in your relationship. Now, see what you want in your relationship. What is happening? Feel it and let it go. See it and let it go. Hold no attachment to what you envision, but know you are programming your mind. This process is helping you to manifest and create the very situation that you want. Do not be afraid if things seem to get worse at first. Healing is simply taking place, and hidden poisons are coming to the surface. As they do, keep the vision you have for your relationship, sharing it whenever possible. This helps you move from where you are to where the healing happens.

Nothing can stop the power of your mind. Nothing can stop the truth, which has to do with joy, happiness, and love.

15.

WHEN I WISH TO HAVE
A NEED FULFILLED,
I GIVE THE THING I FEEL I NEED

All pain comes from what we feel we need and the fear that our needs will not be met. In other words, we're afraid of what we'll lose or what we feel is missing; so instead of accepting our fear, we push it back and resist it, which generates pain. The more we do not accept our fear, the more it hurts; the greater our resistance, the greater our level of fear and pain.

In some situations, the need may be slightly more hidden. For instance, we may feel like we need more sex and that we are willing to give sex at any moment, day or night. What we may be called to give, however, is not the act itself, but more sexual energy. This higher level of giving would create the very thing that we feel we need right now.

Exercise

Today, be willing to look a little deeper into your needs. What is it that you need? Give that to whomever you need it from. Without imposing your giving on them, simply give whatever it is that you feel you need to those people from whom you feel you need it. Give the feeling of that greatest need, give the energy of it. If you have a general need from everyone, give it generously to everyone. If you feel you have a specific need from a specific person, then give it in the same way.

16. THE NEED TO DOMINATE
COMES FROM FEAR

Whenever we are in a situation where we are trying to dominate, or someone is trying to dominate us, it probably comes from the frightened child within. When someone is trying to dominate us, we are being asked to respond as if they were a frightened child. If we respond to that need by reassuring and supporting, we won't end up feeling like we are oppressed.

If we are the one trying to dominate, there is a part of us that is feeling frightened. If we were to communicate our fear, it would not only be a relief of the fear for us, it would also be a great gift for the other person. Communication, reaching out, and forgiveness can heal the fear. It is a great gift for the other person, as well.

Exercise

Today, in every situation where you notice that you are dominating, communicate your fear to the person you are oppressing. Communication heals the fear. In every situation where another is dominating you, reach out and respond to that person as if they were a frightened child. Reaching out heals the fear. In every situation that shows itself as domination, reach out, communicate, and forgive both the other person and yourself.

17. IN ANY CONFLICT, BOTH PEOPLE ARE ACTING IN OPPOSITE WAYS, BUT FEELING THE SAME THING

The beginning of creating resolution, and the key to healing any conflict, is knowing that even though each person may be acting in a different way, the point of joining is a feeling you both have in common. For instance, the feeling of fear can create fight or flight, just as guilt can create withdrawal or aggression. In both cases, the different reactions stem from a common shared feeling.

If communication begins with our feelings, we can create a mood of sharing where both of us have one point to agree on. From this point of joining or agreement, the whole situation begins to unfold in understanding and intimacy with each other. Whatever we are experiencing, we can use it as the barometer for what others are experiencing, even though their behaviour may be exactly the opposite of ours.

Exercise

Today, be aware of the people with whom you are in conflict. Take some time to dwell on what you are feeling in this situation. When you get a strong sense of what the feeling is, be willing to send the other person whatever you believe would heal the feeling that you share. Be willing to bless them.

18. BLESSING IS THE ANTIDOTE TO SACRIFICE

When we are in positions of sacrifice, we feel unworthy. We do not feel good enough to be equal in the situation, so we feel we have to give up who we are and only do things for others.

Blessing is the opposite of sacrifice; it is our desire that things be good for the other person and the situation. Blessing says, 'I have power. I can give in this situation, and my blessing will make the situation better. I don't need to sacrifice myself. I can give forth a blessing.' By giving our energy, love, and best wishes that things be good, we change the situation. Where we felt we had given up on ourself, we can begin to recognise our worth.

Exercise

Today, dispense blessings to everyone, especially in situations where you are tempted to judge someone. Release your judgements, release all temptations to go into sacrifice, and bless everyone with whom you come into contact.

19.   BONDING IS MY TRUE REALITY

We live in a world of illusion where we all seem separate. We are like islands in the sea; if the sea was removed, we would find one firmament, one land. In much the same way, each of us experiences ourself as separate, but in the deepest area of our mind, there is only one mind. It is all Mind, the Mind of Love. Everyone who reaches enlightenment experiences all the world, all the Universe as one. Everyone who has glimpses of Heaven realises that unity, union, and oneness are all truths of higher consciousness. This is why connection and moving aside the illusion of separation is the healing of the world.

Exercise

Today, in the morning, take a moment to close your eyes. Imagine yourself as a little baby in your mother's arms, with your father and your whole family looking down at you. Allow yourself to feel how much they love you. Maybe there are things missing, like money or a nice home, but you are here and they feel grateful for your presence. Feel how much they love you in spite of what you think and believe. The feeling of their love and connection with you is bonding. Beneath the illusion of pain awaits the truth of bonding. Let go of any feelings of separateness. Only feel how much they love you and want you.

In the evening, imagine that you are being held in the arms of God. Let go of all your cares and worries, everything that has been on your mind, and let yourself be held like a little baby. Feel the connection of love between God and you. Feel that force surrounding you, the love moving through you and out into the entire world, creating a network of connection, a network of light. Feel yourself at home. There is nothing to do and no place to go. There is only you, the child, receiving all that love.

20. WHEN I JOIN OTHERS IN THEIR PLACE OF ISOLATION, THEY HEAL AND I RECEIVE A GIFT

When people around us have withdrawn and isolated themselves because the experiences of life have been so painful, we are being asked to recognise that they need us. In fact, any problem of life is a result of this withdrawal. We can find that cave within them where they have hidden, and stand outside, pouring our love toward them, smiling because we love them enough to see where they've hidden themselves.

As we join them, our love will move them toward and into healing. It will get them moving forward once again. As they move forward, responding to how much we've cared for them, they will come out of their isolation, illness, and pain. We also receive a gift.

Exercise

Today, there is one person that you are called upon to reach out to, a person who has withdrawn. Let them come to your mind and, even before you begin to move toward them physically in any way, move toward them in your mind's eye. See yourself joining with them. Your caring, love, and responsiveness will make a world of difference to them. It will make a world of difference to you, too.

21.   CREATIVITY WILL FULFIL
ALL MY NEEDS

Needs make us think that we lack something that can only be fulfilled through a certain situation. They give us tunnel-vision, so we limit the amount of response, fulfilment, or resolution that we can have in any situation.

Creativity is a way of looking at the world or any situation from an expansive viewpoint. It reaches out because it comes from our love for others.

Exercise

Today, some creative project or new thing is calling you, something that would unlock you and release you from your need. What is this creative act or project? What is this form of creativity that would release you, that would give to you and to the whole planet? Creativity is your gift of love to the world. Who are you giving this gift to today?

22. IN THE RIVER OF A RELATIONSHIP, THE IMPORTANT THING IS THE BRIDGE, NOT THE BANKS

Many times in a relationship, we feel that if we moved toward and surrendered to our partner, the point that we wanted to make would be lost. Paradoxically, if we build a bridge to our partner, our point would actually get embodied and integrated with theirs. What is important, then, is not to fight for the bank on our side of the river, but to build a bridge to our partner. As soon as we do this, each person will feel as if they have been heard and responded to. Both feel satisfied because the new form integrates the truth of both banks, creating a form of intercourse.

Exercise

Today, think of someone from whom you feel some distance, and imagine that you are building a bridge from your bank across the chasm. As the bridge reaches the other bank, feel them coming to join you, and feel yourself going to meet them. Feel the energy from their side coming to meet you, and the energy from your side going to meet them. Feel how good it is. Notice the results as commerce begins and increases for both of you, and how it changes the existing situation. When you build a bridge, you not only get your side, you get both banks and, thus, the whole river.

23. WHAT I REJECT IN MY PARENTS, I WILL ACT OUT

The way we have judged our parents is, deep down, the way we have judged ourself. We react to this in one of two ways. By rejecting a behaviour in our parents, we get to act it out as a way for us to understand what drove them to that behaviour in the first place. The other way is where we behave in a totally opposite way as a compensation for how our parents acted. We form roles out of our judgements against our parents, roles that lead us into sacrifice with our children or our partners. Ironically, under the role, we are stuck with the feelings of what we rejected in our parents.

Exercise

Today, take a look at what you have rejected about your parents, and see if you are acting in the same way or in a compensatory way. See if you are acting out a role that makes you do good things, but does not let you receive, which eventually leads to burn-out. Your understanding of their situation, and your willingness to forgive them will release all of you. Allow God's Love to help you forgive them, and say from your heart, 'In God's Love I forgive you, Mum. In God's Love I forgive you, Dad.'

24. IF I HAVE A GRIEVANCE WITH ANOTHER, I APOLOGISE TO THEM AS IF I WERE THE ONE CAUSING IT

The remarkable thing about grievances is that we feel really right about every one of them. We feel so right that we get stuck in them, and do not move forward. We make certain people play certain parts to justify our anger and attack. Unfortunately, we do this so that we can hold onto a belief system that is hurting us. It is like hating gorillas, running and hiding from them until, finally, we inadvertently lock ourself in a cage with one.

Under every grievance is guilt. Our grievances are what we feel guilty about, projected on to someone else. The most powerful way to find the truth of this secret is to apologise for what we thought they were doing to us. Suddenly, we realise that it was us who was doing it. We feel the emotion come back, and along with it an understanding of what we've been doing while hiding it from ourself.

Exercise

Today, reflect on what you feel so right about, and let it go. List three people with whom you have grievances, and visit them, write to them, or call them. Sincerely apologise to them for what you thought they were doing to you. You will find your release in your apology.

25. IF I AM EXHAUSTED, I AM PLAYING A ROLE

Many of us get thrown into exhausting situations in which we burn out, because we are acting out our beliefs about how we should be. When we act out of our roles, rules, and duties, we may be doing the right thing for the wrong reason; acting out of habit instead of choice. This has us do things that are unnecessary, do things to avoid certain feelings, or do things to keep us from receiving good things.

Choice energises us. When we feel most exhausted, we can set small goals for ourself. Each time we reach that little goal, it allows us to gain more energy. To change a role into a place of giving/receiving and energy, we choose to do what we are doing, rather than doing it because we are supposed to. Be willing to do the right thing for the right reason.

Exercise

Today, look at a place where you feel exhausted. Now, imagine that this exhausted self is really some kind of mask or costume. Remove the mask, and see who is there. You may find a family member, a monster, a little child, or even yourself in need of support, dealing with some painful feeling. Ask how you can help and respond to that need. Imagine holding yourself or whoever it is, while supporting and coaching yourself or them. As you love them, let them melt into you. This will fill a gap in you, and some place where you have been in conflict will heal with the energy that now begins working for you.

26. WHEN I AM FEELING DEPENDENT AND NEEDY, I LET GO AND TRUST

The scariest thing to imagine when we are feeling dependent and needy is to let go of what we feel we need. Yet, this is exactly what would bring success. Every time we let go of our attachment, we move into another level of attractiveness and partnership, which takes the relationship forward to a new level of joining and romance. If we don't let go and trust, we become a burden to our partner, pushing them away from us through our dependence and unattractiveness; the more dependent we become, the more unattractive we are. We are pushing them away while trying to grab them at the same time.

Dependency is a form of trying to take without being able to receive. If we really value our partnership, we let go of what we feel we need. We get out of our own way; we trust that as we stand empty-handed, something even better will come to take its place. When we do not need it, it can be given; when we let go, we can finally receive.

Exercise

Today, imagine giving all of what you need into the hands of God. Let your Higher Mind decide whether you need it, and what you will receive. Have expectancy that good things are coming to you. Trust. Your willingness to trust will allow you to move forward.

27. WHAT I RESIST IN ANOTHER WILL PERSIST UNTIL I ACCEPT IT

What we resist will persist. Any time we have a problem with someone or a situation, it is because we have a lesson to learn. The more we try to move away, the more we are stuck in the situation because the resistance is still within us; our resistance holds us back. When we accept what we are resisting, we forgive the other person, move to join them, and free ourself to move forward.

Exercise

Today, bring to mind the person you are resisting the most. Imagine moving across the space between you and them. Feel the light within you moving to join the light within them. When you feel both lights joined, allow yourself to remain in the peace. During the day, check to see if the sense of peace is still there. If the peace has been disturbed, it may mean that you are going on to another layer of the resistance. Again, take the time to feel yourself moving toward them to join your light with their light until you have regained a place of total peace.

28. ABUNDANCE IS THE RESULT OF WILLINGNESS TO RECEIVE

We say that we desire certain things that we do not have. When we look into our mind, however, we realise that what we lack, we do not want. We do not want it because, for some reason, we are afraid to have it. For example, if we believe that a good person should not be rich, abundant, or have too much sexual satisfaction, we will either be good without the riches, or bad with abundance. The fear is stronger than having abundance because our belief says that it is bad. The more we complain about not having what we think we want, the more we are actually afraid of having it. If we check out our belief system and fear level, we may be kidding ourself about what we say we really want.

The problem is neither with the situation, nor is it another person. It is with ourself. The willingness to change our attitude, have courage and open ourself to a new level, find our hidden fears, and look at our belief systems allows us to see and let go of what is stopping our abundance. Somewhere we have valued an idea or a certain feeling (maybe guilt, maybe fear) more than what we think we want.

Exercise

Today, let the negative beliefs that stop you from having what you want come to your mind. Let go of whatever belief or feeling stands in the way of your receiving. Imagine yourself being filled with what you want.

29.   IT IS NOT THE TRUTH
UNLESS EVERYONE WINS

In any form of competition or power struggle, when we win and others lose, it is only a matter of time before they strike back. The only situations that truly work are those where everyone wins, because they are not built on a false economy, but on a movement of energy into a higher form.

Compromising is not the truth; it is each party giving up something to keep something they want. If we stop communication and accept compromise, everyone will feel as if they have lost and as if they are in sacrifice. As we continue to communicate or negotiate, and settle for nothing less than everyone feeling as if they have won, we bring a new integrity into the situation. All sides in a power struggle have at least some of the energy of truth, if not its form. Joined together, they bring an integration of all perspectives into a new vision, which is, of course, what truth is.

Exercise

Today, choose one person that opposes you. Commit to communicating with this person until both of you can get to a point of feeling you have reached a resolution, and achieved a new vision – a place where everyone wins.

30. PAIN IS AN AREA WHERE I HAVE CUT THE LINES OF RELATEDNESS

Pain is a place where we have removed ourself from the situation because it seemed too difficult, where we have pulled back from others because we didn't like what they were doing. By deciding not to recognise the relationship, we cut ourself off and we are suffering as a result. Even years later, we suffer as we get in touch with subconscious places where we cut the threads of connection with old friends and family members, or with parts of ourself.

Exercise

Today, see who comes to your mind as someone with whom you are called to reconnect. Reach out to them and extend yourself so you can remove the pain you are experiencing. Allow yourself to feel the connection with all of those people as you mend the lines of relatedness.

31.   SEX IS COMMUNICATION, NOT JUST THE PLUMBING

Sex is more than just being a good pipe fitter. The very essence of sex is communication. Whatever we communicate is the experience we get. If we are not communicating love, we are not experiencing love. If our experience in sex is just a form of release, of getting our needs met, then we are keeping sex very small. If our energy around sex is that it is just something we were told not to do, it will have the excitement of forbidden fruit; if we do not go past the taboo and the feeling of excitement that comes from it, we will be limiting sex to its first stage and miss all that we could receive.

Sex is a powerful way of making contact and communicating. As communication is one of the great healers, sex is one way of moving through power struggles and reaching out to our partner. It moves us forward through differences to create a new sense of reality, partnership, and release. Communication heals and moves us out of feelings of deadness. Sex can, too, if it is more than just a physical experience. Sex is emotional and spiritual; it is all of the joining and contact that we can make, all of the getting to really know who it is that we are making love to. We get to fully give and fully receive from our partner. We get to totally enjoy them.

Exercise

Today, look at what you have been communicating to your lover. Have you withdrawn from sex? What is the message you are giving to the world, to God? Be willing to reach out once again. Be willing to open the door to sex and move forward to a whole new level of experience. Do not make love, let love make you.

32.   TO HEAL BOREDOM,
TAKE AN EMOTIONAL RISK

Boredom causes us to feel tired, down and out, dead. It also causes us to blame our partner when we cannot be bothered with them because they are *soooooo* boring, as if it had nothing to do with us. Yet, our boredom, like any other emotion, is directly related to us. Boredom is the result of withholding something, holding ourself back in the situation because we are afraid to take a risk, afraid to communicate.

When we communicate what we have been afraid to reveal, there is an excitement and a new emotional energy for us. Not communicating about the things that we are afraid would destroy the relationship actually holds us back from each other and already is destroying the relationship. Willingness to take an emotional risk, work through whatever is necessary, take responsibility for our own experience, and move forward toward our partner, heals the boredom.

Exercise

Today, ask yourself what you are withholding. Where have you been holding yourself back? Communicate this with your partner. Do not stop communicating until both of you feel heard, feel you both have won, feel peace, and feel you are moving forward, together.

33. IN ANY RELATIONSHIP, ONE PERSON
IS THE PROBLEM-FINDER,
THE OTHER IS THE PROBLEM-SOLVER

In any relationship, people polarise into two positions; both serve the relationship and enable it to move forward. It is similar to the positive and negative terminals on a battery; both are needed for the vehicle to operate properly and run smoothly.

One person will seem more pessimistic, or 'negative', though they'll call themselves realistic. They will be good at communication, more in touch with their feelings, and highly discriminating. Their chief gift is to find the problems or possible problems in the relationship. The other person will take on a more optimistic, or 'positive' role, and be more of an idealist. They'll be more diplomatic in their communication, where the problem-finder, or 'negative', will be more out front. Though somewhat naive, the 'positive', or problem-solver, will be able to transform situations.

While the 'positive' will sometimes blithely commit way beyond themselves, the 'negative' will know exactly how much energy, money, and time something will take. Working together, positives and negatives make a great team for success. If the positive and the negative both realise that the other serves a vital function in the relationship, then the two can move forward as a team. The negative can get in touch with the problems and the positive can transform them. It is important to note that in our relationship, we can be the negative in some areas and the positive in others. For example, in the area concerning money, we can be the positive and our partner the negative, yet in the area concerning the children, we can be the negative while our partner has the positive role.

36

Exercise

Today, take a look at your major relationship. In what areas are you the problem-finder? In what areas are you the problem-solver? In these areas, are you appreciating the job that the other person is doing for you? If you learn to value your partner, you can really move forward. Give them appreciation for the function they are serving in the relationship. Learn to value their input, because it is through them that you both move forward.

Giving is one of the best feelings in life. It is to be distin-
guished from sacrifice, which does not allow us to receive.
When we are giving, we are truly feeling our greatness. All
that we give automatically opens the door for us to feel good
and to receive in the moment. This is why so many of the
early native tribes were so generous. Giving allowed them to
feel their greatness of spirit.

Giving is really a form of receiving. The extent to which
we give to a person is the extent to which we feel them giving
love to us. They may be totally loving us, but if we are not
giving, we will not feel open enough to receive what they are
giving back to us. In giving, we recognise what has been
within us all the time. In this recognition is the very quality of
receiving. We get to receive the very gift or feeling that we are
giving; we give, experience, and receive our greatness of
spirit.

Exercise

*Today, your task is to imagine you have all the resources in the world,
and you can bless people with whatever it is you think they need.
Throughout the day, take the time to give to certain people. Support
those around you. Give a little bit more. Go beyond yourself. Smile a
little bit more. Reach out a little bit more. Let one person come to your
mind that you are to give a special gift to, for no good reason, except
that it is your joy. Imagine yourself blessing those around you and
giving these gifts all day.*

35. 'EXPECT NOTHING, AND ANYTHING SEEMS LIKE EVERYTHING. EXPECT ANYTHING, AND EVERYTHING SEEMS LIKE NOTHING.' – SAM HAZO

Expectations are limitations; they are also demands. When we expect or demand something, the getting feels empty; whereas without expectations, anything can be a gift. Anything can provide wonder and offer new ways of thinking.

If we have a picture of how it should be, our expectation leads to disappointment and frustration. Every expectation is a demand of someone else. When we feel demanded of, we sometimes just totally refuse and, other times, we give what is demanded, even though giving because of expectations tends to make us feel oppressed. Our willingness to let go of all our expectations, our ideas of how a person or things should be, allows us and the situation to move forward.

Exercise

Today, notice one area of frustration and disappointment in your life. Be willing to let go of what you expect and how you think it should be so you can move forward. Be willing to have wonder and new ways of thinking that move you toward success. Be willing to learn.

36. THE EXTENT OF MY EXPECTATION
IS THE DEGREE OF MY STRESS

Our demands on others, which are our expectations, come out of feelings of inadequacy and neediness. We try to take care of these needs by controlling outward situations or ourself – imposing the same demands that we make on ourself onto everyone else. In contrast, the closer we get to a goal (something we want that has flexibility around its fulfilment), the more it attracts us naturally. Where we have a large number of expectations, we are working very hard with very little reward because we cannot receive. This is because expectations have to do with the *should's, have-to's, got-to's, need-to's, ought-to's,* and *must's* that rob us of receiving. Stress typically stems from *busyness* in our life. This *busyness* (working hard, but not succeeding) creates stress. The closer we get to an expectation, the more resistance we feel to having it because of all the increasing demands we place on ourself to have it.

Exercise

Today, look at areas where you feel stress, or where you feel resistance to beginning something or to moving forward. You may find an expectation on yourself or the situation that is holding you back. Letting go of it is a way of letting go of the stress.

Consider all of the unfinished projects you have. Let go of the ones that are no longer timely for you, and reset your goals for the others. Take one forward step after another. Do the same thing in your relationship by setting small goals for healing and for having things be better. Let go of expectation, move into and surrender to the flow of life. Stop trying to make things happen, it only creates stress and blocks you from receiving.

37.   EXPECTATIONS ARE TIME BOMBS
WAITING TO GO OFF

The more we expect, the less we receive. Expectations are our picture of what will make us happy, but we are never happy even when we get exactly what we wanted. Happiness is not something we can demand from a situation, it is something that is generated from within.

Our expectations cover our hidden needs while pretending that this 'neediness' (inadequacy) has nothing to do with us, but has everything to do with our partner. This naturally leads to power struggle because when we are caught in expectation, we either make banal small-talk, or we make demands. The latter, of course, creates resistance in our partner. As the resistance builds, it is only a matter of time before there is some sort of explosion or separation – the time bomb goes off.

Our willingness to let go of our expectations opens us to receive expectancy. Expectancy is a positive feeling, a knowing that what is coming is the best thing for us even though we do not know what it is. Letting go of our expectations, or demands, in favour of an expectant attitude allows all good things to come to us. We do not demand, we invite. We do not expect, we know that the best is on its way.

Exercise

Today, get in touch with areas where you are not receiving, and where you have a certain sense of urgency. These, typically, are areas where you have expectations. Be willing to let go of your expectations, and trust that what is coming to you will move you forward.

38. EXPECTATIONS RUIN EXPERIENCES

Expectations ruin experience because they place a demand on the situation to meet our needs. However, there is a good chance that our needs will not be met even if the situation lives up to our plan (our picture of how it should be). Our plan is a way of ritually killing all the inspiration of the event. Expectations are different from goals, which are good to have because they invite us forward, and are much more productive and successful. If we miss the deadline or goal, we simply re-set it, which facilitates moving forward. If we miss an expectation, we beat ourself up and make ourself feel bad, which does not facilitate moving forward.

Exercise

Today, be aware of your expectations. Willingly let go of how you think it should be, so you can be taught by the Universe about what is the best way for you. Trust that, at the very deepest level, everything works out for the best for your healing and growth. If you are willing to let an experience be anything that it is and make full contact in any situation, you will have a much greater chance of happiness.

If you have an event coming up where you might have expectations, imagine the event as a city at the end of a beautiful, emerald river. See yourself getting into a little boat and launching it into this gentle river. As the boat moves out into the current, just relax and watch the scenery go by. The river itself carries you toward the city, your goal, and it feels so easy. There is no effort necessary. As your goal calls you, there is nothing to do — just relax and enjoy.

39.   WHAT I REPRESS,
MY CHILDREN WILL ACT OUT

Sometimes as children we experience certain events that are traumatic or painful, and we fracture off the parts of ourself we thought got us into trouble; we reject them. Typically, any area of failure is an area where we rejected and then repressed part of ourself. In repressing these parts, we forget about them, and then we forget we forgot them. What we have repressed, however, will show up in the people around us as we project our lost selves onto them. This is especially true of our children. For example, if we have repressed a part of our sexuality, our children may seem very precocious with theirs. If we have rejected a part of ourself we considered dishonest, our child will always seem to be lying.

Whatever we have swept under the carpet, our children will act out for us so that we finally have a chance of forgiving it, and releasing our hidden guilt. The parts of ourself we really dislike show up in our family; the parts of us that need to be integrated for our growth and healing will show up in our children.

We cannot divorce our kids. We are always being motivated to work through whatever issues they seem to have in them and, in doing this, we learn to understand and accept them. In forgiving them, we heal ourself. As we learn to get back in touch with our feelings and to re-associate with ourself, our child will be released also.

Exercise

Today, pick a problem your child might have. If you do not have children, pick someone very close to you. Choose a quality you intensely dislike in them. Imagine that you are drifting back through time and space to the point where you pushed away this particular quality. How old were you? Who was with you during this event? What was occurring then that you judged this part of yourself as bad and wrong?

Now, reach out to that little child, that part of you that doesn't understand why it is being pushed away. Take this child into your lap, nurture it lovingly and, then, feel it melting into you. When integration occurs, what is negative falls away and the energy is subsumed into the movement forward in growth.

40. THE MORE I LOVE MYSELF, THE MORE I CAN RECOGNISE THAT I AM LOVED

One of the greatest problems in the world is that most of us feel unloved. Sad as it may seem, this dilemma will continue unless we love ourself. Even as our family and friends love us, we cannot easily experience it when we do not feel any love for ourself. By this, we give the message that we are not worth loving which naturally puts people off, fuelling the problem. The way to begin solving this unloved feeling is to begin recognising our worth. The worth that we give ourself allows others to recognise it in us; if we do not recognise ourself, no one else can. When we love ourself, we feel loved.

Exercise

Today, do something that is an act of love for yourself. Not as an act of indulgence, which won't make you feel loved – it actually wears you out as much as sacrifice does. Start by taking a close look at yourself. Where can you respect yourself more and give yourself credit? Where can you recognise yourself and really reach out to yourself? What could you do that would be a gift to yourself? Cultivate this attitude.

For the most part, you are much harder on yourself than you are on the people around you. Now is the time to give yourself a break and to recognise how much you deserve. If you begin to feel unworthiness or valuelessness, just feel it until it is gone. Don't turn away from the feeling or try to cover it up. The simplest act of healing is to be willing to feel your feelings until they evaporate. Underneath, you may find even more loathsome feelings. Feel them. When they are gone, you will be open to feeling love for yourself as well as receiving love from others.

41.   TEMPTATION OCCURS WHEN A NEW LEVEL IS ABOUT TO BE REACHED

Temptation is a distraction that we use to delay ourself. Anything that delays us from moving forward is our personal conspiracy against our greatness. This only serves our fear, even when the fear is of having it all be so good.

A temptation diverts our mind from the step we are about to take. If we refuse the temptation, we simply allow ourself to move forward. If we bring our energy back into the relationship, the quality of what was tempting us will develop in our relationship within the next two weeks. Our willingness to keep that particular energy flowing toward our primary relationship makes the relationship stronger and more fulfilling.

Sometimes, when we refuse to yield to the temptation on a physical level, our mind keeps lingering on a particular quality the other person has that we think would somehow meet our needs. The ego serves that temptation up to us when the need is just about to be met in our primary relationship. If we take the temptation, our mind is split, our time is wasted, and we move in two directions at once. Problems and pain are bound to ensue.

When we have personal connections there is, typically, a sexual attraction too. Many times when we feel these kinds of energies, we run or jump in to indulge ourself. However, if we choose to move forward with integrity, when we get to a certain closeness, a love energy emerges that makes all of the sexual energy safe. If we indulge ourself without discernment, many times the guilt or problems that ensue cause us to lose the connection. All connection we feel with others is really about a creative energy or project that is there for both of us.

Exercise

Today, look closely at what is tempting you. Be willing to move that energy toward your primary relationship. As you do, your relationship will begin to unfold and give you new gifts; in fact, even the very quality of the gift that tempted you.

42. STAYING OPEN AND FEELING
MY FEELINGS CREATES HEALING

Many times when we are attacked, whether or not what they are saying has any vestige of truth in it, painful feelings like guilt, anger, fear, hurt, frustration, or whatever they happen to be, rise up in us. When we are confronted with these feelings, we either dissociate from them or we use them in retaliation. Neither of these forms of defence truly works to change the situation. The best response is to stand defenceless. Defence-lessness recognises that these feelings are neither right nor wrong, they are simply true because we are experiencing them. With this attitude we stay open to feeling our natural feelings until they are gone, taking a step for both ourself and the attacker. When the bad feeling is gone, the step is completed, and the relationship moves forward.

Exercise

Today, stand as defenceless as possible and take courage in experiencing your feelings. You might go into more dire feelings, but just feel them until they have completely melted away. Take whatever time you need. In the end, there is peace and happiness. This by itself can be the healing that moves your relationship forward.

43.   THE LESS I EXPECT,
THE MORE I RECEIVE

Our expectation covers up a demand which, in turn, covers up a need. This need has a sense of urgency and, whatever we feel we have to have, creates resistance. The very thing we are trying to get, we are secretly pushing away. The more we feel we need it, the more we create resistance to being able to receive it, and the more we create resistance to the very people who might want to give it to us. The more demands we place on them, the more likely they are to pull away.

It takes a person of great maturity not to move away when someone expects something of them. Letting go of our expectations opens us to receiving. Once the urgency is gone, our partner or the people around us are much more willing to move in to fill the gap by responding and giving to us.

Exercise

Today, who is it that you have major expectations of? What do you have expectations about? Get out of your own way. Be willing to let go of any expectation, or demands, you have of yourself and others, and let people give to you.

44. THE INDEPENDENT PARTNER CAN MOVE THE RELATIONSHIP FORWARD BY VALUING THEIR PARTNER

Many independent people who are committed to their relationship do not realise that they have the power to transform it. If we are the independent person in our relationship, learning to value our dependent partner, because they serve a vital function, will move the relationship forward. Be grateful that they handle all of the pain and 'neediness' in the relationship. 'There but for the grace of God go I.' As we value them, they become more attractive and we both win. To reach them, we have to move down through our resistance to our own neediness. With sheer willingness, we can reach out to them and lift them up out of the pain and neediness, moving the relationship forward to a new level of partnership.

After we have reached this new level of partnership and celebrated it, the relationship moves on and, at some future time, we can, once again, play the independent role. As before, we just reach out and back for them, and pull them up. Each time we do this, some of their outward neediness and our hidden neediness is healed, and the relationship continues to move forward.

Exercise

Today, look around you for someone who is needy. Be willing to move toward them. Appreciate them for their part in your relationship and bring them to a new level of feeling good about themselves. Value them by committing to reach out and move through your pain to raise them up to a new level of confidence.

45.   TO HAVE AN EXCITING
RELATIONSHIP, TAKE AN EMOTIONAL RISK

When we feel stuck in a rut, that we are in the same old pattern in sex, communication, or how we live, the antidote is to take an emotional risk. If things have become this dull and boring, we are withholding some vital energies, some vital communication. What we don't want to tell our partner because we think it would hurt them, or it would destroy the relationship, already is.

Communicating about these things can bring new life back to our relationship; the intention is not to wound, but to share with our partner. In effect, to say, 'This has held me back from you, and I don't want it to keep holding me back. I take responsibility for this feeling. This is not your fault. I am willing to experience it fully and share with you so we can make it better together.'

Sometimes, asking for our partner's help will trigger a very painful response in them. At that point, we move toward and genuinely support them. As we reassure them, we will find our relationship has moved to a new level.

With this sharing, there is a chance for new growth and the realisation of a new connection to emerge. When we value the relationship, we are willing to deal with what is not working so the relationship gets better. We are willing to take the risk that keeps generating the excitement.

Exercise

Today, take the emotional risk that would make things better. Who is it you have been hiding from? With whom have you been afraid to

51

share? Remember, when you are standing in great intimacy with anyone, they can receive anything. You can say anything to anyone if you are committed to them because they know your intention is no longer to withhold or make them wrong.

46.   PERCEPTION IS PROJECTION

Whatever we see is a reflection of what is in our own mind. In other words, the way in which we see people and the world around us reflects our belief systems, especially beliefs about ourself. If we change our beliefs, we take away the limits we place on others to be all that *we* are. When we take responsibility for what we are experiencing as coming from our beliefs, we have power to change the situation. For example, if we did not like a particular movie, we would not try to change the image on the screen. We would go to the projection room and change the film. The film is like our belief systems and the projection room is our own mind. With this analogy we can begin to see what kind of movie we are making in our life. It might be a tragedy, a comedy, a love story, an adventure; it might even be a movie that is too boring to watch.

What changes any perception we may have is the willingness to see where we chose a certain event because somehow there was a pay-off. For instance, when we have a major experience in our life, whether positive or traumatic, we decide certain things which create belief systems about life, ourself, relationship, and even God, causing us to have totally contradictory belief systems operating side by side in our mind. Sometimes though, we repress and forget these decisions we made, and our life becomes very complex if the belief system at work is one we have kept hidden from ourself. We hate conflict so much that we will even cover over one belief system if it is in conflict with another belief system inside us. This denial hides the conflict within, but projects it outside us. We can begin to move through this once the realisation of our pay-off (where we decided to be right about life) occurs.

The way is open to forgiveness, transformation, and even miracles.

Exercise

Today, look at your partner. What is your belief about them that has them be the way they are? Be willing to change your belief about them, as well as to see a higher value or belief. This begins to change not only your perception of them, but also yourself. As you decide to examine and change your subconscious beliefs, you will change the film that you are projecting onto the screen of life. When you realise that everything you see and experience is your responsibility, you will be aware of what you are doing in your own projection room, thereby making better choices for a happier relationship and a happier life.

47. WHEN I GIVE AND GET HURT, I AM GIVING TO TAKE

Many of us have the attitude that we have given the best years of our life to old what's-their-name; we feel we have wasted our lives. Then there are the times when we gave and were not recognised; we came away hurt and rejected. The only time this can happen, though, is when we are giving to take; putting a one-sided contract on the person, demanding that they give back to us in the way we desire.

If we give freely, we cannot be pushed away because there is nothing we are trying to get. If we need nothing, we cannot be rejected. If we are giving just for the sake of our pure love, there can be no hurt response. When we give out of our fullness, we get to receive fully. It does not matter how others respond because the joy of giving is the reward itself.

Exercise

Today, choose someone to whom you have given in order to get something in return, and give something to them freely. Give something you feel called to give, something that would release you wholly from the entanglement. Let go of any expectation or demand for a particular response, knowing your giving is your reward.

48. GUILT ALWAYS HIDES FEAR

Guilt is a place where we have made a monument to a mistake and left the path of life to worship at this monument. It has us withdraw and, then, withholds us from the people we love. We may feel we have made a mistake in relation to our partner and now feel guilty about it, but guilt not only reinforces the mistake, it starves our partner of the very love and nurturing they need. Forgiving ourself cuts through the guilt and allows us to give the love and nurturing. Guilt keeps us stuck like the great *super glue* of life; the primary reason for our guilt is so we don't have to move forward and face the next step. Our willingness to allow the next step to emerge cuts through fear in much the same way that forgiveness cuts through guilt.

Exercise

Today, consider how you have used your guilt, or bad feelings, to hold yourself back because you are afraid of the future. Look at how you have been living in the past because you are afraid the future will be the same. Be willing to release your guilt so the future can reveal a greater horizon and call you forward to it; you have no need to be afraid of your future.

Make a choice to no longer be held hostage to a mistake that you have turned into self-punishment by arrogantly belittling yourself and making life all about you. Life is not about you, personally, it is about happiness or the healing that brings about happiness for you. Guilt refuses to learn this lesson. Your choice to release your guilt (and hidden guilt where we blame others by making them guilty) is your willingness to be happy.

49. I AM NEVER DISTRESSED FOR THE REASON I THINK

Typically, we are so out of touch with ourself that when we are distressed we never realise what it is that we really are distressed about. We often confuse ourself, diffuse feeling, dissimulate, and present to ourself different rationalisations about what is going on. We tell ourself and everyone around us a good story.

What we are really distressed about is coming from a much deeper level of the mind (the subconscious or the unconscious mind). When we are distressed in a relationship, it is to our benefit to look deeper. The present upset is just a trigger to get us in touch with feelings that we have carried for a long time so that they can get out to be healed. If we are really in touch with ourself as we feel any sort of pain, we will recognise how much of it is really coming from past situations; almost all of our pain is coming from the past. As we begin to communicate about this original pain and share where it is coming from, we not only heal this pain, we regain our natural self-expression and communication.

Exercise

Today, begin to communicate about at least one event that is distressing you. Share it without any attempt to change the other person. As you finish sharing what it is, reach into yourself and feel the feelings under your complaint, and share these. Continue reaching deeper into yourself to all the feelings you can experience and share them. Sometimes, you may even find a situation coming to your mind where these feelings began. Stay with the feeling. Do not get caught up in the story. The more you share, the more you free yourself from this old pain.

50.   RECEIVING IS GIVING

When we receive, we are receiving not only for ourself, but for everyone else around us. The more we receive, the more we naturally give. We fully enjoy it because as we are fulfilled, we naturally pass this abundance to everyone else. Many people love to give, but have a very hard time receiving and are, instead, thrown into sacrifice and, therefore, burn-out.

In a relationship, until we reach interdependence (partnership), we have a real fear of receiving. Partnership teaches us how to receive. When we learn to receive, our very receiving makes the people around us feel loved; receiving is one of the greatest forms of giving. When our child comes up to us filled with heartfelt love and gives us a little weed as if it were the most beautiful flower in the world, the weed transforms itself, through love, into a beautiful gift for us. Our willingness to receive the transformative power of the child's love is also a gift to the child.

Exercise

Today, be willing to give to your partner and to everyone just by enjoying them and receiving whatever is being given to you. Be willing to recognise how much more you actually are being given than you normally allow yourself to receive. Be willing to accept all that is being given and everything that life is offering you as it comes your way. From sunrise to sunset, receive the majesty of the rising sun, the music of nature's symphony, and the beauty of the setting sun. Today is a day to fully receive and enjoy yourself.

51. WHAT I AM EXPECTING OF
ANOTHER, I AM NOT GIVING TO MYSELF

If we expect others to love or recognise us, it can only be because we are not giving to ourself. Our continual complaining about what they are not giving us, hasn't given it to us; it has actually stopped it being given. If we were to give this to ourself, we would open the door for others to love and recognise us, too. We would find that many people have not only the ability but the willingness to give to us.

Exercise

Today, every hour on the hour, give to yourself whatever it is you have been wanting. Remember, it is not necessarily the form, such as sex, money, and so on, it is the energy of the thing.

52. DEPENDENCE IS TRYING TO GET NEEDS MET IN THE PRESENT THAT WERE NOT MET IN THE PAST

Dependence is trying to remake the past in the present, an attempt that will always be unsuccessful. Dependence tries to take in order to get the old needs met, but since they are old needs, they can never quite be filled in the present situation. For example, if we needed a quarter yesterday to make an emergency phone call and we received that quarter today, it would not meet yesterday's need. Only a realisation of this along with forgiveness will release the past. We can move forward out of dependence by letting go of the past and letting go of those needs in the present.

Exercise

Today, examine the areas where you are seeking approval from someone, or where you feel dependent on someone. Who was it, really, that you were trying to get love from? Imagine yourself as that little child who did not get love, and then, give to that parent or person the very thing you thought you needed from them.

53.   ANY PROBLEM IS A FEAR
OF TAKING THE NEXT STEP

When a problem emerges in a relationship, it is a result of the fear of taking the next step. If we are willing to take the next step, the problem can disappear, or turn into something to be simply handled – no big deal. Basically, a problem is the part of our mind where we are not giving; this part has been fractured and is being withheld. It is the part we have projected as the problem at hand. For instance, if we are giving seventy-five percent of our self, then twenty-five percent of us will show up in problems that seem to be thwarting us. What is between these two pieces of our mind is fear. Our willingness to move forward and take the next step transcends the fear and allows for the integration of these two parts of our mind, which has the problem disappear.

Exercise

Today, say Yes! *to the next step. No matter how big the problem, this allows you to move forward. If you think back, you will realise that any time you have truly taken the next step, life always got better for you. This time is no different. Being willing to move forward is the easiest way to remove yourself from the most complicated problems.*

54. IF MY RELATIONSHIP IS STUCK, I AM AFRAID OF WHAT WOULD HAPPEN IF IT GOT UNSTUCK

Any area in our relationship where we are stuck and not receiving is where we are actually afraid to receive. We have controlled this area and hidden it away. We are probably blaming our partner for not giving to us in this area. We are the ones afraid to receive, afraid of what would happen if this part of the relationship got unstuck and moved forward.

Exercise

Today, investigate the area where you feel stuck and what you might be afraid of receiving. What would happen if this part of your relationship was unstuck? What self-image and what behaviour would you have to give up? What feelings would no longer be true for you to carry around? Ask yourself, 'What is the purpose of me not having this?' Are you afraid that if you did receive in this area, you could not trust yourself? Are you afraid you might be overwhelmed by how good it would be? Are you afraid you would not trust your own integrity? Does your own guilt or unworthiness stop you from receiving?

You are at the heart of this conspiracy; therefore, you have the power to transform any area in the relationship that is stuck. Be willing to give up this control so that you can receive that which would free you and move your relationship forward. It could become unstuck by your willingness to give up control.

55.   MY PAIN MEANS I AM
MAKING A MISTAKE

As a child, if we stuck our fingers into the fire, we would pull them back and learn not to do that again. Emotionally, though, we have stuck every appendage into the proverbial fire and we still have not learned the lesson. Emotional pain is the thermometer to let us know that we are somehow making a mistake. It is letting us know that there is an unlearned lesson calling for our attention. If we paid attention to this pain, we would discover our mistake and, therefore, learn the lesson; we would begin to heal.

Exercise

Today is a day to learn that wisdom does not come from suffering. Wisdom comes from learning the lesson that heals the suffering. Realise you have made a mistake. You can heal yourself if you move past what you are experiencing. Open yourself to it. Spend ten minutes in meditation about any particular area of pain, and ask your Higher Mind for help in understanding the lesson. Be willing to learn it. Ask to be shown the way.

56.   I TRY TO CONTROL ONLY
WHEN I HAVE LOST TRUST

Control is a response to our fear. We try to control others, the situations, or ourself when we are afraid that we will be hurt as we were in the past. In the subconscious mind, under the need to control, there are old heartbreaks, places where we have forgotten faith and lost trust and confidence. Every situation we try to control is one in which we do not have trust.

Trust is the power of our mind when all of its parts are joined together, focused in one direction. Faith is the belief in this part of our mind. Bringing trust into a situation restores our confidence, which allows us to let go of control so things can move forward. If we were to trust, even those things that look tragic or negative would begin to work for us because of the very power of our mind.

Exercise

Today, in any situation, take a look at what you are trying to control. Bring trust to this situation. All problems come from a lack of confidence. Your willingness to trust yourself and the people around you to do the very best means you have the confidence that everything will work for you. Trust is not naivety, it is using the power of your mind to unfold a situation.

57. MY EXPERIENCE AND MEMORIES ARE PERCEPTIONS, NOT EVENTS

In any situation, we are really experiencing the filters that an event comes through, not the event itself. This is why our memories and experiences may seem quite different from others' with whom we shared the event.

We have very little idea what our childhood was really like since we make up stories based on the facts that fit our present mode in which we are operating in the world at the time. As we grow and change, our attitude toward our past changes, and then our experience changes. As we heal ourself, many times our opinions about our mother, father, or siblings are transformed. When we come to a full understanding of any event, including all subconscious elements, we realise no one is to blame, not even us. The hurt in the situation falls away because truth has to do with a level of understanding that releases all pain.

All healing is about changing our perceptions into something even truer. We know it is the truth because there is no pain connected with it.

Exercise

Today, in any situation where you may be experiencing conflict or pain, begin to communicate. Most misunderstandings and pain are healed as a result of clarification. Use communication as a vehicle to clear up any misunderstandings and misperceptions, and to experience the other's perception of the event. Communication brings everyone to full understanding and truth.

58. WHEN MY PARTNER OPPOSES ME, I AM CALLED TO A NEW WAY OF LIFE

In a relationship, two people form and act out one mind that includes the elements of each person's mind. Our partner brings forth aspects of the truth that are very important, both for our growth as an individual, and as a couple.

When our partner seems to oppose us, or has an idea or answer that seems exactly opposite to ours, this seems to threaten us; yet life is just telling us that it is time to move forward. We move forward by learning from our partner's way of doing it, and finding a new way that contains the best of both ways in a higher form. When we integrate both ways, we reach a new level of partnership where both of us have a higher level of confidence and are better able to receive.

Exercise

Today, realise that even though your partner may be acting in a way that is different from you, it is very important for your growth and life vitality to be willing to change, and to integrate what your partner has to give you. Appreciate the fact that your partner is bringing in a difference. As you grow together, this difference will provide more flexibility, a wider perspective, and a more successful path in life.

59. WHEN MY PARTNER IS POLARISED, INTEGRATION WILL TAKE ME TO A WHOLE NEW LEVEL

All healing at some level has to do with integration – recovering the hidden and fragmented parts of ourself, and integrating them. In a relationship when we are polarised, our partner is expressing something that is calling us to integrate, calling us to go to a higher level. When we integrate an opposite, we do not get any of its negative aspects, we only receive its power and energy. The integration always shows itself in the highest possible form, containing both our energies; hence, each of us feels we have succeeded.

Exercise

Today, see yourself actually holding a miniaturised form of your partner in one hand and one of you in the other; your partner represents one part of the truth, you the other part. Now melt them both down to their pure energy so you are just holding two hands full of energy and light – the most basic building block of the Universe. Notice, there is no difference between the energy in one hand and the energy in the other. Now as you bring your hands together so your fingers interlock, the energies join together into one form. You may see a new image, a new symbol, and a new way begin to emerge out of all that energy, or it may stay as a glowing form of energy. Allow all this newness to come into your life, joining you and your partner.

60.
I FEEL REJECTED
WHEN I AM REJECTING

When we reject something, we are the ones feeling hurt. In a relationship where both of us are rejecting something, both of us are feeling hurt. If our partner acts in a certain way in order to get needs met, and we reject this behaviour, we are the ones that will feel rejected. In fact, when we reject anything, we will feel rejected; we feel hurt and even heartbroken.

Notice that we are in charge of our feeling of being hurt, of our rejection and heartbreak. If we are experiencing any of these, it is because we are the one pushing away (rejecting). Our willingness to move toward our partner, whatever the circumstance, to take our judgement off them, to communicate with them, and just give to them will make these feelings disappear.

Exercise

Today, avoid the temptation to reject. In areas where you feel hurt, move toward the other person and give to them without any form of expectation. You may have suffered disillusionment, but nobody else can hurt you; remember, you are in charge of your feelings. Resisting the loss of certain dreams by rejecting something will only create a difficult lesson for you. The beliefs of this event, which come from the decisions you make, can start or reinforce a painful pattern. Getting rid of an illusion is always helpful, even if it is not a happy experience because an illusion cannot sustain you. It is time to make new decisions regarding the event based on the situation. This can be done without resisting or rejecting the other person if you are willing to transform all your feelings of rejection into positive feelings.

61. IN POWER STRUGGLE, THE
OTHER PERSON HAS MY MISSING PIECE

Any power struggle presents an opportunity to win back a
piece of ourself that seemed lost to us. This fragmented or
hidden part is represented by the person who opposes us.
When we quit judging and move toward this person, we join
them in such a way that they are helped. When we reach out
and open the door for them to come through, they can give us
this vital piece that we are missing. Receiving this piece
actually takes us to a whole new level of growth; saving
them actually saves us because of this huge gift.

Exercise

*Imagine your supposed enemy standing before you. Recognise that
they represent the vital piece you are missing. Reach out and pull off
the enemy mask and costume to see the part of you that you thought
lost. When you see that part, ask yourself, 'How can I help you?'
Then give to it. Respond to it with support and love. Hold that part
and acknowledge that part as you. As it is supported and acknowl-
edged, it will begin to grow and mature to your present age, and then it
will melt back into you. Thus, you win back this missing part of you,
which brings more confidence, success and a new ability to receive in
this area.*

62.   MY LONELINESS COMES
FROM PROVING I AM SPECIAL

All our forms of separating ourself from others comes from wanting to be special in some way. Therefore, our loneliness is actually coming from the desire to prove we are special. At times, there is a certain poignancy to loneliness; we suffer quietly by ourself, feeling the pangs of our specialness. We would rather be special than make contact with others, but specialness always leads to pain. Specialness is always a form of separation, looking for special kinds of needs to be met. None of us can be lonely unless deep within ourself we want to be; loneliness is a choice.

Exercise

Today, examine the areas where you are asking to be treated specially. Acknowledge that your loneliness comes out of wanting to be different because you are afraid to be unique – a Leadership gift. Be willing to let go of this veil of specialness, this veil that keeps creating pain for you. Give up your choice for loneliness and make contact with those around you. Move past your need for specialness. Realise that you are recognised and appreciated, and that you have a natural attractiveness.

63.
I CREATE PROBLEMS AS
DISTRACTIONS WHEN I AM AFRAID
TO RECEIVE

When we are in situations where we were just about to receive and suddenly some kind of problem interferes, it is because we are afraid. As we take a deeper look at what fear might be creating these outside problems, we get in touch with the place where we feel threatened, overwhelmed, or where we think we would have to go into sacrifice to settle a debt. We will continue to create problems as outside distractions until we heal the fear of receiving.

Exercise

Today, be dedicated to finding the source of what is keeping you from receiving. Close your eyes and go deep down into yourself and just dwell there. As you rest in this place, allow yourself to begin to imagine what the fear that keeps you from receiving could be. As you get in touch with yourself, let the feelings of where you feel threatened, overwhelmed or in sacrifice come to the surface. Burn through this feeling by just feeling it until it is gone. You may find that the feeling will come in layers big enough that throughout the course of the day, you have to take time to feel it. Be willing to burn through each layer until it is gone. When it goes, you will be free to receive.

64. WHEN I AM AFRAID OF HOW GOOD IT CAN BE, I CREATE PROBLEMS

We create problems because we are afraid of receiving. We are afraid of receiving because we believe we are unworthy of what would come to us, or that it would overwhelm us by being too good for us.

We are the creator of our own life. This means that, ultimately, we are the ones responsible for the way our life is. As we take a look at our problems, we see that this is what we feel we deserve and are worthy of.

Exercise

Today, examine how you attack yourself with all the problems around you. Imagine you have created them because, at a subconscious level, you certainly have. They are all yours. Imagine that fear, the major dynamic of any problem, is at the core. Just sit there dwelling on your problem until your fear begins to emerge. As it emerges, feel it, and burn through it until it disappears.

65. MY RELATIONSHIP IS MY FASTEST PATH FOR GROWTH

We do not always appreciate all the things our relationship brings to us. Sometimes we think, 'I got into this relationship to be happy, and I've been far from it ever since the honeymoon ended.' Many times we complain about all the negative feelings we have to go through, all of the burden, heaviness, sacrifice, and all of the lessons we have had to face. For sure, the one thing a relationship gives us all the time is the path to our own growth. It constantly brings up every unhealed part of us as something between our partner and ourself so that we can mature, grow, and develop as a human being. Our relationship, even though it can be difficult and painful, is a constant invitation to keep evolving, and to move to higher understanding and deeper compassion.

Exercise

Today, do not run away from the unhealed parts. Take the day just to appreciate your relationship, because it leads you to deal with things that you could easily avoid if you were on your own. As negative feelings come up, feel them, communicate about them, and continue to forgive until they are gone. As you do, you will find a new level of trust within yourself and new levels of commitment, giving of yourself, and ability to receive. Your relationship is always calling this forth. Appreciate your partner and all those who've been around you, helping you mature by revealing those pieces in yourself that, once integrated, lead to healing.

66. TO END AN OUTSIDE CONFLICT, CHANGE IT ON THE INSIDE

Any conflict outside of us is an expression of a conflict within us. Often, the easiest way to heal outside conflict is to go within and find the two parts of our mind that are at war. The world around us is like a waking dream that reflects back to us what is going on in our deeper mind.

Exercise

Today, choose a conflict that you are experiencing. Close your eyes and feel yourself relaxing. Feel all the cares and worries of the week melting down through you, out of your feet, and into the floor. Now feel yourself drifting back through time and space to where this conflict began. How old were you when this occurred? Who was with you? What did you decide about yourself and about life? What were the other decisions you made that are now part of your belief system? Your belief system creates your reality. If you do not like this scene, then you can change it. Imagine that you were the writer of this script, and you wrote it for a certain purpose. What would be the purpose for writing this scene?

Now that you have grown and learned, there may be a much better way to succeed in that purpose. Knowing what you know now, how would you make that scene different? Even though you went through that experience, what you decide when you change the scene becomes the software of your mind. What you decide begins to dictate your reality to you. What would you choose to decide now? No matter what the situation or how anyone else acted, if you move forward with love, you will transform the situation.

67. THE LONGER I HOLD ON, THE MORE I LOSE

The longer we hold on, the more we lose. It is really important to know when to let go of our attachments, and allow for a new birth. In any relationship, the more we hold on, the more we lose our attractiveness and, thus, become a burden on our partner. If we are willing to let go of everything we think should be, the relationship can reach a new level of partnership. We may have to let go totally, because if there is any possibility for the relationship to move forward, it will only do so through our willingness to let go.

Exercise

Today, take a look around and see what you are holding on to. Is it a person, an old lover, or someone who's died? Is it a project? When you let go, look for something outside you to show you which way to move. Just let it go, and see what comes to you; be patient, it may take a few days. Remember, even if the person comes back to you, let them go at every turn so your non-attachment allows the relationship to keep unfolding and your attractiveness to keep growing.

68. WHEN I LET GO, SOMETHING BETTER ALWAYS COMES TO ME

When we let go, we are moved forward. If we have been holding on to something, we have been preventing ourself from receiving. When we let go, something much better will come to us. This can be either the same relationship at a new level, or something else much better. Either way, it will be something that is true for us and that will make ourself happier.

Exercise

Today is a day to let go, and to welcome and sit with a certain sense of expectancy. Have the courage to sit there, empty-handed, knowing the Universe abhors a vacuum and wants to fill it immediately. Just wait expectantly, knowing something good is coming your way.

69. EVERY POWER STRUGGLE IS A REMINDER OF A PLACE WHERE I HAVE BEEN HURT

Beneath every power struggle there is a heartbreak. In a power struggle our partner acts out the part of us that we pushed away, hid, or built a defence against because we believe that part hurt us or got us into trouble. Power struggles hold us back because they keep us stuck in a position of trying to defend our old hurt and heartbreaks, so we won't be hurt again. This hasn't worked so far and it won't work now. In recognising that any power struggle is a trigger to help us remember old hurt and pain so as to heal it, we can take the next step by integrating those parts of us that we thought hurt us. The healing of power struggle is really the healing of an old broken heart.

Exercise

Today, in this power struggle, allow yourself to feel all of the negative feelings as old feelings. Feel them through until they are gone and until nothing stands between you and your partner. Feel them through, until you can really embrace your partner as the person who is always giving you back a piece of your heart, a piece of your mind.

70. FEELING MY FEELINGS, THE MOST BASIC FORM OF HEALING

Everyone feels bad from time to time, but whenever we feel anything that is not powerful, loving, and good, it is really an opportunity for healing. Our willingness to feel our feelings until they are gone allows them to evaporate, almost like water on a hot frying pan.

Exercise

Today, as best you can, just feel your feelings. Experience them, even exaggerate them so you can move through them. You may find layer upon layer of negative feelings. These might be feelings of deadness or feelings where you are tempted to die, or you might go into feelings of numbness or emptiness. Whatever the feeling is, just burn it; know that it is not the truth. Don't be afraid to feel your feelings! Feeling your feelings is the most basic form of healing. As you re-associate with your feelings, you learn how to be a true partner because there is a direct correlation between partnership and feeling your true feelings without dissociation or hysteria. You learn how to open yourself to receive and you learn about commitment. Feeling your feelings is a gift you give to yourself and to everyone around you.

71. TO RESOLVE PROBLEMS IN MY RELATIONSHIPS, I FORGIVE MY MOTHER

Mothers are great scapegoats. We can blame them for any-thing we did not receive. As a matter of fact, at some level, whatever is negative in our present relationships is some form of blame on our mother for not giving us what we thought she should have given us. Our willingness to forgive our mother is our willingness to make our relationship, here and now, a lot better.

Exercise

Today, look at the problem in your relationship. You might even write out a number of them. Next to each problem write a response to the question: 'What have I not forgiven my mother for?' In the final column, next to each of the grievances against your mother, write the answer to these questions: 'Would I hold this against myself? Would I use this to stop me now in my relationship?' If the answer is no, you are free, your mother is free, and your relationship is free.

72.   EVERY EXPECTATION
IS A FEAR OF THE FUTURE

Expectations and demands come out of a sense of inadequacy, which is, at some hidden level, always defending against the future. We rush into the future with our expectations, but we have little ability to receive; we demand, but can neither receive, nor enjoy. Alternatively, we do not even bother moving forward at all because nothing could meet the level of our expectation. Both forms of behaviour are ways of defending against taking the next step. Either way, rushing into the future or not bothering to move at all holds us back. Even when rushing into the future, we still have one foot nailed to the floor, and so we go in circles; but at least we know where we're going. Every expectation is a fear of the future.

Exercise

Today, choose to put your future into God's hands. All day long, repeat this affirmation to yourself: 'I put my future into the hands of God.' Put any problem that comes up during the day into the hands of God. Know you are well taken care of and everything is moving forward in your best interest. (Yes, really!)

73. FEELING REJECTED MAY BE A DEFENCE AGAINST FEELING GUILTY

One of the purposes of rejection is it can hide guilt. The guilt may be for something we have done, or it may be from something in the past. For instance, a great deal of feeling rejected in childhood comes about as a result of a child's guilt for feeling attracted to the parent or sibling of the opposite sex. At the same time, the child also fears getting too close to them. As a result, he or she often creates some kind of rejection or separation so as to avoid dealing with the constant feeling of being bad or guilty.

Exercise

Today, realise that any feeling of rejection is really just a defence or a cover to hide feelings of unworthiness. Then, know that these feelings hide feelings of guilt.

Is this guilt coming from something in the past, the present, or both? Somehow, if you were to know what you are feeling guilty about, it probably had to do with you and with whom? If you were to know what occurred between you and that person to create this feeling of guilt that is now holding you back, what it must have been, is? Now, take your guilt and place it in the hands of God. Since God sees you as innocent, it would be arrogant of you to see yourself as guilty. You would then be using your guilt to hold yourself back from moving forward and taking the next step. This is a day to forgive yourself and to allow yourself to be free from the guilt and rejection.

74. THE EXTENT OF MY INDEPENDENCE IS TO THE EXTENT I DENY MY DEPENDENCE

Independence is a stage of growth that we go into after we have been dependent. Typically, there are two primary reasons for becoming independent. The first is because we have been so heartbroken or jealous that it was too painful for us to remain dependent any longer. We decided to become independent so we would not allow ourself to be in a position where we could be rejected again. The second reason is that by being in sacrifice to other people, we burned out. We decided to become independent so as to not allow ourself to be manipulated again.

The extent to which we are independent is also the extent to which we disassociated from our feelings. In other words, the degree of our independence is how much business we left unfinished in our dependent stage before we ran away from it. We can tell how independent we are by how much we move away from people who are needy. The extent to which we are revolted by them is the extent to which we are feeling repulsed by our own neediness. Our independence is our choice to be out of touch with these feelings so we do not have to deal with situations where we could feel hurt because of our neediness.

Exercise

Today, take a look at the extent to which you are independent. By being independent, you have attracted people around you who are dependent because they reflect this part of your mind for you. Reach out to these people, not from a place of sacrifice, but from a place of giving to them as well as the dependent part of you that they reflect. Realise as you are giving to them (reaching out with the truth) that you are also helping yourself by getting in touch with your old feelings. As you help them out of their dependence, you help yourself clear up your unfinished neediness.

75. DEAD ZONE, THE FINAL STAGE OF INDEPENDENCE

In our culture we have been taught that the final stage of growth is independence, but in truth, independence is just a stage along the way to true partnership, interdependence. To move into interdependence we have to be willing to adopt a completely different set of guidelines regarding the rules for the game of life; what was very successful in independence proves to hold us back in interdependence. The final stage of independence, this great stage we have all been taught to aspire to, is a stage of deadness that I affectionately call the Dead Zone. In the Dead Zone we do things because we are supposed to do them, not because we choose to do them.

As independents we are the great rebels of life and won't allow ourself to be captured. However, the extent to which we are the rebel is the extent to which we are hiding that marshmallow of a sacrificer inside us. In the Dead Zone we experience exhaustion and a deep weariness because, as with all stages of independence, we are unable to receive and, therefore, we are unable to refresh and renew ourself.

Independence means our feminine side has not yet fully healed and it is with this that we receive. It is this side of us that nurtures and gives us the fuel to carry on. As our feminine side is valued, it comes into balance with our masculine side and partnership begins. The Dead Zone feels like *stuckness* – being caught up in a pattern. We feel like a failure, no matter how much of a success we are to other people. We also feel tempted to die because we are *soooo* tired.

It is here in the Dead Zone that the essential character of independence is hidden. Competition, here at the final stage of independence, is where we become such a great competitor that we don't even bother to compete; when we are the best, why bother? Competition still drives us forward by making us work, rather than receive our reward.

Exercise

Today, make the choice to let go of independence, and state, 'I am finally willing to go to this higher stage, even if I don't know what it is.' You can ask the Universe or God, 'Please teach me.' Your willingness will allow you to be taught by providing you with relationships where you can begin to learn what true interdependence is.

76. THERE IS NO PAIN MY LOVE
COULD NOT HEAL

Our love has the power to join, the power to support, and the power to heal the world. Every problem is the result of some form of separation, but our love can build a bridge and join us with that person. Our love can fill that emptiness, because behind our love is the power of the universe and the power of miracles. As we give our love to everyone, the world around us is healed.

Exercise

Today, you can make a difference. Someone is specifically calling for your help. Who is it? You do not have to be with or talk to them directly. Visualise them in front of you and pour your love into them. Fill them with your love. See them happy, healed, and whole. Even if you speak no words of love, the love of the Universe will pour through you to your friend who is in need.

77. WHEN THINGS GET WORSE, THEY MAY BE GETTING BETTER

It is important that we learn to live without judgement, because it limits our experience of the truth. Many times when healing occurs, the situation feels more painful and looks messier, but true healing is taking place; it is a birth. When a baby is born, there may be screaming and pain, and it can be very messy, but a new life is coming into the world.

When we sincerely reach out to join our partner and, then, things seem to blow up, we can feel like we failed; we decide not to bother trying again. This explosion, though, is often the very sign that a surface layer has been healed. The next layer of repressed matter is coming up; what was hidden beneath is now at the surface. It is because we have succeeded in joining our partner that deeper pain can now come to the fore. When that occurs, reaching out once again to our partner and joining them will allow what just boiled out to be easily healed. When this occurs, rather than judge the outcome, be aware that having hit the next mountain top of success, it is only a matter of time before we venture down into the next valley of conflict – the very next thing our partner and ourself are to heal. As that gets healed, we will reach a new mountain top, and so on as we evolve forward.

Exercise

Today, change your attitude toward pain. Take a much deeper look at every painful thing you are experiencing because, at the heart of it, there may be a new birth, a new healing, and a new life for you, your partner and the relationship. With the pain that you recognise, be willing to join someone close to you. This will resolve the pain or a layer of it. Recognise that if you are not feeling better or worse, you may have tapped into a many-layered chronic problem. When this occurs, you may only experience a second or two of respite before the next layer hits, but your awareness will let you know that you're moving in the right direction.

78.   THE ULTIMATE GOAL IS
TOTAL DEPENDENCE ON THE UNIVERSE

The initial stages of growth are Dependence, Independence, and Interdependence, but the highest stage is Radical Dependence – dependence on the Universe, on God. This is the form of consciousness where we know that good things are coming to us and that our openness to receiving allows many blessed events to come our way. Like the birds of the air and the lilies of the field, we will be supported, loved, and taken care of as a child of God.

The thought of such radical dependence terrorises us. We have learned to take control and be independent. Now, as we move forward, we are being asked to give up control and to learn greater lessons of trust, and of letting ourself rest in the Hands of God.

Exercise

Today, every time you notice yourself trying to do something, choose that it be done for you or through you, rather than by you. Every time you find yourself trying to get out of a difficulty, get out of your own way and trust that it will be done for you. It is time to be, rather than do. Just trust and open yourself. Allow yourself to be totally loved and cared for in every way, like a little baby, in the Hands of God.

79.   WHEN I FEEL MYSELF CONTRACT,
I REACH OUT AND GIVE

We contract when we feel self-conscious, embarrassed, ashamed, mortified, guilty, fearful, or hurt. One of the simplest forms of healing is to reach out and give. This is an act of Leadership and love, which never allows us to be caught by our own problems because the love for someone else is a stronger calling than our own contraction.

Exercise

When you feel hurt or are in any form of difficulty, realise there may be someone in even greater pain. Ask yourself who this might be, and see who pops into your mind. Feel yourself reaching out to them. As you reach out to give to them, you will find yourself once again in the flow. As you reach out and give, both this person and you are healed.

80. A PROBLEM OCCURS IN MY RELATIONSHIP WHEN I AM AFRAID TO TAKE THE NEXT STEP

Many times problems are just distractions from taking the next step. I have seen major problems fall away when a person becomes willing to take the next step. When a problem occurs the answer comes with it. Our willingness to trust this and move forward allows us to know what the answer is. Once we have taken the next step, whatever the issue is will completely disappear or it may just be something to handle, but it will no longer be a problem.

Exercise

Today, choose the three juiciest problems in your life. Take five minutes in the morning to explore the first problem, and say, 'I will not be fooled by this problem. I know this is just the result of fear, and I can step through this fear by taking the next step. I say Yes to the next step in my life. I trust this next step will come to me. I know that it is better than this. I will not be caught by this problem. This problem is not the truth.'

In the afternoon, choose the second problem, and spend another five minutes on it. In the evening, do this once again with the third problem. You will be very happy with the results!

81. MY EXPECTATIONS COMPENSATE FOR HIDDEN NEEDS

Our expectations come out of our demands which come from our needs; therefore, our expectations are a defence against our needs. They are a way of acting as if we are not dependent. Acting in an independent mode, we demand the situation move toward our picture of how reality should be, but any type of defence, expectation included, always leads to failure, and actually brings about the very thing it was trying to defend against. Our expectations eventually lead us to frustration or disappointment, a place where we begin to experience our own needs and neediness.

Exercise

Today, practice giving up your demands and truly communicating about what you need; often, communicating about it satisfies the need itself. Your demand is a clue to the area of your need. Basically, all of these needs cover up old feelings of sadness, abandonment, and lack of bonding. Your communication is the beginning of bonding again. Even if communication does not succeed in fulfilling your needs, it will give you the confidence to deal with them openly without trying to control others.

82. PAIN AND CONFLICT IN MY RELATIONSHIP COME FROM BROKEN RULES

The pain or conflict we experience in a relationship comes because we feel our partner has broken the rules we established. Our partner will inadvertently or, sometimes, intentionally break our rules just for our healing and benefit. We may not have told our partner that we had these rules, but we think if they *really* loved us, they should have known. We set up these rules to protect us from being wounded again. As we all know though, rules are made to be broken, as all this pain is meant to be healed. If our partner had not broken our rules and triggered our pain, we would never have dealt with it.

This pain needed to come out for our healing and growth and for our ability to partner on a new level. Rather than blaming our partner for not loving us, we could be appreciating them for this. If our rules truly worked, we would not still be experiencing pain or conflict. As we give up our rules and feel the pain we have buried, there will be no need to make rules for protection.

Exercise

Today, write down every rule you have about relationships, about how you should be treated, about sex, about love. This could be one of the funniest days of your life when you see what your rules are and how contradictory some of them are. At the end of the day, after having shared these rules with your partner, who probably will really enjoy them, burn them. In burning them, let them go.

Now, it is time to choose principles for your relationship. Principles create dialogue and they are both resilient and flexible. They are not meant to be broken as rules are, but to be goals that are life-sustaining.

93

83. IN ANY CONFLICT, BOTH PEOPLE
ARE FEELING THE SAME THING

In any conflict, people act out opposite behaviours, but underneath their behaviour, they are feeling the same thing. For instance, one person may be a spendthrift and the other a miser. Both people are feeling the same sense of scarcity, the fear that there is not enough. The spendthrift compensates for this feeling by spending excessively to get over this fear. The miser, on the other hand, pinches pennies to protect against the feeling of scarcity. In any power struggle both people are trying to protect themselves against the same feeling.

If we are in touch with our feelings, we can then be in touch with the feeling underneath our partner's behaviour. Our willingness to begin communicating about this feeling allows us to find a common place, a beginning of something that we share. This is the beginning of healing, because once we find an area of common connection, we are on our way to moving forward together.

Exercise

Today, choose a person with whom you are in conflict, and ask yourself, 'What is the feeling underneath my behaviour?' Now take a look at their behaviour and see if their feeling fits with yours. Naturally, when you are at the most essential feeling, you find that it fits exactly. If you come to a feeling of anger, realise anger is a defence that protects an even deeper feeling. Whatever your deeper feeling, be willing to begin the communication by sharing your feelings with the purpose of moving ahead. For instance, you could start off by saying, 'I'm feeling this feeling, are you feeling it too?'

84. WHEN MY FEAR OR RESISTANCE IS TOO STRONG FOR ME TO MOVE TOWARD MY PARTNER, I ASK FOR HEAVEN'S HELP

We know moving toward our partner is the answer to every problem, but there are times when we are in so much pain, are so exhausted, or have so much resistance that we feel we just cannot take one more step in any direction. This is the time to ask for Heaven's help, to ask for renewed strength to take another step toward our partner. Many times that strength will carry us right to the heart of our partner. Sometimes, the resistance or pain may be so strong, we have to ask for Heaven's help every step of the way. When this happens, it means we are healing a chronic pattern within us, a layer of deep pain. Being willing to ask for help for every step will let grace carry us forward and energise us.

Exercise

Today, in any situation where it seems too difficult for you to move toward anyone, ask for Heaven's help. Allow grace to help you to move toward each of these people until, once again, you feel you have a sense of closeness and a sense of common purpose.

85.   EVERY HERO NEEDS A VILLAIN
OR SOMEONE TO SAVE

When we act out the role of the hero in our relationship, we need to find situations where we can demonstrate our greatness; we need to find a way to save the day. Every hero needs a villain or someone to save. This means our partner has to play the role of the villain, or of someone who constantly needs to be saved. Our hero does not make for a happy choice. Taking centre stage as the star always means setting up a subtle competition where our partner has to play the supporting role. They get to look bad so we can get to look good.

Every role is a compensation for the feeling that we are no good. Therefore, the purpose for playing the hero role is to cover over our feelings that we are bad. On the other hand, to be a villain also comes out of bad feelings, as does the need to be saved. If we feel bad and deny it, we take on roles. In any role, we cannot receive because all the rewards go to the role. As we learn to be more in touch with ourself and our own feelings, nobody has to play the supporting role. Our willingness to commit to our partner also being the star is a step in commitment that moves us both forward. Being willing to give up whatever our role is, to re-associate with our feelings, gives us a greater ability to receive. It allows us to have the capacity to move forward, arm in arm, with our partner. This makes us a true hero, rather than just being in a hero role.

Exercise

Today, begin to look under the hero costume you are wearing. Whether it is the hero, villain, or needy role, bad feelings lie

96

underneath. *The extent of your bad feelings is also the extent your partner feels bad inside. You may have been caught up in this role since you were a child, fantasising or creating situations of saving the day, of helping the needy, or of stopping the villainy in order to fulfil yourself. Be willing to communicate about the feelings your role may be covering, so both you and your partner can move forward together.*

86. I CANNOT BE A VICTIM
UNLESS I AM TRYING TO GET REVENGE

All of us have been victims. Welcome to the human race. Now, as we reach higher levels of consciousness, we try to become independent so we will not be victimised. This does not always work. The truest way to give up being a victim is to give up our need for revenge. One of the most hidden dynamics in any victim situation is the search for revenge. We are in a power struggle where the way to get back at someone is to hurt ourself. As children, when we did not get what we wanted, we sometimes threw tantrums and hurt ourself. We felt rejected, so we did something to get revenge. 'Mum and Dad, you'll be sorry, I'll never eat again'. 'Mum and Dad, you'll be sorry, I'm going to stop breathing.' 'I'll run away for ever and then you'll be sorry.' Sometimes as teenagers in our first relationships, we thought, 'I'll drive my car so fast and crash into the wall and die, and then they'll be sorry. They'll know how much I meant to them, and it will be too late.' Basically, this attitude is still going on in any victim situation. In sickness, injury, or failure we are actually getting revenge on someone.

Exercise

Today, sit quietly and let a present victim situation such as illness, loss, heartbreak, or accidents come to your mind. Then ask yourself, 'Who am I getting revenge on?' Let other victim situations come to your mind, and ask yourself the same question. While it is true revenge is a double-edged sword, the answer here is more than just yourself. Revenge hides under chronic victim situations, yet you are only using someone to hold yourself back. Be willing to see how revenge is a form of avoidance of taking the next step. It is hurting yourself in an attempt to emotionally blackmail someone, and it will not work. Even if you win the power struggle, you may have to go so far as to die as a victim to get your point across.

87. EVERY STEP I TAKE TOWARD MY PARTNER IS A STEP IN PERSONAL POWER

Every time we take a step toward our partner, we reaffirm our own power. If our partner is in need and we step toward them, we do so out of our fullness. If it is too difficult for us, we can take the step by asking for Heaven's help to move toward them. Every step we move toward our partner empowers us. Even in situations where we are in pain and our partner is doing fine, if we step toward them, we feel stronger and begin to move through our pain.

Exercise

Today, consciously empower yourself by continuously stepping toward your partner.

88. EVERYONE'S ACTIONS REFLECT MY CHOICES

A major step in maturity is realising that others' actions reflect our choices. It is also a major step in understanding the power of our mind and the nature of the subconscious. When people realise this is true, they are sometimes tempted to feel guilty for events that have taken place, but this is a mistake because everyone is innocent. Everyone is basically doing the best they can given inner and outer experience, yet we all can do better. Everyone is making these choices mutually, somehow believing that this choice will bring them happiness. Sometimes the choices we make are mistakes, but this is not a reason for guilt, which is a trap of the ego to disempower us. Mistakes actually provide an opportunity for connection, correcting the mistake and joining others.

Everyone involved makes choices, one hundred percent. If one person in the situation desisted from agreeing, it would change the consensual reality, then the situation would not occur. We could choose to see that person as a reflection of our mind and make a choice to help, which would empower them and us at the same time.

This means that, in our relationship, we are responsible not only for our behaviour and feelings, but also for our thoughts – the choices we are making in our mind. Our thoughts create the scenario in our relationship. Most of the time, however, we are totally unaware of our thoughts. In any given two-mile stretch of road that we might drive, we think an average of two thousand thoughts. How many of those thoughts are we conscious of? As we become aware of our thoughts, we become more empowered and we make better choices. Our relationship is the result of some of the choices we are making, even though not all of these choices may be conscious ones.

Exercise

Today, get in touch with what choices you are making in your relationship. Ask yourself, 'What would be the purpose of having my partner act this way? What does it allow me to do? What is it I do not have to do? Who am I getting back at by having this happen? What old debt does it pay off for me?' Let go of any guilt that comes up and, then, consciously choose what you want. All day long let your affirmation be, 'I choose (whatever it is you want in your relationship).' To do that once with full sincerity empowers you to change both the subconscious and unconscious minds. As you choose, feelings and beliefs that stand between you and what you want may come up. Be willing to choose again in the face of whatever feeling is present. Choose what it is you want. Do not stand for less.

89.   MY COMPLAINTS ARE
A DIRECT ATTACK ON MYSELF

Every time we complain, we are saying we do not have the power to make a difference in the situation. Of course this is foolish because we have a great deal of power. When we are complaining, we are making ourself small. There is a risk we are afraid to take, and there is some action we are not taking that we have been called to do. By our complaints, we are becoming part of the problem. We are saying, 'This problem is real, and I'm stuck with it, and I can't do anything about it.' *Au contraire!*

Exercise

Today, see where you can make a difference. Catch yourself in every complaint you make and, instead of complaining, take a step forward and reach out to someone, forgive someone, or take action to make the situation better. Pay attention not only to the complaints you make vocally, but also to those you make in your mind. As the poet e. e. cummings writes, 'I'd rather teach one bird how to sing than ten thousand stars how not to dance.'

90. ANY JUDGEMENT AGAINST OTHERS
IS A JUDGEMENT AGAINST MYSELF

We cannot judge unless we are feeling guilty about something. Otherwise, we would simply see that a mistake has been made and, with our support, it can easily be corrected. When we feel guilty about a mistake or something similar we have repressed, then our guilt will come out as a judgement against someone else. This will keep us stuck with our guilt and what we have judged. If we will only forgive, we will not have to search our subconscious mind to find where all our hidden guilt is. Forgiveness not only releases our partner or the person we have judged, it re-establishes their innocence, and it re-establishes our innocence. What we, or they, have done is not a sin. It is just a mistake.

A mistake can be corrected, but a sin is almost impossible to correct. We obsess about a sin, coming back to it again and again in our mind until eventually we bury our guilt and project it onto others. This, of course, is a situation that keeps us from growing.

Exercise

Today, take a look at the person you are judging the most. Just for a moment, imagine that the very thing you are judging them for is true about you. Dwell on that quality until you actually begin to feel, 'Yes, this is guilt I have hidden away, but this is not true about me, either. I'm not going to hold this against them, because I'm not going to hold it against myself.' Getting in touch with that hidden feeling and burning it, or just refusing to hold it against them so you are set free, allows the whole situation to move forward.

91. TO THE EXTENT I AM INDULGENT IS TO THE EXTENT I AM IN SACRIFICE

When we indulge we are compensating for all the sacrifice we are doing. If we were just truly giving, we would have to be truly receiving. There would be no need to indulge – with food, work, sex, alcohol, drugs, etc. – which wears us out as much as our sacrifice does. A vicious cycle of indulgence/sacrifice is set up as we indulge, then feel guilty we have indulged, and then go into sacrifice to make up for the guilt. The cycle repeats as we burn out from the sacrifice, because we then feel it's okay to indulge ourself and do exactly what we want, with a certain level of rebellion or resentment toward those to whom we feel in sacrifice.

Exercise

Today, look at the areas where you have indulgences or addictions. Are you a workaholic? Are you a foodaholic? Take a clear look at where you feel you are not in the centre of your own life. Where you are not in the centre, where you are not being true to yourself, you are in sacrifice. Come to the centre of your life, and move out of the indulgence and sacrifice. Imagine there is a centre in you. What percentage from 0 – 100 did you get off your centre? (Usually readings of 30% – 80% reflect heavy sacrifice, while 80% – 100% reflect self-destructiveness in the cycle of sacrifice and indulgence.) What experience took you off your centre? Go back there now, and choose, once again, to centre yourself. At this point, from your centre, you can give the gift that the people around you really need. This gift is part of who you are.

92. ANGER IS BLAMING OTHERS
FOR WHAT I THINK I DID

All anger lacks integrity. If we feel angry, however, there is an integrity in recognising what we are experiencing. After we have realised our anger, it is important not to use our anger to try to control the situation. As soon as we communicate about our anger, we can begin to move through it. If we are just openly expressing our anger, we are trying to control the situation by blaming our partner or the people around us for things we feel bad about. As parents, when we get angry at a child for acting in a certain way, we are angry at things we believe about ourself, or we have fears about what the child will grow up to be. That fear, too, comes from beliefs we hold about ourself. By changing these beliefs and healing the fear, there would be more flexibility and creativity within the parent and, therefore, in regard to treating the child. We would treat the child in a more creative or responsive fashion.

Our anger is the attempt to project onto others our own feelings about ourself, to pretend the very quality we are angry about has nothing to do with us. We, of course, are innocent. In truth, we are just projecting our anger at ourself onto others. It is our own fear and guilt that actually drives our anger and our attack.

Exercise

Today, choose to see that all anger covers bad feelings. Be willing to recognise that what the other person is acting out for us is something we feel bad about. Recognising this can be the beginning of communica-tion, and of a new level of honesty and integrity. Recognise that if the person is not acting out of love, they are calling for love, and if we are willing not to judge, we can offer a support that can totally transform the situation. A successful relationship is one that communicates rather than controls by anger.

93. ALL ANGER COMES FROM LACK OF TRUST AND PAST HURTS

At some level all of our anger is about the past. Where we were hurt in the past are the same places we feel hurt in the present; since we imagine the present and past situations as the same, we get angry. If we were to bring trust into the deeper feelings of hurt inside us, the fear and pain in the situation would begin to unfold in a healing fashion. Pain, therefore, becomes a vehicle for communication, which provides a much bigger reward than the anger can bring to the situation. What we get angry at, we reinforce, and we get stuck with it. While anger might allow us to win the battle, it will cause us to lose the war. If we gain control and win the battle, our partner's loss makes them unattractive to us.

Exercise

Today, use your trust to recognise that this situation is not like the past. Even though it looks as if you might be hurt, this is the chance for facing that old feeling, this chronic pattern, so you can step forward with a new level of confidence, knowing it will turn out for the very best.

94. ANGER IS ALWAYS AN ATTEMPT TO CONTROL THROUGH GUILT

Anger, with its aggression and sometimes violence, is always an attempt to control. It is always an attempt to have the situation moved our way and also to make the other person feel guilty. As such, it is always a form of blackmail. Anger says, 'Look at what you have done to me. You should have done it better. It is your fault I am this way. Do it better and take better care of me.' Anger is a form of control whereby we win the battle, but lose the war; the more guilt we sow, the more resentment we reap. We may control a person through our anger or through their guilt for a long time, but eventually they explode, and we lose them.

Exercise

Today, taking a risk will move you forward. If you are using your anger as a tool to hide your fear, instead of exploding at every opportunity to get your way, it is time to start talking about what you are feeling. Talk about your fear so you can move to higher levels of confidence and greater levels of satisfaction. Share that first level of anger, but then immediately share the feeling underneath it; then the feeling underneath that until you feel completely at peace. Sometimes, you might even get in touch with where the situation or feeling began. Sharing about it and the effect it had on you brings a healing balm.

95. ANGER IS A WAY OF CONTROLLING
TO GET MY NEEDS MET

When we get angry, it is because things are not going our way. We use anger to demand things go our way so we get to be right, or get our needs met first. Anger sets up a pattern that locks us into our neediness. When we use anger, we believe others will too, which causes us fear – one of the aspects that creates needs. We fall into a vicious cycle of needs, anger, fear, and needs again; a habit is formed. Often, just communicating about our needs helps to fulfil them by taking that risk in communication. We build up our own maturity. More importantly, whether we get a particular need met or not, we have moved forward and empowered ourself.

When we are honest with ourself, we begin to see that anger does not really work because with it, we alienate those people who could meet our needs. Rather than controlling through anger, we can speak what we are feeling, and move toward our partner to join them.

Exercise

Today, find the person with whom you are angriest. Imagine beside them the person you love the most – it may be the same person. Look at the person you love the most, look beyond their body, their personality, and their mistakes to see the light shining inside them. Imagine your light and their light joined together. Rest in that feeling of peace for a while. Now, take a look at the person with whom you are really angry. Look past their body, their personality, and their mistakes, to see the essence of them – that light, that spirit shining inside them. Now, joined with the person you love, feel the combined light moving to join with the other person's light. When all the lights have joined, feel yourself resting in this deeper place of peace.

96.   ANGER HIDES GRACE

If we care to notice, sometimes, when we get angry at our partner for the littlest things, it is when they have wanted to lavish us with love. Often, in our smugness about really telling them what is bugging us, we choose the anger and do not even recognise we missed an opportunity to feel joyful. If we keep our awareness about us, we will see we really have a choice between our anger and receiving their love.

Anger is generated from judgement. If we pay attention to our anger, we can see we have a choice in the matter. The natural physiological reaction of anger lasts about $4\frac{1}{2}$ minutes. After that, it is something we harbour and choose to feel. The judgement of anger hides the opportunity for grace, for something miraculous. If we are aware and willing, instead of judging, we can use the opportunity to offer support and love, to feel joyful. We can then be a channel of grace in the situation. Every time we offer grace, we have naturally received it in order to proffer it. If we make the choice for grace instead of grievance, we can become an emissary of transformation and healing – an emissary for Heaven.

Exercise

Today, take the time to notice where, in your judgement, you are either withdrawing or becoming aggressive. Make the choice for love and grace. Look back in your life to significant times of withdrawal or attack, and in your mind's eye, make a new choice for grace. In offering grace, the situation is finally transformed.

97.   COMMITMENT OPENS ME
TO RECEIVING

Our commitment is our choice to fully give ourself as much as we possibly can. Giving and receiving are naturally tied together; the more we move into commitment, the more we give to something and the more we receive from it. The more we give to our partner, the more we recognise our partner's beauty, their gifts, and how great they are. Giving to them is what allows us to have the eyes of love that can truly see how wonderful they are. It is our commitment, our giving, our love, that determines how great they are.

How significant a situation is for us depends on how much we have given ourself to it, how committed we are. The extent we are receiving is directly related to our level of commitment in our relationship. Any situation where we have gone beyond ourself and exceeded what we have known ourself to be, moves us into an altered state of consciousness. By giving that much, we are open to receiving great gifts of joy and ecstasy. The greater our commitment and giving, the more we can receive.

Exercise

Today, look at a situation where you wish you were receiving more. Explore how you could give yourself more fully and choose to do so. Sacrifice does not count. Remember, sacrifice is counterfeit commitment. Making the choice to give of yourself allows you to enjoy the situation more. The more you give, the more you enjoy yourself, and the more you receive. Commitment is a choice for giving.

113

98.
COMMITMENT MEANS
BEING TRUE TO MYSELF

It is only when we commit that we really begin to learn who we are. When we commit, we give ourself so much that we begin to know our true essence and what really matters to us. This knowledge comes, not from holding back and complaining, but from giving above and beyond what the contract says – going beyond the call of duty and what is expected of us. Commitment means being true to ourself, getting to know the richness and depth of our being. We get to know the self to whom things come easily. We get to know our best self.

Exercise

Today, remember a time when you felt you had given yourself a hundred percent, with no expectations, a time when you had gone beyond yourself. Go back to that situation. Feel the feelings there. Hear what people were saying to you. What did things look like there? Just revel in that a moment. Now bring that feeling up into your present situation. What is it you would like to do differently now? How much more would you choose to give yourself in this situation? That feeling of joy that comes through giving yourself totally can be yours. Total giving begins to unlock grace and hidden resources. It is the stuff miracles are made of.

99.   NO PROBLEM CAN
WITHSTAND COMMITMENT

Any problem points to a conflict in our mind where parts of us are vying for different needs to be met. No problem can withstand the choice and commitment that join all parts of us together. Commitment is giving ourself one hundred percent. No problem can withstand one hundred percent commitment. When a problem begins to unfold and we take the next step, if we continue giving one hundred percent while taking one step after the other, there is a certain flow. Things easily come to us. Doors open. Opportunities occur. Luck happens. No problem can withstand the power of our choice to give ourself one hundred percent.

Exercise

Today, examine the major problem that is confronting you. Ask yourself what percentage you are giving of yourself in this situation. When did you withdraw the other percentage of yourself? Was it long ago in the past, or just a short time ago? You have the power to totally transform this experience by your commitment. Total commitment, giving yourself this much, creates a state of vision in your life – living for a positive future in the present. Make the choice to give yourself one hundred percent in this situation because nothing can withstand you giving yourself that much.

100. MY PAIN CAN BE A DEFENCE AGAINST MY SEXUAL ENERGY

We may be embarrassed about our sexual energy because we feel guilty about how we have used it in the past, or just about being so sexual. We feel as if we could not handle the attention or that we would not know how to say no. It also certainly would be a clutter if every one of the opposite sex, including dogs, cats, and horses, followed us home. To feel our own energy, however, is to experience something rich and healing, something that *youthens* us and is a gift to our partner. As we move forward in consciousness, so does our sexual energy grow. The growth and evolvement of our sexual energy is a necessary part of us moving into higher areas of consciousness. All joy contains this kind of electrical, exciting energy.

Exercise

Today, you can move through your pain easily by your willingness to feel your sexual energy, and you can make it safe by the amount of love you give with it.

101. HEARTBREAK IS AN ACT OF REVENGE

To experience heartbreak means we have been on the losing end of a power struggle. In these kinds of situations, we often use some form of emotional blackmail to fight back. One of the best forms of emotional blackmail is a heartbreak. Being heartbroken is a way of getting back at the other person. We stand bleeding on their doorstep, saying, 'This person can't be such a good person if this is what they have done to me. I will stand on their doorstep for ever and ever as a monument to what a rotten person they are.' Our heartbreak is a form of revenge.

Exercise

Today, acknowledge your heartbreak as another tactic in the power struggle. Revenge is a place of hardened power struggle. Our heartbreaks are just an example of this kind of calcification. Forgive the people who seem to have broken your heart, including yourself. Do not use another to hold yourself back.

102. WHAT IS MISSING IN MY RELATIONSHIP IS WHAT I AM NOT GIVING

When we want more of anything in our relationship, it is time for us to bring it in. Expecting our partner to bring it in won't work because, if we are the one that sees the relationship needs something and we want it there, then we are the one that is called to give it. It is our function and purpose to provide what we see missing in the relationship. Our complaining will not bring it about; however, giving it will. It is time to stop complaining and start giving.

In a relationship, people bring different gifts. Giving our gifts in the most creative way possible is our joy. With creative giving, we have fun and grow in confidence while opening ourself. We move our relationship forward by what we give it.

Remember, it is not only about giving the form of what we want, like sex for example, but also about giving more of our sexual energy to make sex more attractive. Sometimes, when our partner does not want sex, it signals a place where we may have withdrawn from them sexually. Moving into a higher level of sexual energy will inspire our partner.

Exercise

Today, explore what your relationship seems to need the most. What would you like more of? Romance? Love? Abundance? Then what are you waiting for? Over the next week, give something related to this need in a different and creative way every day. Especially give the energetic feeling of these qualities.

118

103. WHAT I THINK I NEED IS WHAT I AM CALLED TO GIVE

The easiest way to heal a need is to give what we feel we need. Our needs in a relationship are the very things we are called to give. Usually, our biggest complaint against our parents is that they did not meet our needs, but what we needed from our parents is, actually, the very thing we came to give them. When we give to them what we thought we needed from them, our need is resolved.

Waiting for someone else to fill our needs is one of the biggest elements in our conspiracy against our own growth; it stops us from moving forward. Our needs in a relationship show us, if we are willing to see, the very thing that we are to give. Taking this step in Leadership by giving to others what we thought we needed allows everyone to win; by giving, we, too, receive.

Exercise

Today, take a look at what you feel you need. Take the responsibility yourself for bringing it into the relationship. If there is something you need at work or in your family, choose to be the one to bring it there. Being the leader in this will make you very happy because you are in a position where you can really do some good for yourself and others.

104. CONSIDERING HOW HARD IT SEEMS TO BE TO CHANGE WITHIN MYSELF, IT IS FOOLISH TO EXPECT TO CHANGE SOMEONE ELSE

Considering how hard it seems for us to create change within ourself, our desire to change someone else is foolish. We only need look at our own track record in this area to see how well we have done. Even when we do succeed, we lose, because the person loses their attractiveness for us. The easiest way to get someone to change is to change ourself. To move forward ourself is an irresistible call to our partner to join us.

Exercise

Today, be willing to change yourself. Who is the main person in your life that you want to be different? This very person represents an area in you that has been hardened and unwilling to change. Ask for Heaven's help in stepping forward to give this very thing that would have them be different. Take the step forward yourself, and be willing to give what you wanted of someone else. Your happiness is at stake and it is in your hands.

105.   *BUSYNESS* TRAPS ME
IN WHAT IS VALUELESS

We live in busy times. Even though technology is here to save us time, somehow the projects we undertake – business, hobbies and activities we engage in, and the events that we go to – all seem to proliferate. The more technology we gain, the busier we seem to become. Many times this *busyness* can take over our relationships. We move from one activity to another and do not take the time just to enjoy our partner, to receive and experience who they are. In the midst of all this *busyness*, we could take the time to realise what has value for us, what it is that will last us for all eternity versus just a flash in the pan.

Exercise

Today, look at what 'busyness' you have been using to distract yourself from spending time with your partner. You may be doing things together, but you may not be coming together. Be willing to realise that your busyness and your valuelessness may be distracting you from building up your heart, from building up meaning in your life. Think of yourself twenty years from now. What will this activity have meant then? Think of your last day of life. Would this activity have had importance compared with spending time with your beloved? Be willing to let go of the extraneous 'busyness' and to value what is truly valuable.

106. UNDER EVERY ROLE
IS A TEMPTATION TO DIE

Roles cover over a lot of pain. A role is a hard outer shell, a piece of character we began to take on in a situation where we felt like we wanted to die. We felt so valueless, like such a total failure, that we gave up our selfhood and took on a role. A role is doing the right thing for the wrong reason, and because of this, it never lets us receive. No matter how much we succeed, we are not nurtured by the reward. A role may help a child early in life to have a good sense of character, and even to know right from wrong, but later on in life those roles become the armour that weighs us down, the heaviness that exhausts us. We are not being nurtured by what we are doing since we are doing it because we are supposed to. Beneath every role is a sense of tiredness, a sense of worthlessness about who we are. These are the original feelings that helped us build the roles, for roles are compensations and defences. Everyone around us may think we are a great success, but we feel worn out, a mere shell or even a fraud. Roles look good, but they weigh us down and kill us.

Exercise

If you are in touch with these original feelings of valuelessness and worthlessness, know that you are just naturally working through a role and understand what the role has compensated for. One of the easiest ways to move through a role is through choice. Instead of just automatically doing what you feel you are supposed to do, make a choice that, 'This is what I choose to do.' Your choice then creates a true form of giving, an aspect of your life that can heal you and feed you. *True giving, where you really give, not because you are supposed to, but because you choose to, makes all the difference.*

If you are getting to a place of death temptation, which is at the bottom of every role you have, do not be frightened of it. Face the death temptation, knowing it is the way through and that at the other end, there is a place of breakthrough. Running away from the feeling of wanting to die simply empowers it. Face it squarely while choosing to live. Feel the feelings until they are gone to move you past the death temptation. What was a role for you now becomes real; you now have regained the centre you lost so long ago.

107. HOW ANOTHER IS GIVING TO ME
IS HOW THEY WOULD LIKE
TO BE GIVEN TO

If we were to take a look at what the people closest to us give us when they give us gifts, we would notice that they often give the gifts that they would love to have. When we notice how others support us, we see how they would love to be supported. If we observe our partner closely, we will be able to give to them in a way that allows them to feel truly loved. For instance, if our partner is always telling us, 'I love you,' we know to say that back to them. If our partner supports us by doing things, then we support them in the same way. If our partner touches us a lot, touch them back; it is what they would really love.

Exercise

Today, study your partner. When they truly give to you, they give you what they would love to have. To give what others are giving you is a key to helping people really feel they are loved.

108. TRIANGLE RELATIONSHIPS ARISE FROM THE BELIEF THAT I CANNOT HAVE IT ALL IN ONE RELATIONSHIP

We all have limiting beliefs that we cannot have it all in one relationship. We have been told to grow up, and that we cannot live in a fairy-tale world where we are totally happy and have everything we want. The belief that we cannot have it all comes from a deeper, earlier belief that we could not have our mother's and father's love equally. This leads us to then believe that we cannot have all good things in one relationship.

The belief that we could not have our parents' love equally, points to the imbalance of the families we were born into and the lack of bonding we all had to face as children. This, of course, is what our parents also had to face when they were children. Typically, we were fused with one parent and polarised from the other. We did not know the boundaries between the parent we were fused with and ourself; while at the same time we were very distant or independent from the other. Sometimes, though, we will be fused with both parents and alienated from our spouse. This imbalance from our family creates other imbalances. For example, your career may be much stronger than your relationship, or you may succeed in your relationship, but not in your career.

The willingness to give everything to your relationship would allow it to give everything to you. We can rebalance those original relationships and come to know that we can have our mother's and father's love equally.

Exercise

Today, choose to know that you can have it all in one relationship and know that you can help others to have this by your example. Sit quietly and imagine you are a child again. Imagine that between you and your parents there is a perfect balance, a triangle of light connecting to each of you on the points of the triangle. Through these beams of light, feel yourself receiving all of your parents' gifts equally while you are giving all of your gifts and love to them equally. Now add your brothers and sisters to the configuration in a balanced and loving way so that you also receive all their gifts and love equally. In your present relationship, imagine the same thing is occurring between you and your partner and any children you might have. Imagine a perfectly balanced shape, a balance among all of you.

109. WHEN I AM IN FUSION, I AM IN SACRIFICE

When we are in fusion with someone, we do not know the natural boundaries between that person and ourself. We have no sense of where our centre is, so when these people come into our orbit, we are pulled into their orbit and out of our natural movement toward our purpose and living our own life.

Typically, the person we are fused with is someone we feel we have loved all our life. We feel we want to give this person everything, we want to completely take care of them, or make it all better for them. We can fuse with our parents, our mates, our children, but no matter whom it is with, fusion throws us into sacrifice. We become the enabler, the untrue helper – we help, and help, and help. It does not make a difference, however, nobody gets to move forward; we go into a vicious cycle of co-dependence.

If we are fused with a parent, we can feel as if we have to get away from them no matter how much we love them. Where we are in fusion, we are in sacrifice, which does not help anyone. Only by living our own life can we truly help those around us.

Exercise

Today, and as often as you need, cut the cords of fusion between you and others so that you will have a greater sense of freedom and the ability to be more intimate. Sit quietly and close your eyes. Imagine that you are holding the sword of truth in your hand, which only cuts away illusion, what is untrue. See the fusion cords of sacrifice between you and whomever it is, and when you are ready, cut through the cord. The sword of truth cuts through anything and as it does, all that is left behind is what is true. As the untrue is cut away, imagine the lines of true love and bonding growing in its place.

Depending on the type of person you are, you might only need to cut the cord once, or you might need to cut the cord every couple of days. You might even want to cut the cord with a number of people you feel fused to, where you have lost a natural sense of boundary. As you cut the cord tying you to these people, these activities, or, possibly, these addictions, you will find you have a greater sense of freedom. When you end the fusion, you can be more intimate.

110. FUSION HAPPENS WHEN
BONDING HAS BEEN BROKEN

We all have a need for closeness, intimacy, inclusion, and bonding. When our sense of bonding has been shattered or when it seems to be non-existent, we need some type of closeness to survive, so we choose fusion. This way we can have at least some sense of being close to people; however, this is not true bonding.

In fusion, we give up our own centres and our own selves. In bonding, by remaining in our centre, we naturally give the gifts of who we are and receive the gifts of who others are. Our willingness to re-establish bonding through forgiveness and through recognising the love that is there allows us to have our proper boundaries where we can say no when it is true to say no. Most importantly, we can live our own lives.

Exercise

Today, sit down in a relaxed position, and imagine that the cords of true connection, the cords of light and love, are connecting you with all those people with whom you feel fused. As you see these cords of connection, the cords of fusion and sacrifice naturally fall away because they are not the truth.

111. FUSION BLOCKS COMMUNICATION

Fusion blocks communication because we feel so close to the person, we think that we cannot say certain things to them. When we begin communicating, there is a natural resistance, almost a repelling, because we feel if they were hurt by anything we said, we would be devastated; our emotions are blown all out of proportion. We hurt when they hurt, we suffer when they suffer. When they are angry, it is explosive for us, and it is even more explosive when they are angry at us. This over-closeness tends to block verbal communication, so we have a sense of non-verbally communicating everything back and forth. A look can speak of how much we love them or of how much they dislike what we are doing. We feel verbal communication would cause pain, and we are un-willing to create dialogue, so there are just the glances that say it all. However, giving ourself permission to establish dialogue would create healing through communication.

Exercise

Today, think of the people in your life you really have a hard time saying certain things to. These are the people you are fused with and with whom you are really unwilling to take a certain risk. Imagine yourself cutting the cords of fusion with the sword of truth so you can really establish a dialogue with them. If there are things you have wanted to say to these people, now is the time to say them. Whether you are fused with your lover, your mate, your parent, or your child, cut the cord of fusion and take the risk of beginning a dialogue with them.

112.   FUSION BLOCKS LOVE

Love really wants the very best for the other person. In love, we extend ourself in a connective way, in an interdependent way. In fusion, there is a co-dependency with the other person, which stops us from moving forward. If we are the one who seems to be the helper, we are afraid for the other person to get better because our dependency would be uncovered. Consequently, we give to them in a way that keeps them in certain bondage to us. Fusion keeps us in bondage, whereas love gives us freedom. If we feel in bondage to anyone, then all our help cannot truly help them because it is fusion. We cannot confront them or be tough with them for their own sake, even though that is what might be needed. Fusion blocks the intimacy that generates this kind of strong communication. It blocks our ability to say or do what is necessary to really help that person. Fusion blocks intimacy because it is a kind of counterfeit closeness that blocks interdependency. Fusion will not generate the growth, healing and nurturing that love does. In a state of fusion, at some level, both people feel as if they are starving.

Exercise

Today, examine your relationships. Where have you been unable to really feel free because you have not had your own centre? Have you given yourself freely or out of duty? Use the sword of truth to free yourself and communicate what needs to be said. As you communicate, give the gifts and the love you have to give, that you want to give.

131

113. TO BE FUSED WITH SOMEONE
IS TO BE WITHDRAWN FROM LIFE

When we are fused with someone, we have left our centre to move toward a goal that is not a true goal for us. We made the other person more important than our own self in an untrue sense. We made them the goal of our life. While it is true that with love we can find ourself, with fusion we are taken off our centre, pulled back from life, which holds us back from truly giving.

We might seem to be very generous, but actually we are in sacrifice. We might be giving to all kinds of people where really we could be giving to ourself so we could accomplish a much greater work. Fusion blocks our giving and our receiving, so it is an area in which we are not being rewarded. We may have sown a lot, but we are not reaping very much. In fusion, we are an untrue helper. We have withdrawn, but our willingness and commitment will lead us to our purpose and to that which would fulfil us in life.

Exercise

Today, take a good look at the areas of your life where you are not receiving. These are areas where you are not truly giving yourself and may be living someone else's life. Ask Heaven's help to be brought back to your own centre and to really live your own life, so you do not end up in the obituaries under someone else's name.

114.   WHAT I SEE IN ANOTHER
IS WHAT I THINK I AM

We bury the things we do not like about ourself and then project them onto the world around us. What we see in another is what we have projected, what we think we are. If we see something positive in another, but do not believe it about ourself, we then know we repressed that gift out of guilt or fear of being overwhelmed by it. We might have pushed the gift away, but it is still lying within us as potential. If it wasn't waiting inside us, we would not resonate with this gift in another person.

In the same way, the negative things we see in people are what we actually believe about ourself. We know this because as we forgive those things within ourself, they no longer seem to bother us in others. What we see in another is what we think about ourself. If we do not change our judgement on the other person, we will be stuck with what we see in them. If we are stuck with that, we are in sacrifice. As we are willing to forgive them and change the judgements in ourself, a positive gift comes to the surface again.

Exercise

Today, express appreciation to one person who inspires you with their gift. Thank them for having held the vision of this gift so you could know the gift was possible, not only in your world, but in you also. Then, express appreciation to someone whom you have judged. Appreciate them for showing you what you actually believe about yourself. Remember, the greater the risk, the greater the breakthrough you can have. Appreciation moves you through judgement and allows the relationship to begin unfolding again.

115. EVERY TIME I SEE SOMEONE AS INNOCENT, I FREE MYSELF

Innocence frees us. Seeing others as innocent also frees us because, when we see others as innocent, our hidden guilt is released. Guilt keeps us feeling unworthy, in sacrifice, and punishing ourself. When we see someone else as guilty, we are punishing ourself. Our willingness to overlook mistakes and to see our partner as innocent will free us. Our partner has been doing the very best they can, given their inner and outer circumstances and their life story. Rather than complaining, we can help a great deal more by supporting and coaching.

Exercise

Today, observe where you have been considering other people as wrong, bad, or guilty. Ask yourself, 'How have I been punishing myself if I am seeing them in this way?' Take a moment and see what pops into your mind. If this kind of self-retribution is not what you want, then be willing to consider the fact that they are innocent. As a healing statement, say, 'I will release myself today by your innocence. I will release myself today by my innocence.' Then say, 'I see (the person's name) as innocent, and I see myself as innocent so we may be free to walk as allies.'

116. ANGER IS ALWAYS A COVER
FOR ANOTHER FEELING

Anger is a defensive feeling that protects another feeling. The deeper feeling might be sadness, loss, hurt, rejection, vengeance, or it might be a feeling of guilt, sacrifice, frustration, or disappointment. This deeper feeling can be part of a power struggle, or because we feel so dead we think a little anger would at least get things moving a bit. Like anger, rage is also a cover for other feelings. We become enraged so as not to feel our helplessness, humiliation or mortification. We summon rage to protect us from major heartbreak, jealousy, loneliness, and burn-out.

Sometimes, a quick way to move through our anger is simply to ask ourself, 'What is the feeling underneath this?' If we are willing to feel the feeling beneath the anger, the anger immediately disappears, and we move on to the deeper feeling that the anger is defending.

Exercise

Today, examine your anger. Know that every form of anger, including rage, or irritation is just something that is holding you back. Be willing to change and move forward by recognising what you are feeling underneath the anger. Begin a healing dialogue by sharing this deeper feeling with the person who has angered, enraged, or irritated you without expecting any particular type of response from them. Your communication is for your own healing.

135

117. FORGIVENESS IS GIVING FORTH

Guilt keeps us in withdrawal. Every place where we feel unworthy, where we have been in sacrifice, where we have not valued ourself, or where we have suffered loss and not let it go is a place where we are withdrawn. In our present life, all of these losses and feelings of unworthiness show up as judgements on other people. When we forgive those around us, we are giving forth. Areas within us that have been withdrawn for years can now be given forth. As we sow, so shall we reap. Once we forgive, we again move forward into the flow of life and we finally get to receive. As we forgive – give forth – we feel happy. Forgiveness allows us to have all of the hidden parts come back to life.

Exercise

Today, think of three things you are judging your partner for. Recognise that the areas of judgement against your partner are, actually, places where you are not giving forth to them or supporting them. Choose to give to them in these areas. Choose to support your own life in these areas. As you give forth to them, you will find a natural forgiveness, and you will naturally forgive. As you forgive, you will experience a natural flow that restores your ability to receive in these areas.

118. THE POINT OF CONFLICT
IS THE PLACE OF OPPORTUNITY

The direction in which we move is directly related to our attitude toward something. If we see any conflict as a possible end to our relationship, then that is what it may be. If we look at conflict as the point of opportunity for healing, then we can reach a new level of intimacy and integration. Seeing the conflict as a gift, rather than as the beginning of just another place of hell on earth, brings us to a place where we can now deal with this conflict.

Only when a couple has reached a certain stage in strength can they deal with the related areas of conflict. We each have within our own mind all of the conflicts in the world. We are, however, only able to deal with so many at a given time. If we were to truly heal each conflict within us, conflicts around us would also heal. We would then have the answer for our friends and relatives, and even for our acquaintances.

As we progress and move forward, we move away from the personal conflicts in our relationship as well as those that our friends and relatives seem to experience. As we grow in maturity, we are able to face deeper and deeper levels of conflict and to take on more and more in terms of our responsiveness. Our level of responsiveness says that at this point, we can now face this new level of conflict because we realise it is a major opportunity for our learning and our growth. This conflict has been within, just waiting for the right time to surface.

Exercise

Today, examine a current area of conflict as if it is a gift to you. As you change your attitude toward it, the conflict will begin to show you the natural way through it.

119. TO RESOLVE A CONFLICT, GO TO A COMMON, HIGHER PURPOSE

Any conflict degenerates into a power struggle if we do not go to a common higher purpose. Even if we succeed in controlling our partner into doing it our way, somehow our needs still would not be met and we would begin to lose interest in the other person. If we realise that in both viewpoints there is a necessary piece of the puzzle, we can create something greater. We can reach a higher level of purpose and a higher resolution to the conflict. As we begin to examine both sides of the conflict, we discover the common, higher goal that naturally subsumes these two parts of the puzzle within it. It integrates these aspects that now seem to be at odds.

Exercise

Today, bring a conflict to mind. Without necessarily dwelling on either side of the conflict, just rest quietly and ask for the higher purpose that this conflict distracts you from to come to you. The answer may pop into your mind within the first few seconds of letting go of all the cares and worries of the day. Receiving this higher purpose is the automatic beginning of the end of this conflict. What can you lose if you gain your adversary as your ally?

120. MOST NEGATIVE EMOTION
HAS NOTHING TO DO WITH THE PRESENT

Most negative emotion has nothing to do with the present. We usually save up all of the feeling we did not have the courage to finish feeling and, then, create experiences in our present life that give us the opportunity to release the past emotion. If we were to look a little deeper into any situation that triggered us in our life right now, we would realise that most of the pain we are experiencing has nothing to do with the present situation. The pain of the present situation is just a small percent that is needed to trigger off feelings we have been carrying around with us for a long time. These are feelings we need to get out for us to have an openness to life and to be able to receive from life. If these feelings are kept suppressed, they fester inside us and become poisonous, affecting our health and our willingness to enjoy ourself and our relationships.

Exercise

Today, delve a little deeper into any of the conflicts you are having. Realise these conflicts are being put together by old situations that carried emotions you never finished with. Whether or not you get in touch with those old situations, feel the feelings until they are completely gone. Be willing to recognise that your partner and the people around you are not to blame. They are actually helping you to create this healing for yourself. They are helping you to be more open to life so you can receive and enjoy your happiness.

121. PARTNERSHIP LEADS TO CREATIVITY

In a relationship, when we move past the power struggle stage and out of the Dead Zone, we enter an area where we become more and more gifted. It is an area of partnership where we constantly receive new and greater vision. This stage of a relationship is called Co-creativity. Of course, as love is the major dynamic in this sense of creativity, it is an area of fulfilment and great satisfaction. Love and creativity bring happiness. When we partner and bond with someone, we create a kind of juice or electricity in the relationship that unfolds new gifts, talents, and opportunities for each person.

Exercise

Today, think of ways to connect with your partner. Spend the day dwelling on a campaign of love. Feel your connection and love for them. In spite of any debris that might be in the way, the love and connection are still there. The love and connection are what is important in your relationship and in life. The more you connect, the more your relationship opens itself. There is more and more abundance, happiness, love, and all of the good things in life for you to enjoy.

122. PULLING AWAY FROM A FEELING
IS WHAT MAKES IT HURT

As we pull away from a feeling, as we resist it, another feeling that might not have been there to begin with comes up – a feeling of hurt. If we try to escape pain, resisting it causes us to work twice as hard and bury twice as much. When we are unwilling to feel the loss of a loved one, for example, we avoid going through the natural mourning and anger about the loss. When we pull away from it, we actually add another feeling to the loss, the feeling of hurt or rejection. The same thing happens when we don't want to feel our guilt. As we push away from the feeling of guilt and add a feeling of hurt to it, we then have to dissociate all that much more. If we choose to feel the feeling, instead of burying it inside, and experience it totally, it is soon gone, and we have a new beginning. We leave behind the disappointments that were gradually making us old and wearing us down.

Exercise

Today, take the opportunity to feel any feeling that comes up, negative or positive. Fully experience it. If it is a negative feeling, by feeling it, it will eventually burn away into a positive feeling. Fully experiencing a positive feeling makes it even more positive.

123. ANY PROBLEM IN MY RELATIONSHIP IS A SIGNAL THAT A GIFT, TALENT, OR OPPORTUNITY WANTS TO EMERGE

A problem is a form of distraction and shows us there is a fear. Our fear is of receiving a new gift, talent, or opportunity that is being offered to us. It is something that we have always wanted. With the courage to accept it, we would have it. Our willingness to choose the gift, talent, or opportunity is the very thing that lets it come forward and makes the problem, which is just a distraction, disappear. The easiest way to take care of our problems is by looking at them in a new light. In doing so, we recognise that every time there is a problem, a new gift, talent, or opportunity wants to emerge for us and our relationship.

Exercise

Today, imagine that pouring down from Heaven is this new gift, talent, or opportunity that would dissolve your problem. Imagine the energy of it entering you and, at the same time, emerging from deep within you. As you let yourself know what it is, you feel it becoming embodied in you. Even if you do not know what it is, your problem begins to fall away, for its only purpose was to distract and delay you.

124. THE PERSON I LIKE THE LEAST IS SHOWING ME WHAT IS HOLDING ME BACK

The person we like the least is showing us what is holding us back. This person is called a shadow figure. They embody the shadow side of ourself – what we have hidden away and repressed in ourself. As long as we keep it repressed, people who embody these same qualities will tend to come at us in our life. The way through is to look beyond our repulsion and remember that these individuals are there to let us know about the invisible block that has been holding back our progress.

When our experience is one of working very hard, but making very little movement forward, the situation is the result of a belief we have about ourself, a quality we hate about ourself. We buried the quality and, then, projected it onto someone else, which completely blocks us by setting up an invisible shield to our progress. When there is a shadow figure around us, or when we have projected a certain quality that we just cannot stand onto our partner, this quality drags behind us like an invisible anchor and holds us back.

Exercise

Today, ask for self-forgiveness. Ask for a feeling of innocence and resolution for both of you. Your willingness to have your Higher Power handle the needed forgiveness with this person releases the invisible block in your life and allows you to move forward at this very moment.

125. THE HEART OF COMMUNICATION IS RECOGNISING THAT PRESENT PAIN IS ROOTED IN A PAST RELATIONSHIP

When we begin to share about what is not working or what is painful in a relationship, we eventually realise the pain is not coming just from this relationship, but has its roots in another. If we are willing to support each other, we find neither one of us is the bad guy in the relationship. The pain is not something either we or they have caused, rather it is something we can help our partner with as we are willing to share the mis-understandings and the past pain.

Exercise

Today, imagine a situation where you felt your partner caused you pain. Recognise where that pain is really coming from because it had to have some antecedent to be this big. Now be willing to share this recognition with your partner. Share the beliefs that have come from past relationships, the rules you made because you thought you needed them to survive. As you share these things with the willingness to let them go, you will find your partner much more willing to communicate and support you.

126. REFUSAL OF WHAT IS UNTRUE
IN A RELATIONSHIP ALLOWS
THE TRUTH TO EMERGE

Something we can constantly use in our relationship is knowing that if there is something untrue, something that is not love, happiness, or abundance, we do not have to stand for it. If it is not the truth, we need not accept it because it does not belong in our relationship. With the power of our mind along with the truth, we can refuse it and choose something else.

Exercise

Today, choose at least two areas of your relationship that are not the truth because they are not happy or joyful. For this exercise, you can also choose aspects of your relationship that are neutral or just 'blah'. Using the power of your mind, say, 'This is not the truth. I will not accept this. What I choose is the truth. What I choose is say whatever it is.' Saying this once with sincerity sometimes has the power to remove the entire conflict, or at least the power to remove one layer of the conflict. Use this time and again so you can recognise this as a principle: If it is not the truth, do not adjust to it. Do not compromise. If it is not the truth, do not choose it. Keep asking for the answer, the resolution.

127.   TO ANALYSE A PROBLEM
IS TO RESIST THE SOLUTION

The answer to every problem comes at the moment the problem began. We actually do not have to waste any time finding the solution to a problem. We just require the courage to accept the answer. Analysing a problem is resisting the solution because to analyse is to break up the whole into little pieces by thinking we will find the answer there. 'Analyse' is really 'anal lies', while 'rationalise' is really a form of 'rational lies' because thinking always happens after the fact. The solution comes through our intuition, through inspiration. Most of the great inventions were discovered in a state of reverie, a state where answers just pop in. The answer to any problem can just pop into our mind. When we stop thinking about the problem, we allow ourself to receive the answer.

Exercise

Today, take the time to allow yourself to sit quietly. If the answer to your problem has not popped into your mind in the first ten minutes, allow yourself to sit there and observe every thought that comes up – things you have to do, sexual fantasies, anything. To each of these thoughts, say, 'This thought reflects a goal that's keeping me from my answer.' After you say that, the thought will fall away. Then, at the end of ten or fifteen minutes of doing this, state, 'Now let the answer be given to me.' Your willingness to receive the answer will clear the clutter of all your thoughts. Your willingness to receive the answer is the only thing between you and the solution.

128. TRUST HEALS ALL

Trust is one of the great healers. It is the power of our mind used to build ourself. To trust means that whatever problem we have begins to heal, because any problem is a sign of a lack of trust. By bringing our trust into the problem and using the power of our mind, we can feel and see the situation with a positive expectancy. Every time we think of the problem and choose to see, feel, and hear it working out, we are no longer obsessed by it. Rather than reinforcing the problem, we open for the answer to come in. The power of our mind naturally seeks solutions. Trust is our answer. Trust heals all.

Exercise

Today, take some time to use trust for any problem that seems to be holding you back, especially in your relationship. Remember, moving your relationship forward also moves every other area of your life forward.

129. WHEN I OPT FOR INDEPENDENCE,
I THROW AWAY PASSION

There are two types of passion. One type comes from urgency, the other from giving ourself totally. When we opt for independence, we are opting to move away from our needs and away from the sense of urgency, but we still have not come to the point of giving ourself one hundred percent. Dissociating from our needs and our pain means we have unfinished business with things we are unwilling to look at within ourself. These places of unexamined pain hold us back from giving ourself fully.

Exercise

Today is a day to find your passion again. Recognise your needs, give up your defensive independence, and give yourself one hundred percent to your partner, your life, and your work. Give yourself in spite of whatever holds you back. As you give yourself fully, moving through the painful feelings, you emerge with a new sense of love, power, and passion.

130. GIVING UP A JUDGEMENT KEEPS ME FROM BEING STUCK WITH WHAT I HAVE JUDGED

If we judge, we are stuck with what we have judged. Judgement gives us a sense of being right, but it does not move us forward. Our willingness to be wrong allows things to keep moving forward. Our willingness not to know all of the answers means we can be taught something; if we are a full glass of water, nothing can be poured into us. Our judgement says, 'Nothing can be taught to me. I have all the answers, and I am stuck.' Choosing to give up our judgement and recognise that there may be more to this situation than meets the eye allows us to see with greater perspective and be shown the way in this situation. If we have the answer, we cannot be taught; however, there is always something to learn.

Exercise

Today, take a moment to discover what you are judging and, therefore, stuck with. Be willing to let it go. Imagine that you placed your judgement on a little boat that went down a swift river, flowing out to sea and moving out of your mind. There, coming toward you from upriver, is the answer, the next step in the situation. Only when you let go of the little boat carrying your judgement can your ship come in. One powerful form of affirmation might be: 'I hope I'm wrong, because if I'm right, this is what I get.'

131. IF THE PAST IS UNFINISHED, GHOSTS OF OLD RELATIONSHIPS WILL COME TO HAUNT ME IN THE PRESENT

Everything we have not finished with our parents, siblings, or other significant relationships will interfere with our present relationship. We bring every unlearned lesson forward to be learned now in our present relationship. The healing in our present relationship heals past relationships and we can see them in another light. Sometimes, it is easier simply to make contact with these significant people, understanding the old situation in the light of maturity, letting go of the problem, and moving forward. When the old ghosts are dispersed, the blessings and good times of the past will empower you.

Exercise

Today is a day for finishing old business. Contact anyone with whom you have outstanding feuds or misunderstandings. Be willing to reach out and take the next step, apologising where necessary in order to move forward. Healing can take place even if the person has died. Just imagine them present, and speak to them, or if you prefer, write a letter to them to clear up the old business.

132.   RULES COVER GUILT

Every rule we have covers our guilt. If we did not have the guilt, there would be no need to make rules. We would be flexible and responsive in that area. The reason we made a rule in the first place is that, at some point, we believe we made a big mistake, and to never make that mistake again, we set a rule for others and ourself. Many times the rule later becomes the problem and stands in the way of our responsiveness, and of our ability to consider what is needed in present circumstances. Of course, that is exactly what guilt does; it keeps us unresponsive. Guilt keeps us acting in the same old ritualised manner.

Exercise

Today, take a look at the areas where you are rigid in your relationship. These are the areas where you feel, 'It has to be this way for me.' Realise that hidden under each of your rules is a sense of guilt. Be willing to let go of the rule and the guilt.

133. A RULE IS SELF-PUNISHMENT FOR A MISTAKEN BELIEF I HAVE ABOUT MYSELF

Our rules are our disciplines. Unfortunately, though, these disciplines are a form of self-punishment. Somewhere we made a mistake and we feel guilty about it; now we are punishing ourself. How we punish ourself is that every rule is a place where we cannot receive; rules prevent receiving. They prevent receiving because where we feel guilty we cannot receive. Where we have a rule, we cannot have true contact with our partner because of something that we feel really bad about. Our rule covers our guilt.

Exercise

Today, write down every rule you have in your relationship. In a column next to it, write what you have decided about yourself in relation to the rule. You can be sure that if anything in this second column is negative, you are punishing yourself in some way. In a third column, write how you are punishing yourself. When you take a good look at what the rule is, what the mistake is, and how you are punishing yourself, you might want to make a new decision about the rules you have in your life. Awareness and making new choices are keys to healing.

134. MY PRESENT RELATIONSHIP IS THE PROCESS BY WHICH OLD PAINS CAN BE HEALED

The love in our present relationship allows us to let go of old ideas about ourself as well as old pain. In the process of growing together, everything between our partner and ourself will surface so it can be healed. All of us have nice self-concepts, yet these can sometimes hide very dark self-concepts. Beneath these dark and painful images of ourself, we have a more authentic self-concept of our true goodness, self-images that are not merely compensations for the darkness we feel inside.

Exercise

Today is a day of recognition for how far you have come. Acknowledge yourself for uncovering all these nice self-concepts that never let you receive anything. Appreciate yourself for getting down to the darker ones so the healing work could continue. Feel your gratitude for your relationship that has brought you the awareness of these darker self-images so that you could heal them and reach your true sense of goodness that allows you to receive.

135. IF I HAVE A PROBLEM, I AM HOLDING ON TO OLD PAIN

The problems we have now have roots in old problems. Even if we were to cut away the current problem, the root would still be there ready to just grow other problems. It is really helpful, therefore, to realise where the root of our current problems comes from and how it has grown into many different problems in our life.

Exercise

Today, write down three present problems in your relationship. Then, beside these, identify from whom in the past this problem stems. Next to that, write what the problem was with that person. Trust what pops into your mind for each category. Your intuition will give you answers that your thinking and memory could never give you because they are in collusion with the ego, and they would never give something the ego does not want to deal with. Your intuition will constantly bring you answers. By using your intuition, your answers can be inspired.

Now, look at what you have written. If these problems you've identified come from unfinished business, would you like to finish the business now? This could be as easy as forgiving the people in the situation, blessing them, or just letting the whole thing go as not being true any more, as not being worth holding you back at the present time in your life.

136. APPRECIATION ELIMINATES
POWER STRUGGLES

The problem with power struggle is that we polarise into opposite camps. We take an issue that is between the two of us, but instead of seeing it as something that is up for healing, we use it against our partner. The bottom-line dynamic of power struggle is that its whole purpose is to keep ourself from moving forward. To use something that naturally moves ourself forward would end the power struggle. Appreciation moves us forward; therefore, it ends the power struggle. If we are in a conflict with our partner, as we begin to appreciate them, we are once again in the flow.

Exercise

Today, spend some time in the morning and evening thinking about the things you really love about your partner. Also reflect on the things your partner gives you. How does your partner bless your life? Sometime during the day, communicate these things to your partner. Even if you are not in a power struggle, use this time to appreciate your partner, to tell them the things you love about them, and the ways they have helped you. Even if there is only one thing you can find to appreciate about your partner, appreciating that one thing will move you forward, and it will bless and open you.

137.   BE WILLING TO LET GO OF
THE NEED TO CONSUME
THE OTHER TO MAKE UP FOR THE PAST

Where we have past needs that weren't met by our parents or our life situation, we have a tendency to want to consume our partner, to swallow them alive. We take every little thing they can give us, overwhelm them, overshadow them, fuse with them, and smother them so we can get these needs met. Of course, if we haven't noticed, this kind of consuming pushes our partner away. If we let go of our past needs, we find a natural balance and openness in our relationship. If we are always trying to grab our partner, we never find our partner moving toward us. As we are willing to let go of any way we are trying to consume our partner or anyone in our life, we receive the answer to all of our prayers. Now is really the time to give to our partner and these people in our life.

Exercise

Today, give to the person that you feel you are trying to consume the most. Give them everything you are trying to get from them.

138.   THERE IS NO SUCH THING
AS A BROKEN HEART

Broken hearts are really a form of tantrum. We feel broken-hearted because our loved ones have not acted in the way we wished them to. We take our hearts out and threaten to break them because they do not listen to us. We smash our hearts into a thousand pieces, thinking, 'They'll be sorry now.'

We are the only one who can break our heart. Nobody can make us feel anything we do not choose to feel or that we are not already feeling at some level. If we were willing to let the situation be different from what we think it should be by acceptance, then we could take the great amount of emotion that comes and give through it. We could enter a new birth in our life. We could step into a whole new level of love, with a sense of confidence and empowerment.

Exercise

Today is a day to regain yourself. Go back to your heartbreak situations and, this time, use them as an opportunity for healing. Imagine that instead of pulling back from the person, or going into another layer of power struggle, you are giving through all that pain, whether they did what you wished or not. At this level, you find yourself reconnecting wires in your heart, your mind, and, sometimes, in your genitals that have long since been cut. You feel a new surge of vitality as you renew yourself and come to a new birth.

139. THE MORE UNLOVEABLE THE BEHAVIOUR, THE GREATER THE CALL FOR LOVE

When we find unloveable behaviour in our partner, family, or work situation, it is crucial to realise these behaviours are really a call for love. Our willingness to support people through what may be the worst time of their life allows them to progress, to keep moving and growing. Letting them know that even though we do not approve of or like their behaviour, we value who they are, who they are truly becoming. This is a great test of someone who loves. It is the great calling of Leadership – someone who is willing to move through their own discomfort and respond to people who are using unloveable behaviour in their call for help.

Exercise

Today is a time to be a true leader in your relationship and in your life. Look for ways you can reach new levels of responsiveness, both at home and at work.

140. AN ATTACK IS A CALL FOR HELP

When we are attacked, we tend to put up defences, run away, or attack back. If we chose to realise this attack as a call for help, hence responding with openness and moving toward the person, we would enlist this person as one of our greatest supporters.

When a person attacks, they are going through some of their hardest times and because they are frightened, they do not expect someone to move toward them. To move toward them, however, it can only be with a certain sense of confidence and love. As we are moving forward to support them, they feel the love, even if nothing else happens. If we just pour love into them as they are attacking, the next time we are with them, we notice that both of us have moved forward and that they somehow feel bonded, feel connected with us. Attack is a perfect opportunity to establish bonding with the person who is attacking.

Exercise

Today, be the leader in your relationship. One of the greatest acts of Leadership is realising an attack is a call for your help. Many times, in supporting people who attack you, they later become one of your best supporters.

141. A ROLE IS THE COSTUME FOR AN UNMOURNED LOSS

If we do not deal with our losses by experiencing all the feelings, we do not make a new beginning. Instead, we costume the loss with the role of dependence, independence or being the untrue helper. If because of this loss we take on the role of dependence, we will now act very needy, but the role itself does not allow us to receive. If we adopt the independent role, we act as if the loss did not matter to us and that we do not care. Saying we do not care, though, really hints of how much we do care. If we mask this unmourned loss with the role of the untrue helper, we are always helping everyone with their pain, but covering up our own. Somehow, this never quite helps us move forward because we limit our capacity to help others.

Exercise

Today, take a look at what you have used to move away from your old losses. Are you in a state of dependence, independence, or in the helping role? What is the loss you have not recovered from? Allow yourself to feel the feelings of loss, not as the adult you are, but as the child inside who still mourns that loss. Allow yourself, as that child, to finish the mourning process, and birth inside you what this role has hidden. As you are willing to move past your roles and allow this birth to take place, you will move forward and have a greater capacity to help others in your life.

142. A BAD FEELING IS RELEASED
BY TRUE GIVING

When we feel self-conscious, embarrassed, or criticised, we tend to contract. If at the very time we felt bad, we gave, we would be expanded. We would step through the wall of our personalities and know ourself as bigger. The easiest way to move through a bad feeling or even just a *blah* feeling is to truly give.

Exercise

Today, ask yourself, 'Who is it that needs my help?' Whomever pops into your mind, ask yourself, 'What is the best way for me to help them?' What comes into your mind? You could send love to them by calling, writing, or supporting them in some way. It might be a certain thing they need. You could just imagine that thing is pouring down from the Universe, filling you, and pouring through you to them. As you reach out to them, you break through the invisible wall around you and you feel good again.

143. JEALOUSY IS REVENGE ON MYSELF

Jealousy is one of the most unpleasant feelings we can have because we have attached our happiness to someone else's behaviour; this certainly causes us pain. It is a combination of dependency (neediness), a sense and fear of loss, as well as feelings of hurt, rejection, unworthiness, valuelessness, and anger. This is enough to drive us into independence because it hurts so much.

Jealousy, however, is a form of emotional blackmail because we are trying to control another person through our bad feelings, whether or not they know what we feel. By being willing to take our criteria of self-value away from another's actions, we release ourself from jealousy. We then recognise that they might be behaving the way they are out of their own needs or compulsion. As we let go of the situation and move forward, the situation will change and naturally unfold.

Exercise

Today, the exercise is one of letting go. You can be jealous only when you are competing for someone, which means you have a belief in loss and that you are the one who is losing. Be willing to let go of your attachment and step forward. The more you step forward, the more you find a place where everyone can win by finding their natural relationship. If this is not your true partner, you will find someone who is. When you have let go and moved forward, you find greater peace in your committed relationships and you find your attractiveness comes back. This does not mean throwing the person away or running away from the situation; it means letting go of your attachments about how the situation should be.

144. THE EXTENT OF MY JEALOUSY
IS THE EXTENT TO WHICH
I FEEL UNTRUSTWORTHY

One of the most hidden aspects of jealousy is that we are projecting onto our partner how we believe we might actually act in a similar situation. When we feel that we could indulge in this way, in spite of our protestations to the contrary, we feel very jealous. The extent to which we feel untrustworthy is the extent to which we punish our partner and ourself with jealousy. To become more trustworthy, in other words, to heal our old broken hearts, gain more trust in ourself and experience ourself as more valuable, means we are able to feel more committed. We then feel more worthy of committing to ourself and others. We give up being such a *fickle-fuckle,* and we are more willing to allow ourself to receive, thereby knowing ourself as worthy.

Exercise

Today, remember that the key to healing jealousy is in becoming more trustworthy, not more dependent. Find the negative beliefs of yourself that led to your jealousy. As you become aware of these, change them by making a new choice about yourself. While you may have thousands of negative beliefs about yourself and relationships, each one you choose to change moves things forward in a positive direction. Begin to value yourself, because valuing yourself allows you to make commitments.

145.   EVERY FANTASY
IS AN EXPECTATION

Every fantasy is an expectation and, under that, a demand. A fantasy says, 'This is the way it would be if my needs were met.' We make a picture to receive some kind of nurturing from a situation in which we are not receiving enough nurturing. Then we bring this fantasy into the present situation so we can feel more nurtured, but the situation becomes less exciting. We now have to keep making our fantasies bigger and bigger to create more and more excitement.

Like expectations, fantasies block receiving. They block the nurturing that the situation could give us. As we are willing to let go of our fantasies, we open to what is really there and we are more able to enjoy it; otherwise, our fantasy locks us into one certain reality. We can take a trip down a side path, but we remain locked in at this one step in our life. As we let go of our fantasies – the castles in the clouds and the pipe dreams – we find ourself receiving more.

Exercise

Today, take a look at how much fantasy is in your life. Look at romance, sex, career, the lottery, etc. Begin to let go and move closer to the situation, into closer contact with your partner. As you get to know your partner and make more contact with them, there is a natural electricity of sexuality in your relationship that allows you to receive the nurturing that your unfolding relationship has for you.

146. THE GOAL OF EVERY
RELATIONSHIP IS INTERDEPENDENCE

When we move out of the romance stage in a relationship, one partner polarises more into independence and the other more to dependence. Sometimes, the power struggle stage in a relationship is primarily the fight for who is going to be the more independent one. The goal of every relationship, however, is to move into interdependence. This is where both people are equally balanced in relation to each other; and each has balance with their masculine and feminine energies – natural interdependence.

If we are the independent person in our relationship, our goal is to reach out and value our partner. If we are the dependent one, our goal is to let go of our attachments and pain, and feel our true feelings until we move the relationship up to a whole new level of partnership. No matter what position we are in, we can constantly move our relationship ahead.

Exercise

Today, take time to set the goal for your relationship. If you do not have a goal, you can end up anywhere and be stopped by anything. No matter where your relationship is, set the goal for interdependence. Every time you think in any way about your partner, your relationship, or your experience in the relationship, see and move toward the goal of interdependence and balance in your relationship.

147.   MY MOTHER AND FATHER
ARE EMBODIMENTS OF MY
FEMININE AND MASCULINE SIDES

Our mother is the feminine within us, and our father the masculine. If our parents were out of balance, the masculine and feminine within us are likely to be out of balance, too. Sometimes, if our parents are at war, we find that our masculine and feminine energies are also at war. As we heal the masculine and feminine within us, our father and mother are healed. As we learn the value of the masculine and its ability to give and initiate, as well as learn the power of the feminine and its ability to receive and nurture, they will naturally come to balance within us.

When we are independent, the feminine within us is wounded and we need to learn how to respond to our own needs. As we do, we have a much greater ability to receive, and our masculine will move out of the independent, the untrue masculine, and find its natural initiating stance in the relationship. When the masculine and feminine are out of balance within us, our relationship is out of balance.

Exercise

Today, imagine the man and woman in you. Which needs help? If the man in you needs help, let the woman receive Heaven's grace to empower the man. If the woman needs help, let the man go to her and sustain, protect, love, and foster her. As you do this, you will find the masculine and feminine within you come to a greater healing balance. This will have an effect both on your parents and on your own relationship.

148. EVERY OLD LOVE FROM THE PAST
I AM HOLDING ON TO KEEPS ME
FROM TAKING THE NEXT STEP
IN MY PRESENT RELATIONSHIP

The mind is a funny thing; if we are fantasising about something, it does not know if it is real or if we are just fantasising about it, because everything in the mind is an image. When we are thinking about the good things in an old relationship, the mind says, 'Hey, we're satisfied, we already have it. Why create it now?' Our willingness to let go of all the good things that we have ever received from anyone in the past allows this very thing to grow in our relationship now, and to be even stronger and more generative in the present than it was in the past.

Exercise

Today, see who it is you are still holding on to from the past. This holding on is keeping your present relationship from moving to a new level. It is also keeping you from moving forward. Be willing to let go of those old loves. They are great gifts from Heaven, but not gifts to be used to hold back your present happiness. Be willing to let go and receive it all now.

You may find that you are not holding on to an old relationship as much as a quality from that relationship. Be willing to put any of these qualities into the hands of your Higher Mind to let go for you.

149. WHEN I FEEL OVERWHELMED BY MY PARTNER'S NEEDS, I BECOME A CHANNEL FOR HEAVEN'S GRACE

Sometimes we feel just too tired, as if there is not enough of us to satisfy our partner, to really help or take care of them. When we feel burned out, it is time to ask for Heaven's help, and to let the energy of the Universe pour down through us and into our partner. When we do not have the strength to move forward, we allow our partnership to move us forward. Allowing all the love of Heaven to pour through us and fill our partner keeps us from feeling sucked dry. If we try to use our own energy, sometimes we can feel sucked dry within a few minutes, but by tapping into the Universe, we have enough grace to feed everyone.

Exercise

Today, think of someone around you who is needy. Imagine the energy of the Universe pouring through you and filling them up. Imagine this energy is constantly running through you all day for anybody who has needs around you. Notice that as the energy pours through you to other people, you are also filled.

150. IF MY RELATIONSHIP FEELS DEAD, THERE IS HIDDEN COMPETITION

Deadness in a relationship hides a subtle, or not so subtle, form of competition. Take a very, very close look because with competition, we consider ourself just a little bit better or more right than our partner. It also has us feel that we are the best one and deserve to be supported in a better way. All of these feelings really hold us back because competition sets up separation. Where there is separation, there is a lack of contact, and this is what creates deadness. As we are willing to move out of competition into co-operation, we naturally move in harmony with our partner.

Exercise

Today, explore the deadness in your relationship. Be willing to recognise that these are the areas where you are in competition with your partner. Where are you the better one, the best one? Be willing to communicate these to your partner, and let go of them. Commit to your partner so you, your partner, and your relationship move forward.

151. ALL RELATIONSHIPS
ARE NO-FAULT RELATIONSHIPS

Everyone is doing the very best they can given their inner and outer circumstances. If we begin to look at relationships as no-fault, where no one is to blame, then we begin to look at relationships in a true light. Any time there is blame, a relationship stops growing and begins to die. The faults we see in the world or in others are really the reflection of the hidden, or not so hidden, faults in ourself. If we look at all of our relationships as no-fault relationships, then we will keep progressing in every relationship we have.

Exercise

Today, make a decision for all of your relationships to become no-fault. Make a list of all the places where you have blame going towards someone. You will probably find you have some sort of judgement or blame going toward everyone around you. Your willingness to see them and yourself as innocent allows everyone to move forward and receive more.

152. EVERYTHING THAT HAPPENS
IN A RELATIONSHIP HAS TWO SOURCES

Many times we hold grievances against our partners because we believe they did something to us. As we become familiar with our subconscious mind, we realise no one is doing anything to us that we are not already doing to ourself. Everything that happens in a relationship is a form of collusion. When a relationship gets ready to end, at some level, both people are choosing for it to end. At a subconscious level, they are choosing who's going to be the independent one, the bad guy, and who's going to be the dependent one who carries the heartbreak or dependence. Both people choose the role they can best use to end the relationship. Everything that happens is the result of choice.

Exercise

Today, consider three situations you think you did not want to happen. Take the first situation and imagine for a moment that you did actually want it to happen. Now you know you did not want it consciously, but given all the circumstances, the reason it happened is that a part of you chose it as the very best way for you. Talk to that part of you. Find out what was going on that led you to make the choice you did. What was the purpose behind the event? What did it allow you to do? What did you not have to do? Just pretend you are that part. Listen to what comes to your mind, and you will find the underlying motivation for your co-creation of that event. It is time to let all that go and move forward so you can be happier in your present relationship.

153. THE AMOUNT OF RECOGNITION I RECEIVE IS TO THE AMOUNT I RECOGNISE MYSELF

The approval we receive from others directly relates to how much we approve of ourself. Along the same lines, the amount of recognition we receive is to our own self-recognition. Other people mirror our experience of ourself back to us, so if we are not valuing ourself, we are certainly not going to recognise the amount of recognition that is coming toward us.

Exercise

Today, spend time to see how much approval or recognition you seem to be receiving from the world around you. Then spend the rest of the day just valuing yourself and giving to yourself.

154. THE AMOUNT OF APPROVAL I RECEIVE IS THE AMOUNT I GIVE TO OTHERS

To the extent we give approval, friendship, or love, these gifts will come back to us. When we are giving out of recognition to others, we are recognised. When we share our gifts with others, we feel gifted. The extent of approval we are receiving in our life is really the extent to which we are not judging those around us, therefore naturally giving forth to them. As we naturally give forth to others, they naturally respond to us with their approval, recognition, and love.

Exercise

Today, give to others where you find any lack of recognition in your life. Especially give to those from whom you believe you need it the most.

155. GUILT HOLDS BACK MY POWER

To the extent we feel guilty we are withdrawn. When we are withdrawn, we punish ourself and we hold back our own power. If we feel guilty, at some level, we feel we are bad. We do not allow ourself to move forward because our badness might show, so we keep ourself withdrawn or, sometimes, we attack. Attack, however, is a form of domination that shows our lack of power and how much we fear.

Exercise

Today, take any bad or guilty feelings, and place them in the hands of God. In God's hands you can only be innocent. Imagine that you are taking your guilt and sending it out on a little boat. As the boat floats down a swift river, the river cleans all of the guilt out of your mind. It frees you and allows you to step forward. Take a deep breath. Feel all that air coming into your lungs. Feel how much you can receive from life. Feel how much you can allow yourself to naturally be yourself, to express yourself and your power.

156. ANY PROBLEM OUTSIDE ME
CAN BE HEALED WITHIN MY RELATIONSHIP

Anything that is happening outside our relationship can be healed within it. Everything outside our relationship is a metaphor, a mirror of something happening in the mind and heart of our relationship. If scarcity surrounds us, there is scarcity within our relationship. This means it is time to give and receive truly, not just in sacrifice and burn-out. Any problem around us points to a place within our relationship that is yet to be connected. As we connect and find new joy within our relationship, we reach a new level of partnership and co-creativity. Correspondingly, we find the problem outside our relationship begins to heal. One of the deepest and most powerful secrets about a relationship is that it has the power to heal whatever problems surround us, no matter from what depth they come.

Exercise

Today, choose a problem you want to heal. It could even be one your partner and you would like to work on together, although you can do it in your own mind. Imagine the problem is somehow between your partner and you. Begin communicating with your partner about the problem as if there is a joining in your relationship that the problem is meant to hide. Communicating moves you towards each other and through the problem. Make being connected more important than the problem separating you. Sometimes, you are even able to find the area in your relationship that has not yet been connected, such as intimacy, communication or sexuality. When you move to connect in this way, you find creativity flowing through you and your relationship, not only healing it, but also healing the world.

157. IN MY RELATIONSHIP I CAN CHOOSE DRAMA OR I CAN CHOOSE CREATIVITY

There are two reasons drama gets created in our relationships. Either we are in a power struggle where one or both of us find more and more dramatic ways to express our point, or the relationship seems dull, so we create drama to relieve the deadness. Unfortunately, though, every power struggle and every form of deadness in our relationship is just an avoidance of our creativity.

Exercise

Today, concentrate on an area in your relationship where you are either in conflict or have a sense of deadness. Imagine you are floating down inside yourself, past the conflict or the deadness and into a deeper layer. In this deeper layer, there is a place where there is something creative you are being called to do, something that would really help you feel fulfilled. Feel the energy of this creativity juicing inside you while, at the same time, rushing out to be expressed in your life.

158.　THE HELPER ROLE COMES
FROM BELIEVING I AM DESTRUCTIVE

Within the psychodynamics of everyone who has felt com-
pelled to adopt a healing role – doctor, nurse, therapist,
minister, priest, psychic – is a belief that long ago we were
guilty of causing some kind of pain. We felt guilty because,
somehow, we could not help at a time of great need. As
children, we tend to blame ourself for the destructiveness,
illness, and death around us and then later, we take on the role
of healer.

Now all of us, at some point, take on this sacrifice or helper
role because it comes out of our own guilt. This is why at
times we can help ninety-nine people, but if we miss one, we
feel as guilty as if we had missed them all; a sure sign we are in
a helping role.

Belief in our guilt is a misunderstanding, yet the child
within does not know this. The role we play is a compensation for feelings of guilt, wrongness, or destructiveness, and it
stops us from receiving and moving forward to help even
greater numbers of people. The best way to truly help others
is by helping ourself. In taking a giant step forward from
being the helper, we become the healed healer where we can
finally receive. This allows us to have the strength and the
vision to help a great many more people than we are
presently. It allows us to move out of roles in our relationship
and to be more responsive to our partner. It allows us to
receive more love and gratitude from our partner and the
world.

Exercise

Today, take a look at the helping roles you are playing, and ask yourself, 'Where did I begin to believe it was my fault? Where did I begin to believe I was helpless? Where did I begin to believe in my own destructiveness?' Take your adult mind back to those childhood places and look at them again. Choose to stop condemning yourself for what occurred. Realise that what you blamed yourself for is not the truth. Instead, recognise that you have come to be the antidote for it. Since this can only be done from the centre that you left so long ago, ask your Higher Power to carry you back to your centre and, from there, radiate what is needed to all those around you. This antidote comes from you being who you are – not what you do. Now is the time to let go of the past so you can become more effective by finding the vision and love that wants to express itself through you, as you. You begin receiving and are more naturally effective as you become the healed healer.

159. APPRECIATION IS ONE OF THE EASIEST WAYS TO HEAL ANYTHING

Any pain, problem, or wound is a place where for some reason we have stopped moving forward. When we seem stuck in lack of abundance or in any area, appreciation begins the healing process that moves us back into the flow of life. As there is no pain, problem, or wound that can withstand the power of appreciation, they dissolve and we move forward. It is amazing how much more we enjoy our life just by our appreciation.

Exercise

Today, appreciate as many people as you can. Appreciate the world around you. Appreciate the senses you have been given to enjoy even the breath you are taking right now. If there is a problem between your partner and you, keep telling them everything you appreciate about them until it completely melts away in your warmth.

160. THE PURPOSE OF EVERY ENEMY IS TO BRING BACK A LONG-BURIED PIECE OF MY MIND

Enemies are of great benefit to us as we recognise that they embody a piece of us that we lost long ago. As we realise this, they can be a partner for us. Our willingness to forgive and trust in this brings the split part of ourself back for us to fully integrate. The force of the energy that this enemy brings against us is always brought for our own healing. If we do not resist the energy, but allow it to move into us, we leap up to a higher level of consciousness. The amount of energy they throw against us actually reflects the amount of our own energy we use against ourself at a deeper level in our mind. The first step to healing is in recognising what our enemy is showing us. Then, as we appreciate them as someone who is giving us a signal about a long-lost piece of ourself that we have judged, it can be recovered.

Exercise

Today, take a look at your enemy. What quality or qualities about them are you fighting against? Have you ever acted in this way? If you cannot remember acting like this, was there anyone close around you who did act that way? What feeling would it take for you or anyone to be acting in this fashion? If you cannot identify with the feeling, then ask yourself what is the feeling underneath it that drove the behaviour? When you finally get to a feeling you can identify with, recognise you and your enemy are feeling the same thing. Allow this to be the bridge of compassion and commonality that joins you to this person who had been your enemy. The more you use the bridge, the more you understand and find your common purpose.

181

161. MOST CONFLICTS ARE HEALED
BY CLARIFYING MY EXPERIENCE

Every conflict is a form of misunderstanding. Explaining our experience to our partner, and listening carefully to their experience and what they were feeling to act the way they did, can resolve the conflict. Clarification of our own and the other person's feelings effectively deals with about eighty-five percent of all conflicts. As we fully understand our partner's experience and as they fully understand ours, we naturally join together and move forward.

Exercise

Today, in any situation that you feel is not completely resolved, begin to talk about what is going on for you. See what is going on for your partner, too – what the meaning is for them, why they are acting and feeling the way they are. Do not forget to reaffirm your partner and the value of your relationship in this conflict, because without them, you would still be suffering.

162. IF I DON'T HAVE A RELATIONSHIP, IT IS BECAUSE I HAVE CLOSED THE DOOR

Sometimes, at the end of a relationship, we shut the door because of our feelings of pain and anger. Then, we shut the door on all relationships and completely repress the fact that we did so. After a certain amount of time, when we go out looking for a relationship, no matter how long, how hard, or in how many directions we look, no eligible person seems to be around. We cannot seem to find anyone eligible who interests us; it is because we have shut the door. The good news is that we can open the door right now – flinging it wide and beginning again.

Exercise

Today, if you are not in a relationship, when did you close the door? If you are already in a relationship, you might take a look at what seems to be missing, because where you are missing something, you have closed the door to that particular quality. Why did you shut the door? Imagine you are swinging the door wide open. It is your door, so if it is locked, guess what? You have the key. As soon as you open the door, what you are missing will come your way.

163.   THE TRUTH ALWAYS HELPS

If we are in a dead or conflicted situation, and do not know what could help, we can try the truth! The truth moves us forward by pulling us out of withdrawal because it is a form of giving. Truth is not just unloading on your partner, it is sharing the deeper feelings we have around the situation. The truth is vital because it sets us free.

Exercise

Today, get yourself out of prison. What truth are you not telling? What truth are you holding back from your partner or the situation around you? Go tell the truth.

164. KEEP TELLING THE TRUTH
UNTIL EVERYONE WINS

Truth is not a weapon with which to bludgeon the people around us. Truth allows everyone to win. Truth is the integration of all perspectives in the present situation. When all perspectives are added, everyone is motivated to move forward. What always hurts in a situation is that people have not told enough of the truth to come to full understanding and resolution. Unless everyone wins around us, it is not the final truth.

Exercise

Today, keep communicating until everyone feels as if they have won. Do not stop at compromise, because then you will feel as if you are in sacrifice, and then everyone will feel as if they are losing. Keep communicating until everything is resolved. The truth means everybody wins.

165. THE ONLY PROBLEM IS
SEPARATION. LOVE HEALS SEPARATION

If we followed every problem down to its most basic dynamic, at the very bottom we would find fear and separation. Love heals separation, so whatever the problem is, the solution is simple – love. As we heal the separation, make the bridge, and create the bonding, we move through the problem and join with our partner. Whatever the symptom is – guilt, fear, sickness, or any form of conflict that causes us to feel separate – use love, use forgiveness, use bonding as the glue to make everything come together and the problem disappear.

Exercise

Today, choose two of your greatest problems, and look for the place of separation in each. When you discover the separation, choose love as the way of healing it. Give the love, the forgiveness, which creates bonding and heals the separation. Practise love as the answer to all your problems so the separation heals and the problem disappears.

166.   COMMITMENT ALLOWS FOR
GREATER SELF-EXPRESSION

Commitment creates safety, freedom, and ease. With these, we have a greater opportunity to find our gifts and to express them. When we feel that we have the kind of safety net a committed relationship provides, we go on to find greater creativity and higher levels of self-expression within ourself. Our commitment opens us to ourself, to our giftedness.

Exercise

Today, value your partner for the new things that have developed in you since your relationship began. Appreciate your partner for what they have given you. Express your gratitude to them that, as a result of the commitment in your relationship, these new aspects of yourself had a chance to grow so that you could recognise them.

167.   A BROKEN HEART IS REALLY
A BROKEN EXPECTATION

A broken heart is really a broken expectation that another would fill our needs. Our heart can only be broken if we are rigid in our expectations and rules about how our partner should be. When we are willing and let go of our expectations, we have a certain flexibility, and our heart cannot be broken.

Exercise

Today, take a look at where you are experiencing some form of heartbreak, or where you are still suffering from an old heartbreak. Realise this was your unspoken demand for the relationship to be according to your rules, and that the person wasn't acting in a way to meet your needs. Be willing to let all of this go so you can move forward and receive, so you can feel the love you have been missing.

168. IF I AM ATTRACTED TO A PERSON, I HAVE A GIFT FOR THEM

Being attracted to someone lets us know that we have a gift for them. Often, when we are attracted to somebody, we think they are supposed to give us something, but our joy comes in realising that if we give the gift, a creative project comes to both of us as a result of that connection. If we are willing to give our gifts with integrity, we enjoy a creative connection with many, many joyful people.

Exercise

Today, as you recognise yourself being attracted to someone, ask yourself, 'What is the gift I am to give them that would really move them forward?' It might only be a blessing or a feeling of support, but whatever it is, give it without any expectation of receiving anything in return. Give your gift with integrity and love, and enjoy this creative connection you now have with them.

169. IF I GIVE UP BEING RIGHT,
I WILL BE HAPPY

Being right closes us off and does not allow any new information to come into the situation. We have our answer and we do not want to be confused with any of the facts. Being right is a way of actually hiding how wrong we feel inside. Where we are being right is where we have stopped unfolding by our own choice. This choice is ours – we can be right, or we can be happy, but we cannot be both.

Exercise

Today, write down the areas where you are stuck and not receiving in your life. Next to each area, write down all the ways you are being right about this situation. Be willing to let these go, and let new answers come to light. Be willing to give up this futile defence you use to hide your guilt, and allow yourself to be happy.

170. THE ROLE GETS THE REWARD, WHILE I REMAIN IN SACRIFICE

A role is a place where we give, but cannot receive. In a role, we deal everyone a good hand, but we are not even dealing ourself into the game. Roles lead to tiredness and burn-out. Whatever we are trying to prove by this role is already true about us, so there is no need to prove it; there is just the willingness to recognise it as being true of us. As we accept this, we allow ourself to receive the reward for all of our work and to enjoy our partner, our family, our work, and our life. We allow ourself to enjoy the air we breathe, the food we eat, and everything we do, while enjoying the natural good feeling that comes from giving. We then make the choice to do the right thing for the right reason; not because we are supposed to, but because we choose to. Whatever we are supposed to do becomes a role which gets our rewards while we reap burn-out. Whatever we choose becomes our commitment and we reap the rewards for ourself.

Exercise

Today, take a look at any area where you do not seem to be receiving or getting anything out of what you are doing. See whether you are in a role rather than just naturally giving out of your own choice. Just by choosing to give, you can totally correct the situation. Choose again. Even in a difficult situation, your choice will empower you and give you energy.

171. ALL HEALING COMES
FROM JOINING

If separation is at the heart of every problem, then all healing comes from joining. It follows, then, that moving towards people allows the situation to begin moving forward and unfolding rather than staying stuck. Joining is the easiest way to heal the most complicated of problems. It is as simple as just going to our partner and establishing rapport with them, which allows us to come to the point of natural bonding in our relationship. It allows the intimacy necessary to overcome and overlook the little things that seem to come up and get in the way of our natural joining. When we experience natural joining, all the little grievances that make big problems fall away.

Exercise

Today, choose one big, juicy problem. Who are the key people in this situation? Move toward them until you feel as if you have joined them. Be willing to use communication, forgiveness, moving off your 'position', or whatever it takes to join with them. Even though you may not agree with everything they are saying, you will, once again, feel personally close to them, which allows a new answer to come through for both of you.

172.   EVERY BIRTH FEELS
LIKE A DEATH

If we woke up in the middle of the night and were being born, we would feel as if we were dying. Every place of birth, every new beginning in our life can feel like a death. In situations that seem to be closing in around us, we tend to mistake the end of a chapter in our life as the end of it all. As we realise that as one aspect of our life closes, another one begins, it makes it easier to let go of the old so this new birth can occur. As we trust what seems like death, it becomes our birth. When the ego is dying, at a certain level, it always tells us that we are dying.

Exercise

Today, take a look at your life and see if a situation seems to be ending, or if something seems to be closing down. Realise what needs to finish so the new beginning can occur. Keep your faith in the birth process because a new chapter is about to begin for your life. Trust the closing-down process. It is happening for you to discover the new life that is building on the ashes of the old.

173. I HAVE THE RESOURCES TO MEET THE NEEDS OF EVERY SITUATION

We are never placed in a situation that is beyond us. Every situation we face comes to us at the point where we are able to transcend the situation and come up with the healing answer that assists everyone. There is a place in our mind that knows the answer, however paradoxical, to all our major conflicts. When we are ready for the next lesson, it appears, and we have the resources within to find the way out.

Exercise

Today, choose a problem area in your life that seems beyond you. Ask for your Higher Power to take over and handle it. Just watch. Over the next twenty-four hours, observe what seems to occur in the situation. Get out of the way, trust the solution will happen, and watch as the situation unfolds. Either the entire problem area will disappear, or a major layer of it will dissolve. If it is only a layer, keep asking for help until every layer of the entire problem is healed.

174. I CAN EXPERIENCE GUILT ONLY IF I AM USING SOMEONE OR SOMETHING TO HOLD MYSELF BACK

The purpose of guilt is to protect us from feeling our fear of moving forward. We experience guilt only when we need someone or something to hold ourself back. As we realise the purpose of guilt is only to hold ourself back, all the situations where we felt guilty were because of our fear. Making the choice to move forward in our life allows us to recognise and accept our giftedness.

Exercise

Today, examine what you are still feeling guilty about. How are you using guilt to hold yourself back? Maybe at a certain point in your life you did not feel you could handle a particular gift, ability, or aspect of yourself. Now you have the maturity and the wisdom to do that. Choose to move forward in your life, no longer using guilt to hold yourself back.

175. I AM RESPONSIBLE FOR MY OWN FEELINGS

If we are feeling the feelings, they are coming from inside us. Nobody can make us feel something that is not already within us. Saying somebody makes us feel angry or hurts us is like saying that someone can unscrew the top of our head, climb down inside us and grab our anger throttle or push our hurt button. This is simply not true. We have the choice about what we are feeling. It is a split-second choice because most of us are reactive to outside situations. If there is pain inside us, situations arise that naturally trigger it forth.

If we try to make someone else responsible for our feelings, we belittle and victimise ourself. They are our feelings; therefore, we are responsible for them. As we take responsibility for them, we no longer have to manipulate others to do things differently so we can feel good. In taking responsibility for our own feelings, we recognise that we are the one who can change them.

Exercise

Today, accept responsibility for your feelings. Being responsible for your feelings takes all forms of manipulation and emotional blackmail out of the situation so it can heal. Your negative feelings point to a lesson you need to learn, something you are called upon to change, and something that wants to be healed. You can change your feelings to heal yourself and the situation.

176. FEAR IS ATTRACTION

Psychological tests have shown that as fear increases, so does sexual energy, which is part of our creative power. At a deeper level, what we are afraid of, we are also attracted to. If we are afraid of death, at some level, we are flirting with death. If we are afraid of something happening to our partner, at some level there is a desire for it to happen. This is one of the most hidden parts of our mind and, of course, we naturally want to repress it. Repressing it, though, keeps us in the dark from what we are creating because fear creates just as love and hate create. Our willingness to bring this hidden part of our mind into the light creates healing.

Exercise

Today, take a look at what you fear. What is your hidden attraction to it? Examine your fear as something that you would like to happen. As you bring your fear into the light and see what, at some level, you wanted to happen, you can change it to what you really do want to happen. With this choice you no longer have a split mind and fear of the outcome; rather you have the knowing that bringing what was the darkness in your mind into the light created healing.

177. THE EXTENT OF MY OPENNESS IS THE EXTENT TO WHICH I INSPIRE OTHERS

Many of us are afraid to reveal ourself; we only show others the nice and sweet things about ourself. If we were to share our real feelings, including the places where we are afraid, ashamed or feel bad, we would find that our realness and integrity would inspire others and move them toward us. It is a paradox that we hold back this side of ourself so that people will like us, when it is the revealing of this side that actually allows us to have real contact with others.

Exercise

Today, get real and share what you are experiencing. Do not homogenise it, pasteurise it, or wrap it up in 'nice' cellophane. Do not share to manipulate or change anyone, instead, share to change yourself and to reach out to others. Share the very heart of your experience and the people around you, after the initial shock, of course, will feel inspired to move forward.

178. TO CLEAR UP A PROBLEM IN MY CAREER, I FORGIVE MY FATHER

When we have a problem in our career, there is a place where we are holding a grievance against our father, a place where we have not yet forgiven him. As we are willing to forgive our father, and every time we do, we move forward in our career.

Many of us feel unsupported, unrecognised, and misunderstood by our father, as if we were attacked. We can feel our father's competition only if we are competing. We can see our father's failure only if, at a very deep level, we wished him to fail. With the understanding that our father can only be what we give him to be, we can choose to give forth to him. As we give forth to our father, we discover that all our authority figures are seen in a new light. Our father and our career are representative of our masculine side and, therefore, interrelated. As we forgive our father, give forth to him, our career blossoms and opens up for us.

Exercise

Today, take a look at your father in this new light. Remember that what you give to him spells your success. Even if he has died, you can still forgive and give to him. As you give to him, the father in you increases, and your masculine side supports you. Wherever your father is, he will feel blessed by your understanding.

179. THE PURPOSE OF RELATIONSHIPS IS TO BOND ALL THE FRACTURED PIECES

Every time we were crushed or traumatised is a place in time where we failed to learn the lessons we were given and, instead, created fractured pieces in our mind. These are places where we actually had an opportunity to step into a much higher level of love, understanding, and bonding. The opportunities are not lost, however, because all of those tests are recreated and again presented to us in our relationship. Our relationship is the workshop in which we are, once again, given the lessons so we can learn them and bring all the broken pieces back together again.

Exercise

Today, look at any conflict situation, and realise that it is, actually, a situation where you are being re-tested. You flunked the first time, but now you are being given the opportunity to re-take the test and this time pass. Sometimes, when unlearned lessons are presented again, they can feel more like a trial than a test, but you can succeed. Ask for Heaven's help, respond to the situation with as much communication and responsiveness as possible, and apologise if necessary. You will find yourself having learned the lesson and moving forward.

180. EVERYONE WHO COMES TO ME
FOR HELP IS COMING TO SAVE ME

When someone comes to us for help, they are coming to help us heal a piece of ourself that we ordinarily would not know is wounded. Many times, when we have healed something on the surface, something within us is unfinished. With awareness that the other person has come to save us, as we are helping them we discover that the advice we are giving is the very thing we most need to hear. Listening to this advice, also, as a message to ourself, heals our wounds and everyone is saved.

Exercise

Today, be especially grateful to anyone who comes to you for help. Be responsive to them, realising they are actually bringing back a missing piece of yourself, a piece that will lead you on to a new level of success.

181. WHAT I REJECT IN MY PARENTS MY PARTNER ACTS OUT

What we rejected in our parents are, actually, parts of us we projected onto them that we did not like about ourself. Our parents represented our inner world, our subconscious mind; they are projections of two of the most vital parts of our mind available for healing. Whatever we reject is an unlearned lesson that will continue to plague us until we learn it. As these parts of our mind are unhealed, we project the same things onto our partner who gets to act it out until we get the lesson. If we continue to reject, the problem continues to haunt us and becomes even bigger so we can't ignore it. Now is a good time to forgive or integrate our rejected parts so the judgement and self-judgement fall away.

Exercise

Today is the time to learn this lesson. Ask for help, open your mind, be a little bit more responsive and hold back your judgements. Now, feel your heart flowing out to meet your partner so you can take off the mask you have made them wear. As the mask falls away, you find a part of yourself that has needed love. Give this part the love it has been craving. If it is a child, love this child until it grows up and reaches your present age. It will then melt into you, reconnecting wires that were cut long ago. Now, as you no longer hold against yourself what you held against your parents and your partner, everyone is free.

182.   WHEN A PROBLEM IN MY RELATIONSHIP FEELS BEYOND ME, I ASK FOR HEAVEN'S HELP

We have all had problems that felt beyond us. These conflicts are so painful that, when in them, we feel we do not have the resources at hand, the strength or the courage to face them. This is the time to ask for Heaven's help to heal our problem. As we learn to partner with our partner, we are also learning to partner with our creativity and with Heaven. Asking for Heaven's help allows us to clear whatever problem faces us, no matter the difficulty.

Exercise

Today, be willing to receive from Heaven. No matter how big the problem looks, ask for help, open your heart and receive the grace that Heaven has for you. As you do, you and your partner move forward.

183.   IF I WANT THE BEST IN MY
RELATIONSHIP, I GIVE MY BEST

What we are receiving in our relationship allows us to recognise what we are giving. Since we want the best in our relationship, to have it, we give it. Giving the best of ourself allows us to enjoy the best in other people. Giving the best in ourself opens doors that, otherwise, would not be opened, and provides the opportunities for new gifts, new fun, and new enjoyment to arise in our relationship.

Exercise

Today, give your very best. Give your heart, give your all, and notice what a great day it is.

184. PAIN IS THE ENERGY I NEED TO HOLD ON TO NEGATIVE THOUGHTS ABOUT MYSELF

If we are willing to release our pain, the negative thoughts or self-concepts we have about ourself will naturally shift. Pain is the energy that fuels our negative self-concept; so without the pain there is nothing to support self-destructive patterns. Our willingness to experience the pain until it is gone frees the energy that is constricting us. Conversely, letting go of the negative thoughts easily releases us from pain.

Exercise

Today, be willing to let go of the pain you have been using to hold on to negative thoughts about yourself. Realise you have been using the negative thought or self-concept to keep from moving forward, because you are afraid to face something that will make you much happier. Let go of these negative self-concepts and discover a greater capacity to receive and enjoy yourself more.

185. WHAT I RESIST IN ANOTHER IS WHAT I AM RESISTING IN MYSELF

What we do not like in someone else is what we do not like in ourself. Our resistance is showing us what is happening in our own subconscious mind; it is showing us what we have judged about ourself and buried inside. We rejected a part of ourself and then projected it onto another. If we are willing to stop resisting this part and to understand it, the other person will seem to change before our eyes. We then find that both ourself and the other person move forward, together.

Exercise

Today, examine your resistance to another person. Be willing to recognise that your resistance is, actually, one part of you resisting another part of you. Acknowledge this part that you have buried. Feel it totally inside of you and keep acknowledging it until your discomfort moves to acceptance. As you accept it, you will feel free, and the other person is also freed.

186.   HAPPINESS THAT COMES
FROM WITHIN CANNOT BE LOST

The happiness that is generated within us cannot be taken away. If, however, we depend on outer things for our happiness, we lose it when those things change. As we are willing to keep generating the happiness within and give it, even in difficult times, the happiness in our relationship will never be lost. When we give love and happiness, especially in difficult situations, we heal and grow immensely; our joy is increased.

Exercise

Today, look at any situation where your happiness seems to be dependent on outside things. With a little shift, give that happiness from within you. When you are generating happiness, everyone gets the benefit, everyone is nurtured, and everyone moves forward.

187.   IF ANYTHING I DO IS HARD
WORK, I AM STUCK IN A ROLE

If anything we do is hard work, something is not working. A role sets out to prove how good and virtuous we are, but in the proving we have to work extra hard. We find ourself explaining how tough it was, and how we got over it, just to win some admiration from those around us.

Hard work is relying too much on our own independence, trying to do it ourself. Taking it all on our shoulders, though, only covers our guilt; in the long run it is a way of holding things back. We are a much more vital resource when we are not doing the work of a mule. We are already that which we are trying to prove. In our essence, we are truly good. As we stop trying to prove it and let go of our guilt surrounding it, the difficulty falls away. Everything is so much easier.

Exercise

Today, examine the situations that seem difficult in your life, the areas where you are working extra hard. Ask for Heaven's help and allow the grace to move through you into the situation. Ask and allow the people around you to also help. Let go of your guilt and free yourself. Give what you can, what you are called to give, but do not take it all on your shoulders. The power of grace and the openness of your mind brings through a resourcefulness that frees everyone.

188. THE BIGGEST SECRET OF AN INDEPENDENT PERSON IS THAT THEY HAVE NOT LET GO OF SOMEONE FROM THE PAST

The reason we are independent is because we are still attached to a person from the past. If we are negatively attached to this person, perhaps we experienced a heartbreak and have not yet let go. Our rejection of the experience keeps us independent and blocks us from moving toward interdependence and true love. If we are positively attached, at some level of our mind, we are still fantasising about remaking the past or having a particular person turn up at our doorstep. Of course, holding on to these positive things keeps them from occurring right now in our present situation. As we let go of the attachment, whether positive or negative, we are able to receive the joys of a relationship that is alive and well in the present.

Exercise

Today, let go of the people you are attached to. As you let them go, open yourself to new opportunities and the return of the feelings you lost. Feel the fear and loss, or any painful feelings until they disappear. When these painful feelings are gone, you can begin to feel the good things that are coming your way.

189.   ALL PAIN COMES
FROM ATTACHMENT

When we lose what we are attached to, we suffer. What we are truly connected to, however, can never be disconnected; the love we give is never lost. Letting go of our attachments is the key element in keeping us out of pain. Our willingness to be connected to the person, rather than attached to them or the circumstances, allows us to enjoy the people we are with. We then experience situations without feeling pain as they change and move forward. Non-attachment takes the pain out of our experience because we can receive and enjoy.

Exercise

Today, in every place where you are suffering, ask yourself, 'What is it I am attached to?' Then, take a look at where you are attached now, because this is a place of future suffering. Be willing to let the attachments go and be connected to the people involved. Be willing to give them your love and you will feel yourself moving forward.

190. IF IT HURTS IT ISN'T LOVE

In spite of what all the songs, books and movies tell us, if it hurts, it is not love. Only our needs hurt; only not getting what we want hurts. Love cannot hurt because it is a feeling of contact that brings joy. When we shrink, contract, or pull away, that is what hurts. When we do not get our needs met, it hurts. When something in a relationship brings up our old pain, we hurt. Love does not hurt us, it expands us. Sometimes when our heart expands, it can feel a bit like hurt, but it is poignancy – the richness of our heart growing in love and appreciation. Poignancy is your heart beginning to dance again after having been crippled a long time. There is a real sweetness to this feeling as our heart expands with love.

Exercise

Today, look at the situations where you have tried to measure your love by your hurt. Where have you disguised your needs as love and, then, tried to get the other person to respond in a similar manner? Be willing to let go of these needs so you can move forward and make contact with your partner, not as you want them to be, but as they really are.

191. THE LESS I DEFEND MYSELF, THE SAFER I AM

Every defence creates attack. The more defensive we are, the more we create attack coming at us. Our defences are there to protect buried pain, but buried pain poisons us. When we are attacked and are not afraid to feel the feelings that come up because of it, the attack helps bring about our healing. The greater majority of this pain is from the past, and the attack has brought these poisons into our awareness. When we are attacked, the extent to which we stand undefended is the extent to which we will eventually succeed. The truth does not need defending; only our ego, the hider of all pain and the essence of separation, needs defence. Openness is the heart of communication. It is the ability to give and be ourself without an excuse. As we remain undefended, we find another gift is also being given to us – the support of those around us.

Exercise

Today, as best you can, stand undefended to everything that moves toward you. Everything that comes to you serves as your teacher. Your openness allows these teachings to be brought to you in the most gentle way possible.

192. FEAR IS ALMOST EXCITEMENT

If we pay attention to fear, we notice it is energy that is trying to move through our body. Our fear is a resistance to this energy coming through. If we are willing to let it move through us, it will pour through us as excitement. Millions of dollars are spent every year trying to get excitement in our lives. We jump out of aeroplanes, climb mountains, go to horror movies, anything to create some kind of excitement, but all we have to do is to take a look at what is frightening us. When we stop resisting it, we let it flow through us, and the energy provides us with the thrills.

Exercise

Today, spend some time looking at what you are afraid of. See where the energy is trapped in your body. Then, be willing to let it move up through your body until it overflows from the top of your head. This could be a most exciting day for you.

193. LOSS IS ALMOST A NEW BEGINNING

Loss comes to clear the decks. It teaches us that what we were attached to could not really sustain us. Loss is the first step to a new beginning. If we do not finish our mourning, if we hold on to the past, or if we go into depressions so as not to move forward, then we do not have our new beginning. We do not see the dawn coming up after the dark if we resist the night. We are being asked to grow, mature, and move on so we can birth a new life for ourself.

Exercise

Today, recognise that all your losses were really about new beginnings. Be willing to let go of all these losses so the new birth shows itself. Now the next good thing can come to you.

194. HURT IS ALMOST TENDERNESS

If we do not resist the feeling of hurt, and if we do not move into contraction, then we can experience a great feeling of tenderness. Unresisted hurt creates an opening in our heart where old pain can come forth and be healed.

Exercise

Today, do not resist the feelings of hurt. Let the lips of your wounds sing the songs of your heart.

195. GUILT IS BLOCKED WISDOM

Guilt is a way of removing ourself from the lesson to be learned. We attack and punish ourself in an attempt to pay for the mistake, but guilt stops us and keeps us stuck. If every time we made a mistake as a child we beat ourself up, we would never have learned how to walk. Every lesson is here to be learned and our guilt shows us a lesson, as yet, unlearned.

Guilt is almost wisdom, but until the lesson is learned, it is a form of punishing ourself for not making a simple correction. Our willingness to learn the lesson corrects the mistake, which adds to our knowledge and wisdom.

Exercise

Today, look at where you feel guilty. Ask for help to see the lesson life wants to teach you and be willing to learn it. As you learn this lesson, you are released into greater wisdom.

196. SACRIFICE IS ALMOST LOVE

Sacrifice contains a desire to give, but it leaves out one very important element – ourself. Since sacrifice happens through a role where we are not really present, it gives, but it cannot receive. Sacrifice cheats our partner out of their ability to give back to us. It cheats our partner of the value of our gift because, if we devalue ourself, there is nothing of worth for them to receive.

Valuing ourself changes sacrifice and *almost love* into being truly love. Giving ourself in what we give is the greatest gift because it allows us to receive also. This means there is always more to give, and always more to receive.

Exercise

Today, look at the areas where you are in sacrifice. Realise that part of you is being withheld and choose, instead, to give fully. As you give yourself fully, you can fully receive all the love that is meant for you.

197.   DISAPPOINTMENT IS
ALMOST RELEASE

Disappointment is the first step on the way to release. Unfortunately, most of us stop here and forever remain disappointed because things did not turn out the way we felt we needed them to. If we are willing to experience the disappointment and the need within it, and let it go, we move out of stress into success; we stop pushing the proverbial river. We listen to life's rhythms rather than trying to squeeze life into our concepts. Disappointment lets us know that our picture of life is not a true one, and as we let it go, we are taught what life is really about. We become like an empty glass ready to be filled, rather than full and unable to take in anything more.

Exercise

Today, imagine you are like a glass. Clear yourself of all disappointments and stand ready to be filled with what life will teach you.

198. FRUSTRATION IS ALMOST UNDERSTANDING

Frustration comes from things not turning out our way, which we think is the right and the best way; we are disappointed that our expectations were not met. As we are willing to move past our frustration, we have an opportunity to reach a full understanding of our situation. Frustration shows us that we have an incomplete understanding, something about our partner, the situation, or ourself is not fully understood. As we choose to not stop halfway, to not settle for an *almost understanding*, we complete the cycle and unlock the door to our prison of frustration.

Exercise

Today, in areas where you feel frustrated, look for a deeper understanding. Ask for the deeper awareness that could be teaching you. All awareness creates a flow and moves you forward. Your understanding is your key.

IT IS IMPOSSIBLE TO FEEL
FEAR IN THE PRESENT MOMENT

Fear can only be experienced by living in the future. Trying to live the future now, which is impossible, only creates strain and fear. Even if we only move five minutes ahead in a difficult situation, we create a lot of fear for ourself. By living in the future rather than the present, we can only expect our future to be like the past, because the past is all we have to give our future. However, if we fully live in the present moment, we give this to our future and fear disappears. When living fully in this moment, no matter how difficult it looks, we are not concerned about our future; therefore, there can be no fear. The moment is a moment of release and giving, which opens the door to eternity and love, the opposite of fear.

Exercise

Today, look at ways where you are living in the future and creating all kinds of fear for yourself. Be willing to be in the present so the future can take care of itself. As it says in A Course In Miracles, *'Place your future in the hands of God,' and just live moment by moment, enjoying it fully. Be present, be here and receive the richness and nectar of each moment. Happy sipping!*

200.   BEING A VICTIM IS
A FORM OF ATTACK

All of us have been victims at times. Typically, these are the
most painful, traumatic times of our life because they seem to
come from situations that surprise us, even blind-side us. We
seem to be attacked from an unexpected quarter. It is true,
however, that we reap what we sow; therefore, more is going
on in a victim situation than meets the eye. There is as much
violence in a victim as there is in a victimiser. A victimiser
sends the violence outward, while the victim directs the
violence, firstly, against themselves and, secondly, towards
someone else.

Every time we are victimised, we attack some person who
is significant to us. We might even be attacking someone who
died long ago, but we typically attack the people who are
around us now. Being a victim is a state of unawareness, a way
of being and staying angry. To take it to its deepest meta-
physical level, it is a form of attack that says, 'I'll show you,
God. I'll show you that you are not such a good God. I'll
suffer and be unhappy here on your earth.' As we let go of
being a victim, which is to stop attacking others through
attacking ourself, we become willing to receive. We are then
surrounded by abundance, love and support.

Exercise

*Today, take some time to sit down and write out ten major incidents
where you were a victim. Next to each incident, write down who it was
you were attacking and, then, what it was you were attacking them
for. Recognise how being a victim was just a natural part of your power*

221

struggle with them. Make a choice about whether or not you want the attack to continue. If you have kept who you were attacking a secret from yourself, there is still an element of being a victim, and attack is still going on. It is holding you back, so ask for help to realise who this is. Choose to stop attacking, thereby freeing yourself and everyone concerned.

201. TRUST MENDS OLD HEARTBREAKS

In any frightening problem situation, trust is the answer. Trust is the most important element in confidence. Trust is using the power of our mind to choose the very best, knowing that what appears to be dark or painful will be transformed. The healer of dissociation, trust returns feeling and allows tenderness and safety in our relationships; trust mends our old heartbreaks.

Trust heals anything, but do not confuse trust with controlling the outcome, or how the answer will come about. Our job is only to choose and then know that everything will turn out for the best. When doubt or pain creep in, make the choice that brings peace. Trust is not being naive. Trust sees the potentially painful elements and, unlike naivety which usually leads to heartbreak, it denies they have any final or lasting power over the situation. It recognises that, sometimes, these elements are actually helpful in the long run. Trust is the recognition of how powerful we are in any situation. It both nurtures us and makes us safe. It can be the mother we always wanted.

Exercise

Today, use the power of your mind to transform any situation. Choose a situation that needs transforming and trust it. Bring in the power of your mind, knowing no matter how the situation looks, trust will make it work for you.

202.

ALL HEARTBREAK
HIDES COMPETITION

Heartbreak is a way of trying to take something from our partner. We cannot be heartbroken if we are truly giving, but we can if we are giving to get, which is taking. Heartbreak is a way of trying to take something from our partner. When we compete with our partner to get our needs met, one or both of us begin to act in very independent ways so when they do something against us, we withdraw, attack or ambush. This continual competition creates greater and greater pain until, finally, somebody has a heartbreak.

Our willingness to acknowledge that we are secretly, or not so secretly, competing begins to shift these power struggles, so both ourself and our partner win and get each of our needs met. This can happen through dialogue in any situation that is difficult. Fully giving ourself, and letting go, creates places of major birth. It also opens the door for receiving, instead of taking.

Exercise

Today, look at areas where you are competing with your partner. Choose to let go and truly give to your partner. As you do, you will really enjoy them and you will know the joys and safety of partnership.

203.   ALL SABOTAGE HIDES
A FEAR OF GREATER SACRIFICE

When sabotage occurs, it looks as if we have failed, but, actually, we are succeeding at the sabotage. This is, naturally, at great cost to ourself. While everyone else may see us as successful, we are feeling the off-the-ledger costs, and these costs are getting too great for us. Sabotage occurs just at a point where we are about to step into a whole new level of success. To us, of course, this means a much greater level of sacrifice. We feel we just cannot do it any longer, we cannot take on any more than we already have. Sabotage is a result of not being able to stand the thought of greater sacrifice. We blow up the future successful situation, and when they find the plunger that detonated the explosives, our fingerprints are all over it. Our willingness to give up sacrifice and to deal ourself into the game, making more room for ourself to breathe and enjoy life, allows greater courage to step into the future and succeed at a new level.

Exercise

Today, let go of sacrifice. It is the only roadblock on your way to a much higher level of success in your relationship and in your career.

204. DEPENDENCE IN THE PRESENT POINTS TO JUDGEMENT IN THE PAST

Wherever we are dependent, we have judgement. We think someone or the situation did not meet our needs. To get our needs met in the present, we become dependent in the situation, thinking that if we become full of needs, surely, someone will meet them. Where we have judgement in the past, we also have guilt. Needs, which arise from lack of bonding, loss, or fear, are tied in with feeling guilty. Instead of trying to live in the past, we could simply move forward and, by so doing, find that our needs would naturally be met. Dependence simply creates a bad feeling which becomes a vicious circle: 'I'm needy, I feel bad about myself, I feel even more needy, I feel even more bad about myself.'

Exercise

Today, let go of those judgements about how things or someone should have been. Be willing to forgive the past and more openly embrace the next step. You will find that your needs are naturally met.

205. EVERY RELATIONSHIP IS A REFLECTION OF MY RELATIONSHIP TO MYSELF

Every relationship around us shows how we are valuing ourself. If someone is mistreating us, it can only be because we are mistreating ourself. If somebody is abusing us, it is only because we are abusing ourself. Even to experience rape is showing us how strongly we are, somewhere, forcing ourself against our wishes. If we do not like our relationships, the way to change them is to change how we are treating ourself. If people are not respecting us, there is something about us that does not ask for respect. People can only be punishing us if at some level we feel guilty and feel we deserve to be punished. Whatever that is, it is a mistake. We deserve the very best; so let's treat ourself that way.

Exercise

Today, take a look at your life. How are you treating yourself? Take the ten most significant relationships, and ask yourself, 'What is the key quality in their treatment of me?' Then, take a look at how you are treating yourself. If there is a negative aspect in your treatment of yourself, explore where that began. Knowing what you know now, how would you choose to change what you decided or how you acted in the past that helped make this self-concept? What are you worth to yourself? It is only what you are worth to yourself that the world around you will recognise.

206. GRIEVANCES
DESTROY RELATIONSHIPS

Many of us do not want to share our grievances with our partner because we do not want to have to deal with the mess and the pain. The problem is that grievances destroy relationships. The more we hold on to a grievance, the more we hold ourself back. This builds up a wall between us and our partner, until there is an area of deadness in our relationship. We can share our grievances with our partner. Our willingness to share these grievances, take responsibility for them, and let them go moves our relationship forward.

Exercise

Today is a day of communication, of new motivation to not let the backlog of grievances weigh you down and wear you out. What grievances do you have? What grievances are you still holding onto from the beginning of your relationship? In truth, no grievance is true. It only serves to make you righteous and unwilling to move forward, while hiding your own guilt. Begin taking down the wall between you and your partner, grievance by grievance, so you can find who your partner really is behind all of the grievances you have set between you both. Be willing to move yourself and your relationship forward.

207. EVERY TRAUMA OFFERS A CHOICE

Most of us have had traumatic things happen to us. At the time of a trauma, we have a choice as to what the experience will become for us. Either we choose for this experience to become the thing that wounds us so mortally that it eventually kills us because we never get over it, or we choose for it to become the grain of sand around which we produce a great pearl.

A gift is hidden in every trauma, but it takes a deeper vision to see it. In terms of the healing that needs to be done, everything works for the very best. If we look at our past traumas with new eyes, we see the gifts they offer. If we do not receive the gift from the trauma, the trauma itself will become part of our defences, part of the character armour we use to keep pain away from us. Our willingness to see the gift allows us to take down the armour. It lets the energy flow that can then be used for our health, vitality, happiness and fun.

Exercise

Today, imagine that you are taking one of the traumas you have had and are putting it in the Hands of God. As you do so, a gift comes to you from the Heavens. Feel the gift really coming into you. Accept this gift, this peace, this new understanding, and, where you had closed down, you will feel your whole life growing again.

208.
THE ROLE OF THE
LOVER LIMITS INTIMACY

If we are acting out the role of lover, we limit love, because love comes out of our spontaneity. It comes out of our willingness to be born every day once again, to no longer follow the recipes, or go by rote, but to let love teach us and unfold us. When we follow a recipe, we are just acting out the way we think a lover should be. Of course, at some level, the role of lover hides unworthiness and prevents receiving. Acting out the role of lover stops us from really being in the fire of love, which melts us down, heals and purifies us, and shows us the way. The fire of love takes us into ecstasy and flow, where we are more ourself than we have ever been.

Exercise

Today, look at the things you do just because you are supposed to. Take the oldness and tiredness out of your love situation, and do something new. Surprise your partner. Let them really feel love. Give them something that is essentially you, which they will always remember.

209. DEADNESS IN SEX OR MY RELATIONSHIP IS HEALED BY MOVING INTO A PLACE OF BIRTH

Deadness is a defence to protect ourself from our unconscious mind. One of the fastest ways to move out of deadness is to find the major feeling hiding beneath it. This feeling has such strength and power that when seen correctly, it automatically moves us into a new birth. The kind of feelings that knock us to our knees, like heartbreak, jealousy, terror, violence, anger, emptiness, nothingness, and futility, are truly birth situations.

When we are in deadness, simply asking for the birth situation will take us to the pain that the deadness hides. Typically there is so much pain here we lose our awareness, so when we hit this place, remembering that we asked for the birth helps. This place of sacred fire pain, of purification, is the place of our birth. All it takes to move out of the pain and into the birth process is to give. Typically, at this point, we are in so much pain that we often forget or feel resistance to giving. Remembering to give creates an easy birth. It can be the simplest type of giving – sending love to someone, supporting someone or helping someone in the simplest possible way. Just giving moves us into a new birth, into a place that contains things like a much greater love, a higher level of sexuality, passion, creativity or art, a new level of psychic ability, a new sense of vitality in health, new confidence or power, and a greater sense of peace, vision and purpose.

Exercise

Today, get out of deadness and move into a place of birth. Ask yourself what is the feeling beneath the deadness, and when it comes, begin giving to take yourself out of the pain. Create the new birth by giving.

210. DEPRESSION IS THE FEAR
THAT SOMETHING NEW WILL LEAVE ME

Depression is fear of future loss because we are holding onto a loss from the past. This keeps us from moving forward and welcoming life because we have a fear that the loss will happen again. We refuse to go on and trust the present or future. We refuse to put our faith into anything because we are afraid our faith will be broken and that we will lose something very important. We feel, 'Better to have never lost than to have loved.' We refuse to move forward and take a risk, or trust that life has something better for us.

Exercise

Today, recognise that your depression hides a place of birth. It is time to let go of your past losses and claim the faith to move forward. As you let go, you find the new birth that is waiting for you. You find yourself moving into a whole new resurrection in your life.

211. EXPECTATIONS GIVE ME NO REST

Expectations give us no rest because no matter what the situation is, it does not satisfy us. Our lack of satisfaction reflects how we are not satisfied with ourself, how we feel inadequate.

Expectations are related to perfectionism. To a perfectionist, anything less than perfect is failure. Not having walked on water lately, we have probably always thought of ourself as a failure, and never allowed ourself a reward. This is what expectations do – they never give us a rest. When we complete a job, instead of giving ourself a time and place of rest and reward, perfectionism drives us on to the next thing.

By not having a rest, we cannot have the vision to see a much higher perspective. We keep worrying, always doing every little, last thing, always trying too hard and doing too much so we keep making little changes, instead of seeing what the next giant leap is for ourself.

Then again, there are some perfectionists that never try at all. We think that if we cannot do it perfectly, why even begin? Even if we do nothing at all, in our mind, we are still under so much stress and pressure that we still do not have any rest within ourself.

Exercise

Today, let yourself come to reward. Allow yourself the rest that would give a much higher perspective and the celebration that would motivate you to move to the next level. Let go of all your expectations, and find the ease of life carrying you forward.

212. IRRESISTIBILITY IS ONE OF THE BEST GIFTS I CAN GIVE MY PARTNER

Irresistibility is feeling our attractiveness to such an extent that our charisma draws the people around us closer. This is one of the gifts or acts of Leadership. As we draw people to us, with integrity, we can then lead them forward. It is also a great gift that we can give to our partner; it is a way of inspiring them. Irresistibility makes any job go easier because it is full of playfulness. Irresistibility knows that no matter what, 'How could they not love me?' It is the essential feeling to create loveableness and flow.

Exercise

Today, practise your irresistibility, which is really an inner knowing. It is an energy you provide to the world around you. People love attractiveness because it moves them toward something. As you irresistibly draw your partner toward you, you are offering a gift to yourself as well as to them.

213. THE PAIN OF REJECTION IS ALWAYS OLDER THAN THE PRESENT RELATIONSHIP

The experience of rejection in our relationship is to trigger off old heartbreaks. The pain of rejection is always older than what is happening right now. Heartbreaks we had as children, or in our beginning relationships, will be part of our present relationship until they are healed. If we are willing just to experience the hurt and realise it is really old pain, if we can be in touch with what the old pain is and share it, we correspondingly create a movement forward and a certain responsiveness in our partner. Our willingness to communicate about where the pain is coming from frees and opens us.

Exercise

Today, dwell on a present hurt in your life, and see if you can find its root. When you do, go back to the situation, and imagine Heaven pouring through you to meet everybody's needs. As the courage of Heaven is pouring through you, give love to everyone in that situation. Notice how everything changes. Notice how you are freed in a very easy way from having to go through all the pain.

214. MY SEXUAL DESIRE CAN BE
A COVER FOR MY PAIN

Sexual desire can be a great defence and, sometimes, we use it as a cover for pain. If we entice our partner into having sex with us, we do not have to deal with all the pain. When we have the type of sexual desire that is hiding pain, our partner does not seem interested, is busy, or just does not feel like it. This is the time to take a look at what the sexual energy is hiding. Letting go of pain always wins back our attractiveness.

Exercise

Today, take a look at what your desire might be hiding, especially if you do not seem to be requited at this moment. Your willingness to feel the pain or the feelings beneath your sexual desire, just by feeling them all the way through, would motivate your partner to move toward you. Your willingness to burn through the feelings creates great success where you most want it.

215. COMMITMENT MEANS I KNOW THERE IS TIME FOR THE BROKEN THINGS TO HEAL

When we are committed, we are in for the long haul. We have set a goal of joint purpose and mutual growth together, the coming of wholeness for both of us in the relationship. This means we do not run away from conflicts or broken feelings, but move forward to heal these things. Commitment means we do not have to worry that every little conflict may be our last. Instead, we feel, yes, there is a conflict here, but we are just moving through it on the way to finding greater happiness and deeper love. Commitment means we know there is time for the broken things to heal.

Exercise

Today, reaffirm the goal in your relationship. What do you want to occur? What do you want with your partner? If any problems confront you now, close your eyes and naturally feel yourself moving through those problems, and on to the higher goal. Feel the energy of your partner beside you as you move through each block and step over each hurdle on the way toward this final goal. This is a growth of your own maturity and a realisation of wholeness and greatness. This is a growth of love and beauty in your life.

216. DEADNESS IN A RELATIONSHIP CAN BE HEALED THROUGH GIVING

Deadness in our relationship means we are stuck, tired, and that we have been in sacrifice. We can make a new choice here. We can choose to give ourself more and move out of some of our *busyness* to make truer contact. True giving moves us forward and allows us to receive. Our giving allows us to feel the greatness of our generosity; it allows us to feel our best self. The more we give, the more we know who we truly are. Sometimes, when we feel we have nothing left to give, if we ask for Heaven's help, we find we have just what is needed, just enough to move us forward and get us back in the flow again.

Exercise

Today, take a moment to close your eyes, and imagine the Universe pouring down all kinds of energy and light. As you are filled with this energy, feel how you are motivated to give, especially in certain areas. What are they? Maybe you are called to give very simple things. Even the simple things can show your love.

217. FANTASY IS A WAY OF NOT COMMUNICATING MY NEEDS

When we are in fantasy, we are hiding what we need. We are imagining what would nurture us, excite us and make us feel good. We fantasise to compensate for what is missing in our life, but the fantasy actually comes between us and our partner. It supports the status quo of our mind. Fantasies do not really satisfy us because they do not allow for change in our life; they are trying to give us relief while the real relief is in moving forward. By communicating about and giving through our needs, we can begin to change the situation.

Exercise

Today, check out the fantasies you have in your life. Do you make pipe dreams about what you are going to do later, or what you are going to do with your partner? Now is the time to let go of all those things you are going to do in the future, or all the things in your mind you are using to excite yourself. Really communicate with your partner. Really make contact, because this is the way to move through your needs into a sense of satisfaction and a new level of receiving.

218. THE EXTENT TO WHICH MY HEART HAS BEEN BROKEN IS THE EXTENT TO WHICH HEARTS WILL BREAK AROUND ME

When we have had our heart broken a number of times, or even just one good time, we move into independence so as not to be hurt any more. This dissociation is an unwillingness to be captured, an unwillingness to be, once again, thrown into sacrifice or be a *love slave*. In this unwillingness to deal with our feelings, we take the independent role and, because of this independence, we become very attractive.

Self-sufficiency fosters a certain attractiveness that moves people toward us, but it also has a way of bringing out their dependency. Of course, when their dependency comes out, they try to get us to meet their needs, and they try to capture us in a relationship; all the things we vowed would never happen again. Naturally, we move away from these situations where we can be manipulated or where we have to deal with our own feelings and, then, hearts begin breaking around us.

The extent to which our heart was broken is the extent to which we will not be responsive to the needs of the people around us. When we are willing to deal with our own heartbreak, our old hurts, and our own needs, we find within ourself a greater willingness to be responsive, and to communicate to the people around us so they do not hurt themselves. Communicating our truth, what it is we want, but in a responsive way, helps and supports others to move through their own painful experience.

Exercise

Today, be responsive to someone around you who is in need. Your responsiveness to them heals you both.

219. UNDER EVERY POWER STRUGGLE
IS AN OLD HEARTBREAK

We have power struggles to protect ourself from old heart–break. In a power struggle, two people are polarised. The other person acts out behaviour that got us heartbroken before; it might not be the exact literal behaviour, but something metaphoric or essential to the old heartbreak situation. Our unwillingness to move toward the other person is really our unwillingness to move toward and through this old heartbreak. Even though we are afraid the same thing will happen all over again and we will get hurt, if we are willing to uncover the heartbreak under this power struggle and to communicate about it, we will begin to heal the power struggle.

Exercise

Today, look at a place where you are in power struggle, and be willing to share your side of it. What is going on for you? Be willing to talk about what broke your heart long ago, because communication is the beginning of healing and the end of power struggle.

220. INTIMACY CREATES HEALING

Intimacy creates the safety for communication to occur and the closeness by which old pain can come to the surface. Intimacy creates healing because the closer we get to a person, the less any problem can stand between the two of us. The word 'intimacy' comes from the Latin terms *in* and *timere,* which means, 'not to fear'.

All of us have a basic primordial fear that, 'If a person gets to know me, they won't like me.' Often after the beginning stage of a relationship, people quickly drop their partner because of their fears of being unlikeable, and that once people know them, they will lose all their attractiveness. The willingness to maintain intimacy, however, creates the courage to move past the initial fear, finding new levels of honeymoon and intimacy.

Exercise

Today, think of someone with whom you could create a greater sense of closeness. It might be your partner, one of your parents, or a friend. Be willing to move toward them and create the atmosphere of safety, warmth and intimacy that leads to healing.

221. IF I REACH A PLACE OF MEANINGLESSNESS, I ASK FOR HEAVEN'S HELP

Sometimes, the circumstances of life throw us into a state of meaninglessness, a place where we experience a loss so severe that we are knocked out of the game of life, or a disappointment so deep that we are thrown into the ashes. We have set our mind on some goal, and when the goal is reached, we realise that it is nothing like what we thought it would be. Sometimes, people spend their whole life working on a project, and when they get to the end of it, they feel it was all useless. This feeling can also just surface for no apparent reason.

Meaninglessness is a state of consciousness just this side of enlightenment. When we reach meaninglessness, all we need to do for a major breakthrough is to ask for Heaven's meaning. Meaninglessness is the battleground of the ego and our Higher Self where our ego is trying to take us down into another useless crusade. It tries to lead us into thinking that we can find meaning somewhere in this world. When we ask for Heaven's meaning, we will hear a quiet voice saying very simple things, like 'give', 'love', or 'be happy'. These words carry with them the grace to move us forward and experience the directive. In this place of anguish and of meaninglessness, this place of ashes, ask for Heaven's meaning. While meaninglessness is one of the most painful of experiences, it is easily transcended.

Exercise

Today, whether or not you are in a state of meaninglessness, take time to clear your mind. Whenever a thought comes up, just say, 'This thought reflects a goal that is keeping me from true meaning.' After about ten minutes, when your mind is cleared, ask for Heaven's meaning for you. The words that come in will bring true peace to you, and following them will bring true fulfilment.

222.   THE GRASS IS ALWAYS
GREENER OVER THE GRAVEYARD

The grass is always greener over the graveyard speaks about the conspiracy the ego has for us, how it tries to trap or delay us. There are two common traps with this conspiracy, both of which have us believe our happiness lies elsewhere.

The first is where we are with a partner that we have been in relationship with for a while, and all of a sudden, we see someone new coming along who seems much more attractive to us. Now, if we have been in a power struggle with our partner, or working through the Dead Zone, anyone will look more attractive. After all, the first stage of a relationship is the romance stage, so anybody new will look more attractive. Of course, if we went on with the new person, we would eventually reach power struggle and the Dead Zone with them, too.

The second common trap is when we are in a relationship with someone and our mind begins thinking about someone we were with in the past. We dream about them and, consequently, make our present relationship tasteless, in which case, we move on, and later end up fantasising about the relationship we just left, as well as the one before.

The key to both traps is that we think our happiness is some place other than where we are. The ego works to trap us and keep us out of our present, possible happiness.

Exercise

Today, appreciate the situation you are in now. Really appreciate your partner and everything about your life. With integrity, you can enjoy the connections with everyone who is attractive around you, without losing your present happiness. Do not fall into the trap of thinking the grass is greener someplace else.

223. ALL RELATIONSHIP TRIANGLES COME OUT OF THE COMPETITION IN ONE'S ORIGINAL FAMILY

The purpose of all triangle relationships is to keep us from moving forward. A triangle relationship is a form of competition rooted in our original, unbalanced family. Imbalance creates a sense of scarcity where we feel we have to compete for love, and fight for needs to be met; we have to grab our share before everyone else does. This unhealed family situation throws unhealed people out into the world where the old competition for our Mom's or Dad's love is replayed through triangle relationships. Although this is one of the best traps of the ego, almost all families, at this time, can be better balanced and come to a greater state of bonding.

Exercise

Today is a day to heal the imbalance in your mind. Imagine that as an adult, you go back to your original family situation and support yourself as a child to be strong enough to support the rest of the family. Support brings balance and ends competition. As you heal this imbalance, you bring healing into your present situation. You are no longer looking back trying to get the needs of the past met in the present.

If you are in a triangle relationship, your willingness to move forward will allow the person who is true for you to move forward with you. Trust in yourself and in Heaven that your true partner will come forward, ready to be with you, one that has the best qualities of both people. You will no longer fear that you might lose something or someone in the triangle. It is extremely difficult to attempt to pick between two people, but to choose the truth of the next step allows your true partner to come forward to join you.

224. ALL SACRIFICE IS UNWORTHINESS

Sacrifice comes from the illusion that if we give up our own self, we can let the other person carry us forward. We are willing to do anything for a person just so we can use their selfhood for our sense of identity. All sacrifice is unworthiness. It cheats our partner as well as ourself because we cannot receive their gifts, and they get what we consider to be damaged goods, something picked up at the discount counter. As we value ourself, we find we are creative enough to reach a solution without having to give up our position or our selfhood.

Exercise

Today is a day to begin to value yourself and find your true centre. Choose to live your truth rather than someone else's. Ask your Higher Mind to carry you back to your centre. It is a place of peace, innocence, true value and relatedness. Give yourself the most valuable gift of all – you.

225.
WHAT I GIVE
CREATES MY EXPERIENCE

Meaning and value in life come from how much we give. If we are giving very little, we will find that the situation has very little for us. If we are giving all of ourself, we find that the situation brings us back to ourself multiplied.

Exercise

Today is a day where you can increase the value of what you receive by totally giving yourself. What you give creates your experience. What you give to your partner allows higher meaning to emerge in your relationship. The more you give, the more you will receive.

226.   FEAR COMES FROM
MY ATTACK THOUGHTS

Many of us think fear comes from something outside us. Fear really begins as attack thoughts, grievances, or complaints in our own mind. Since the mind works in terms of projection, we naturally see the world responding to us as we are thinking. When we send out attack thoughts, we see the world as attacking us back; we see the world as a threatening place and we feel frightened, but the fear began in our own mind. Our willingness to acknowledge this allows us to change our mind, to change our fear into love, which naturally extends ourself to the situation and people around us, and creates healing.

Exercise

Today, be willing to change your fear, your attack thoughts, into love thoughts, into blessings. Bless someone around you. Wish the very best for them. Give them a gift of your energy, which in the giving multiplies for both of you. Any blessing you give is a blessing you get to receive. Blessing heals your attack thoughts and your fear.

227.   EVERY POWER STRUGGLE
HIDES A BIRTH

Every power struggle hides a place of feeling so painful that we will do anything to avoid it. We would rather have a war on the outside and suffer this pain over a long period of time than experience it in a few short hours or, sometimes, even moments. We can, however, if we want, get over this long, drawn-out war, this power struggle. With courage, we can choose to move into the pain under the power struggle; our willingness to go to this depth of feeling takes us to a place of new birth. Choosing to give to someone from this place of pain uses some of the most creative energies of our mind to bring about a whole new situation of love, transcendence, vision and purpose.

Exercise

Today, if you choose, you can take a giant step. Your awareness of this place of birth and the willingness to find it allows it to show itself. As soon as you experience it, give to someone. Your giving transforms the pain into a new area of transcendence.

228. EASE IS HOLDING NOTHING BACK

The extent of our ease is the extent to which we hold nothing back. When we venture everything, we receive from ourself and from life. Ease is a living partnership with our Higher Power, our family and loved ones, and everyone we work with. When we give one hundred percent, everything moves into ease.

If we are withholding ourself in any way, things become difficult. Difficulties come from guilt with a certain belief that we can pay off our guilt through giving ourself a hard time. For instance, we would typically have the thought, 'I must be a good person. Look at how hard my life is.' We compensate for our guilt by our roles, rules, and duties, which are defences and do not allow us to receive; they only lead to difficulties, *stuckness*, and feelings of deadness. Giving ourself fully, one hundred percent, in any situation, brings ease that moves life and opportunities toward us.

Exercise

Today, rather than doing things out of rote and habit, choose to give yourself fully. Allow ease to move you forward in partnership. It always says, 'You can do this together. You can move forward together in such a way that no one loses.' You know this because you have given yourself fully. Together, in partnership, nothing can stop you.

229. SACRIFICE IS COUNTERFEIT LOVE

Sacrifice looks like the real thing, but it is bogus. It is a way of giving without receiving, therefore it is not a true giving. Sacrifice says, 'I'm not okay. You are okay,' thus cheating someone out of the greatest gift we can give – ourself. Sacrifice is tied to feelings of unworthiness, guilt, and failure. It always tries to prove something it does not even believe itself; it is compensation, doing something to make up for old feelings of failure. Sacrifice is based on giving up our identity to steal a more worthy self, the person for whom the sacrifice is being made.

Sacrifice is counterfeit love because while love extends itself and creates, sacrifice arrogantly abases itself. At the same time, it discredits any gift that is offered, for nothing is received. The feminine (the side of us that receives) remains unredeemed; there is no opening, no release. Sacrifice, the most common form of counterfeit love, is a surreptitious holding back, and unwillingness to move forward and change. It is counterfeit commitment which withholds the most needed element in relationships, our giving and receiving.

Exercise

Today is the time to move out of your sacrifice. Ask your Higher Mind to carry you to your centre. Tell yourself the truth. Know what it is you really want to do. Recognise that what comes to you today comes out of your true giving.

230.   FANTASY IS A WAY OF
NOT UNWRAPPING MY PRESENCE

Fantasy is a way of costuming everyone around us to fit our needs. Though all of us have fantasies, it is important not to get caught there, because the more we are caught in fantasy, the less we show ourself. Only after unwrapping and giving ourself can we really receive the gifts of life. While we may play a little bit in fantasy, we need to remember that it is who we are that gives us our real satisfaction. Giving ourself, revealing ourself and opening ourself with all our desires, wants, needs, joys and satisfaction is what allows life to give to us.

Exercise

Today, take a look at all of your fantasies – sexual fantasies, hero fantasies, fantasies about how life is going to get better. Be willing to let all these go. When you catch yourself in fantasy, just ask yourself, 'Who is it that really needs my help?' Pour your love out to that person. As you do, you will feel a much greater sense of satisfaction and a much greater openness to receiving the gifts of life.

Do not wait for retirement to enjoy yourself. Do not wait until it is too late to begin to enjoy your partner. Look at them, drink them in, feel them inside you, enjoy every gift they have. Do not wait to say how much you love and appreciate someone. Think of the people who have really meant something to you in your life and contact or call them. Just say thank you from your heart because appreciation brings enjoyment. Do not wait to take a full breath of the air of life, to take such a bite out of life that when the juices run down your face, everyone will lick their lips. Open yourself and drink in life. It is all being given to you now.

231. MY RELATIONSHIP IS NOT
A FIFTY-FIFTY DEAL,
IT IS A ONE HUNDRED PERCENT DEAL

The things we complain our partner is not giving in our relationship are the very things we have come to give. If we give fifty percent and wait for them to give their fifty percent, we could be waiting a long time. By giving only fifty percent of ourself, our partner seemingly is not giving anything at all. When we choose to give ourself one hundred percent, the relationship will move forward. As we give fully, our partner also begins to give what they have come to give the relationship. Any area that is not succeeding is an area where we are not giving one hundred percent.

Exercise

Today, examine your life. See where you could make the simple choice to give one hundred percent, and make your life and your relationship easier.

232. IN MY RELATIONSHIP I CAN CHOOSE DRAMA OR I CAN CHOOSE CREATIVITY

If there is drama in our relationship, it means we are misusing our creative energy. We have drama so we do not feel bored, so we can feel alive and that something important is going on with us. In power struggle, we sometimes create even greater drama, but we could be using all this energy to find the solution rather than making the situation more dramatic. Our creativity is an act of love and contact with others. It will create all the excitement we need.

Exercise

Today, use your energy in a positive way. Look for creative solutions. Your creativity allows you to feel your best self. Rather than creating more and more drama, problems, or hysteria in your relationship, use your creativity to find the answers.

233. CREATIVITY IS THE ANTIDOTE TO LOSS

When we feel we have lost something, we tend to move into areas of fear, sadness, bad feelings and, sometimes, guilt. We could use this situation as an opportunity to become creative, which would free us from the sense of loss. By taking all of the energy in this painful situation and transforming it for our own healing, it would be a gift of love to those around us, and an antidote to their loss also.

Exercise

Today, take any situation where you feel a sense of, or a fear of, loss and become creative. Just sit back, close your eyes, and allow to come into your mind how you might give out of your love to transform the situation through your creativity.

234.
TO HAVE A NEED
FULFILLED, I FORGIVE

When there is something we need, one of the easiest ways to move out of the need is to forgive. Forgiving takes away the judgement and the guilt, both of which keep us stuck and unable to receive. Removing them allows us to move forward, and as we do, our need is fulfilled. If the situation seems beyond us, the need impossible to fill, we can ask our Higher Mind to come in and help complete the forgiveness so we come to peace and feel our own wholeness. Our forgiveness is a giving forth; with every giving forth, we both give to ourself and fulfil our need.

Exercise

Today, list three major needs you have in your life right now. Ask yourself, 'Who is it that I have not forgiven?' Whatever it takes for you to forgive, do that so these needs can be fulfilled, and you can come to peace. Remember, forgiveness is a true function of your Higher Power, so allow your forgiveness to be handled easily by turning it over to your Higher Power.

235. WITHOUT COMMITMENT TO A COMMON GOAL, ANY CONFLICT COULD DESTROY A RELATIONSHIP

If you do not have a common goal, then any conflict could be the last one in your relationship, the thing that brings your relationship down. When we have a common goal or commitment that we have chosen together with our partner, then any conflict that comes up is just something to move through on the way to that goal. As we resolve each conflict, we build another layer of partnership.

Exercise

Today, take some time to close your eyes and visualise your purpose in the relationship. What is it you want? What is it you have chosen? Feel your partner arm in arm with you, moving forward in confidence toward this goal. Know that you can step through each conflict together on the way to the goal. As you commit, the power of the conflict is lessened and the power of the relationship is increased.

236. I CAN ONLY ENTER HEAVEN
NOW, NEVER ON AN INSTANT REPLAY

Many of us think back to idyllic times in the past when we felt like we were in Heaven, but thinking back to those times is just something our mind uses to help make up for the lack we feel right now. Heaven is a state of consciousness that can only be entered now; trying to live in the past does not make us happy. Replaying those idyllic times is really a lie, because, even during those times, there was something missing that drove us on, searching for something more. We now have a chance to fully learn the lesson and gain a much greater sense of happiness.

Exercise

Today, choose to be present in the moment so you can experience the Heaven within you. Close your eyes, and imagine that all the joy and happiness in the world is filling you up right now. Let it fill everything within you, your toes, feet, ankles, legs, genitals, hips, body, heart, lungs, all your organs, your arms, neck, face, head, eyes, ears, and to the very crown of your head. Feel it overflowing. Heaven is within you now. Don't get caught up in some self-concept that demands a certain amount of doing and, therefore, stress to fulfil. A self-concept is part of your attempt to fill a need or prove a point that is really unnecessary. At the deeper part of your mind is only Oneness, there is only Heaven to be experienced now.

237.   MY JUDGEMENT THROWS
ME INTO SACRIFICE

Our judgement throws us into sacrifice because when we judge, we feel bad. The more we judge, the more we feel bad and unworthy and, therefore, the more we sacrifice. We act out a role to compensate for how we feel, to prove we are not like this. Every role is based on a judgement and becomes a compensating role that does not allow us to receive. Our willingness to let go of judgement is our willingness to let go of sacrifice; every judgement we let go of and every person we forgive saves us lots of time as well as saving us from lots of unhappiness and unrewarding work.

Exercise

Today, free yourself by making a new decision not to be bound by the past. Every judgement you have on your parents locks you into roles and sacrifice. Imagine your mother as just a little girl, sitting on your lap and telling you about all the hopes and dreams that she had for you when she dreamed of having a baby. Then, imagine your father as a little boy, sitting on your other knee, telling you of how he dreamed of growing up to be a man, and having children of his own, how he was going to take care of them and give his very best, so these children would feel loved. Now for a moment, remember how it was for you as a child with your desire to have things be better, your desire to have children you would love, and your desire to give the very best to the people you love. If you are willing, let go of your judgements on your parents. Given their upbringing, background, and inner and outer pressures, they did the very best they could. Your willingness to let go of your grievances with them frees you.

238. IF I DON'T HAVE SOMETHING IN MY LIFE, IT IS BECAUSE I AM GETTING REVENGE

All of us complain about what is missing in our lives, what we don't have or what we would like more of. Our willingness to take a deeper look at why we do not have this thing would bring us our answer. The answer is that we are getting revenge on someone. It is always true that we are getting revenge on ourself, but that is not the whole answer. Revenge is always about getting back at someone beside ourself. As we are willing to let go of our power struggle with this person, we are no longer robbed of our present happiness.

Exercise

Today, it is time to stop getting revenge and let yourself receive. Ask yourself, 'By not having this thing, who is it I'm getting revenge on? Who is it I am getting back at?' Close your eyes, and imagine this person standing in front of you. Is the power struggle worth more than what it is you want? Be willing to forgive them for whatever wrong you perceived them doing. Now, give to them the very thing you want. As you do, you will feel yourself receiving and being filled with the same thing.

239. PRESENT SACRIFICE IS A PAST JUDGEMENT THAT MY NEEDS WERE NOT MET

Judgement about people in the past who have not met our needs creates sacrifice. There are two reasons why sacrifice is created. When we have judgement that our needs were not met in the past, we either go around in the present looking for people to meet these needs, which actually makes it impossible to have the needs met, or we try to show those people who did not meet our needs how it should be done. We do this by taking on a compensating role that is the opposite of how we judged them to be. On the surface it might seem as if we are doing things so much better than they did, but what is actually occurring is sacrifice because we cannot receive. Without receiving, we go into greater sacrifice and burnout. Once we understand this and forgive the people in the past, we can move on.

Exercise

Today, look at the areas where you are still in sacrifice. Ask yourself, 'Who am I still judging?' Be willing to forgive them. Ask that part of your mind that is in charge of forgiveness and illumination that forgiveness be accomplished. Ask your Higher Mind to free you from working so hard and receiving so little. Ask to be freed from those past hungers which you cannot seem to satisfy in the present.

240. MY HAPPINESS IS THE
BEST GIFT I CAN GIVE THE WORLD

Many of us think our happiness depends on things outside of us. We think that we have to wait to be happy until some of these things are taken care of, but happiness comes from within. It is the best gift we can give the world because happiness is infectious. Happiness is enlightening, and it gives hope. As a form of love, happiness spreads around. If a situation seems stuck, bringing happiness to it moves it forward, because there is so much creativity in happiness.

Exercise

Today, for no good reason, be entirely happy. Be that hidden agent. Give happiness for no good reason, for every good reason.

241.   IF MY PARTNER LOSES,
I WILL END UP PAYING THE BILL

When we fall into a power struggle with our partner, if they lose, we end up paying the bill, because we are the other part of the team. It is really important that we concentrate on moving through all forms of competition and power struggle into areas of support and co-operation so our partner always succeeds. Our partner's loss demonstrates hidden, or not so hidden, areas of competition. Either we get the benefit of every success our partner has, or we end up paying the bill.

Exercise

Today, give extra support to your partner. No matter how you feel, give a little bit more to make sure your partner succeeds. Their success is your success.

242. LOVE STOPS TIME
AND STARTS ETERNITY

In eternity there is a sense of pure creativity where joy abounds and overflows. The extent to which there is love in our life is the extent to which we do not have to travel to go anyplace. We do not have to work to get anything, because love is here, love is now. With love there is never a means to an end. Love is always both the means and the end; there is no place to go. Love begins right now. If we could love powerfully enough, we could stop time. The place where time stops is a place where we could save ourself years and years of hard work and pain.

Exercise

Today, use the true sense of time, which is learning about love and healing yourself. Allow that healing to come into your life now. Who could you be loving more? Who is right there before you? Yes, it is your partner, to whom you could give so much love that time seems to stop and eternity begins.

243.   JUDGEMENT IS ALWAYS OF
A PERSON'S BODY, PERSONALITY,
OR MISTAKES

Judgement can arise only if we are looking at a person's body, personality, or mistakes. If we look beyond that to the person's essence and gifts and to what is likeable about them, our judgement falls away. When we look to what we appreciate, our judgement cannot stand up. To see and join with this part of them is to free ourself, because judgement is always a two-edged sword that we use to attack others as we attack ourself.

Exercise

Today, bring someone to mind that you have judgement on. Close your eyes and imagine yourself looking past the person's body, personality, and mistakes to what you appreciate about them. Then, look beyond that to their gifts. Now look even farther, look beyond their gifts to the place inside them where their light shines. Sit before that light a moment and notice that you cannot judge them as you look at the light of their spirit. In seeing this part of them you have freed yourself.

244. WORKING TOO HARD IN THE PRESENT MEANS I HAVE NOT LET GO OF THE PAST

Working too hard is a compensation for bad feelings. Often, we become so good at our work that when we work, we feel we are our best self, but workaholism points to something from the past we have not let go of. It means there is some kind of judgement, conflict, or pain; there is some kind of old feeling that we are still hanging on to. As we let it go, we naturally move into a place of balancing our work situation where we work just enough, and have the courage to deal with whatever feelings come up from within us. Our willingness to find what we are still hanging on to from the past and let it go allows us to work in a way that is much truer and more effective.

Exercise

Today, examine situations where you seem to be working too hard, where life seems to be too much of a burden. Realise that this is an area where you have not let go of something, where you carry a grievance. Ask yourself what that is. Be willing to let it go, now, because your grievance is killing you.

245. WHEN SOMEONE GETS ANGRY AT ME, THERE IS A LESSON FOR ME TO LEARN

When someone gets angry at us, if we just listen, we will hear the lesson that this person has come to give us. We have a certain responsibility for their anger, so we cannot say, 'Oh, it is just their problem.' On the other hand, regarding others' anger, it is just a lesson for us to learn, so taking on their anger and making it the end of the world will have us miss an important opportunity. Being aware and using every opportunity, no matter how negative, helps us to grow. If we let it, this anger will awaken us to something about which we were asleep, something that would help us move forward.

Exercise

Today, do not fight against anger. Do not run away from it, rather listen to see what truly applies to you. Use the anger as an opportunity for self-examination; the anger may be entirely misplaced, yet it can still serve to get you in touch with something that is vital to you. Someone's anger focused on you can help you to find an area of self-attack that you are called to let go of.

246.
PARTNERSHIP IS
COMMON PURPOSE

We are partners with many different people. We are partners with each one of our original family members, we have partners in business and our relationships are partnerships. In partnership, achievements and opportunities naturally come our way, but the success of the partnership depends on our choosing a common goal. Moving together with a common purpose creates ease and flow, and allows grace to be present. With all partnerships, the extent to which we live in a common purpose is the extent to which we succeed.

Exercise

Today, starting with your most important partnership – the one with your love partner – see your common goal, and imagine yourself moving together with your partner toward it. Repeat this with all your other partnerships – your children, parents, siblings, business partner, creative partners and anyone else. With each partnership, once you see the common goal, notice how strongly it attracts you, how it calls you and how you effortlessly move forward.

247. MASTERY IN A RELATIONSHIP IS A WILLINGNESS TO BE INNOCENT WITH THOSE I LOVE

Our innocence is one of the greatest gifts we can give to the world. To achieve innocence is to achieve mastery because we do not have to go anywhere; it always happens where we are, in the here and now. Innocence means no longer having to punish ourself or prove ourself. Proving takes lots of time and does not really work because it is a compensation for a negative belief. Once we know our innocence, we have freedom from the vicious cycle of pain and compensation; we allow ourself to receive and invite the world into our heart. Through our innocence, our partner becomes a source of healing, wonder, and enjoyment. Innocence allows us to give the best gifts of life by our being. Innocence is fun and playful; most of all, it is the very truth about us. As we are willing to live this truth, we create a power that is a source of healing for the world.

Exercise

Today, let go of anything that stands in the way of your innocence. Close your eyes and imagine that you stand before God, who knows you to be truly innocent. For that which is Love knows only Love and that which is innocent knows only innocence. It is only your arrogance that would judge you otherwise. The more innocence you have, the more you can give and receive all the love around you, and the more you can see how much is being given to you.

273

248. ALL HOLDING ON IS FANTASY

When we are holding on, we are living in the past. When we are living in the past, we are just living in a fantasy that we made up. Holding on can never make us happy because fantasy is an illusion. As we are willing to let go of the ghosts of yesterday, we allow ourself to receive what life has for us now, which is better than what we are letting go of. Life has something that is true for us that would move us forward. It is something that would let us really make contact and be satisfied.

Exercise

Today, look at what or who you are still holding onto. Who is it? If you are still holding onto a certain quality about them, let it go. Otherwise, your mind will be satisfied with the image and will not create that experience in your life now.

249.   ALL PROBLEMS ARE
THE RESULT OF AMNESIA

Happiness, healing, and forgiveness are all about remembering who we truly are and what we have come here to do. As we join with other people, we begin to see no separation, judgement, or fear between us, we remember ourself and our oneness. Amnesia means that we have forgotten who we are as a child of God, which is the very thing that would fulfil us and make us happy; we are all amnesiacs. We are the spiritual prince and princess of a kingdom we left long ago. We have forgotten that we have a rich Father.

As we remember who we are and what we have come to do, we find the peace that is full of empowerment, the peace that heals. We know everything is coming our way, that all things work for us, and that God is always looking out for us, loving us, and taking care of everything.

Exercise

Today, it is time for remembering. Close your eyes, and go to the deepest part of yourself. Remember who you are and what you have come to do. Remember the kingdom you left so long ago that still awaits you. Remember that you are the light, the light is your ally. You serve the truth and you have come to touch the world. Remember the legacy and all the joy that belongs to you.

250. IF I DO NOT HAVE SOMETHING IN MY LIFE, IT IS BECAUSE MY GUILT BLOCKS IT

Guilt is the great spoiler. It blocks our receiving because we feel we do not deserve to receive. Of course, our natural tendency when we do not have something in our life is to blame someone else, especially our partner. We believe they are not doing something they could be doing that would, somehow, give it to us. If we took a deeper look, we could see that what really blocks us from receiving is guilt. When we feel guilty about something, we have a sense of unworthiness and feel we do not deserve all the good things of life.

Guilt is a mistake. Imagine, for instance, if our own child made a simple, little mistake and then spent the rest of their life blocking out our love, and all the gifts we and everyone else wanted to give them. What then would be the feeling about this guilt? Would we not want to intervene and help our child find their innocence? Most of our guilt comes from similar circumstances. Most of it comes from patterns generated from mistakes in childhood. When we know our innocence, we can help those we love to find theirs.

Exercise

Today, talk to the child within you. Tell that child of its innocence, and help it see that knowing what it knew, it did the very best it could. Forgive your child. In doing so your child will set you, the adult, free. This will allow you to receive the love and gifts you so richly deserve.

251.   PLEASE TOUCH

Touch confirms, validates and heals. When we are in the midst of a power struggle and we touch our partner, we reaffirm that there is something greater than the misunderstanding. The more we can touch our partner, the more *connectedness* we create. Our touch is so healing and reaffirming that it alone creates the intimacy needed to resolve the problem. Our touch gives hope.

Exercise

Today, be willing to touch your partner, your children, your parents, and your friends. Shake hands, hug, or just put your hand on someone's shoulder, which gives the sense of confirmation that touch brings. Caress your partner. Give them the touch that reaffirms life and says, 'You did a good job. Thank God you are my partner.'

252. THE GUILT I ACCEPT FROM OTHERS IS ONLY THE GUILT I AM ALREADY FEELING

People can accuse us of all kinds of things. They can accuse us of being a bank robber, a sexual pervert, being too selfish, or not being a good parent. The only accusations that bother us, however, are the ones we are already feeling guilty about. Nobody can make us feel guilt that we are not already holding in some part of our mind.

Exercise

Today, when someone triggers your guilt, use the opportunity for healing. Know that this is a place where you felt guilt and stopped yourself from growing. Now you have the opportunity of transforming your guilt. No one has power over you that you are not giving them. Nobody can make you feel bad except where you already feel bad. Say to yourself, 'Now that I am in touch with this feeling, I can do something to change it. I know this guilt is an illusion and that it is based on a mistake. I will learn the lesson now and move forward in my life. I will feel it until it disappears. I choose to receive.'

253.   WHAT I FIGHT AGAINST,
I BECOME

The more we fight against something, the more we take on the qualities of whatever we are fighting against. At some level, a rebel always harbours a tyrant within. In our personality, when the rebel knocks off the tyrant who has been running us, the rebel becomes the leader. Unfortunately, given time, the rebel within will manifest traits similar to those of the tyrant. Everything we resist persists because we reinforce and empower whatever we fight against.

Exercise

Today, see what you are fighting against, particularly a quality within you. Close your eyes and allow yourself to drift back to that place in your life where you believed, before you hid it away, that you had the same quality. Naturally, in believing something about yourself that you hid away, you will create someone in your life to act out the particular quality. The more you fight against it, the more this particular quality will come to the fore in your life. Go back to that part of you that you hid away. Take it in your arms, reassure and accept it. Understand what a difficult situation that part of you was in. As you foster that part, you will find that it will begin to grow until it reaches your present age and naturally melt into you. You will find that this resistance or fight that has been outside you just disappears.

254. FEELING MY FEELINGS IS A BASIC FORM OF HEALING, LETTING GO, AND MOVING FORWARD

Feeling our feelings is the most basic form of healing. If we feel our feelings until they transform, the negative becomes positive, and the positive becomes even more positive. It is the simplest healer there is. We know that the pain we are feeling is an illusion, that it is a mistake, but because it is our experience we are willing to feel it. When the negative emotion is gone, we come to a whole new level. Every time we feel our feelings, we end denial, let go of the past, and allow ourself to move forward.

Feeling our feelings re-associates us. By the time we get to independence, we have dissociated thousands upon thousands of feelings. Dissociation is the counterpart to hysteria. Although hysteria seems to feel lots of feelings, it still avoids the true feeling that would move us forward. Our willingness to be aware and experience our true feelings leads us out of deadness and into partnership. By our willingness to feel our true feelings, we can then feel joy and receive.

Exercise

Today, remember that feeling your feelings is the key to enjoying life, so just allow yourself to feel more. You may notice a time lag between choosing to do this exercise and becoming aware of your true feelings. This merely speaks of the amount of dissociation that you are in. Some people even take a week to really get in touch with what they feel. Whatever your time lag, be willing to start becoming aware of your feelings. The extent to which you are truly re-associated with your feelings, is the extent to which you will allow success and its enjoyment into your life. Feeling your feelings allows you to know yourself and to embrace life fully.

255. DEADNESS IN MY RELATIONSHIP IS HEALED BY ASKING FOR HEAVEN'S HELP AND MOVING TOWARD MY PARTNER

When we feel dead in our relationship, so stuck, weary, or disinterested that the resistance seems beyond our ability to get through, we can ask for Heaven's help. Asking for Heaven's help is asking for that part of our own mind, our Higher Self, to give us enough energy, at least, to take the next step. The key in taking this next step is to move toward our partner, because once we have finally reached our partner, we find both rest and energy. Sometimes, we are in a place of such chronic exhaustion that we have to ask for help each step of the way. Any time we get to a place of exhaustion where we feel there is nothing left to give, just asking for Heaven's help and moving toward our partner until we join them will give us a sense of release.

Exercise

Today, look at a situation in which you feel stuck or too weary to move. Ask for Heaven's help to join your partner, and to move toward them so you and your relationship move forward.

256.   I CAN EXPERIENCE GUILT
ONLY BY LIVING IN THE PAST

Living in the past does not work because it no longer exists. When we feel guilty, we are living in the past, spending time in our mind instead of making true contact with those around us.

Exercise

Today, let go of the past. Let go of the guilt and allow the lesson to come forward so you can move on. As the guilt falls away, you make better and more satisfying contact with everyone around you. Without guilt you naturally become more attractive and life seems to treat you better.

257.   SHOULD'S ALWAYS
EXPRESS A CONFLICT

The reason none of our *should's* happen as they should is because they express a conflict in our mind. One part of us wants to do what we feel we should do, but another is resisting. There are hidden demands and needs within '*should's*,' so the closer we get to what we feel we should do, the greater the resistance. Also, we receive no reward for doing the things we feel we should because we feel we have not chosen it; it is something that we ought to do, have to do or must do.

Exercise

Today, let go of all your should's. Allow yourself to choose. Your choice and goal-setting heals the conflict and creates flow in your life.

258. LOVE IS GIVING EVERYTHING
WHILE HOLDING ON TO NOTHING

Love totally gives. It wants to give everything it has; when it is truly love, it holds on to nothing. Love has no expectations and no conditions because it is not a contract – 'I'll give you this, if you'll give me that.' When we give everything and hold on to nothing, a great sense of power, love and creativity emerges in us. Our heart opens and time is transcended. We seem to move into a higher state of consciousness where everything becomes vibrant with colour and full of love.

Exercise

Today, remember that love is giving everything while holding on to nothing. Anything you hold on to, any contingent deals or attachment, blocks your enjoyment and receiving. Holding on is just a way of trying to make yourself safe. Love not only makes you safe, it makes you real and alive. Love makes you remember God and how much it is everything you ever wanted.

259.   BEING TRUE TO MYSELF
MEANS I CANNOT BE FALSE TO ANYONE

When we are true to ourself and stand in our own centre, we
have a natural direction and purpose to our life. Sometimes,
people around us become uncomfortable when we are in our
centre because living our truth reawakens them. It asks them
not to live comfortably in areas where they are stuck in roles
and duties. Even though we make them uncomfortable, we
are not being false to them. Being truly committed to ourself
makes it impossible to betray anyone because truth for ourself
allows us to extend the truth to others; it allows them to take
their next step also.

Exercise

*Today, take a look at all the different areas where you could be truer to
yourself. Where something is difficult, you are not being true to
yourself. It is also important to note that it is not necessarily what you
are doing that may be untrue, it may be how you are doing it.
Sometimes, you may be doing something for approval that seems to
help you in the short run, but will lead to failure in the long run. In
areas where you are true to yourself, you are receiving, and things
naturally flow with a certain ease, so now is the time to be true to
yourself. By living this truth, you are true to everyone else.*

260. IF I DON'T HAVE SOMETHING IN MY LIFE, IT IS BECAUSE I AM IN A POWER STRUGGLE

When there is something we think we want in our life, and we don't have it, it is because we are in a fight with someone. Power struggle is just a way of holding ourself back because we are actually afraid of what we think we want. This power struggle is really a place where we are using this person to avoid the real issue, which is the fear beneath it. Letting go of the power struggle would allow us to have that something in our life.

Exercise

Today, let go of the power struggle. It is not true anyhow. Sit down, and divide a sheet of paper into three columns. In the first column, list what it is you want in your life. For each item, ask yourself, 'Who am I in power struggle with? Who am I fighting?' (The answers 'myself' or 'everyone' is a form of avoidance.) Whoever comes into your mind, write it in the next column beside the item. (It could be your parents, someone who is dead, your partner or God.) Now, would you rather have the power struggle, or all of these things you really want? In the third column next to each person, write down what the fear is that holds you back from what you want. Be willing to move through the fear, because as you do, you are opening yourself to have what you want in your life.

261. SEXUAL DEADNESS IN MY RELATIONSHIP IS HEALED BY TAKING THE NEXT STEP

When sex in our relationship is dead, it is an indication that, somewhere, we are stuck. At some level, we are afraid of moving forward, but our willingness will move us forward. It takes us out of this place of weariness, so for at least a little while, we are moving forward. Taking this step forward might not be the answer for the rest of our life, but it will be the answer for tonight; for now, that is just enough.

Exercise

Today, take time to sit and close your eyes. Imagine that you are sitting on the ground in this place of deadness in your relationship. Now, feel yourself begin to sink through the ground until you pass all the way through the place of 'stuckness'. As you move through the last layer, you find yourself in a place that seems really open and free, a place where you can breathe again. No matter how stuck you are, every time you are willing you will be carried forward.

262. JEALOUSY IS A BIRTHING PLACE

Jealousy is one of the worst feelings to experience. When we are feeling it, especially strong jealousy, theta brain waves are perking through our mind. These are the brain waves of tantrums, but they are also the brain waves of our most creative states. With willingness, we can turn this tantrum into a place of birth. We can take ourself out of the livid pain of jealousy and create a birth by totally giving ourself. As we give through our jealousy, the place where we are stuck becomes a leaping-off place into our future, into higher consciousness and love. As we leave our attachments and needs behind through this birth, the pain of jealousy can create a whole new level of love for ourself. When we give through this birthing place, we find out more of what unconditional love truly is. No one can stop our love.

Exercise

Today, allow a new birth to be brought about in the easiest way. Imagine a wall of jealousy between you and your partner – a wall of tantrum. Give through your jealousy by pouring your love through this wall or by being in service. Service helps you extend yourself through the wall. In this way, the pain is transcended without the necessity of suffering.

263. MY SUCCESS IN LIVING MY PURPOSE IS DETERMINED BY THE EXTENT TO WHICH I FORGIVE AND INTEGRATE MY PARENTS

Living our purpose is not necessarily something that we do, it is who we are. To the extent we forgive and give to our parents, we give the gifts that free us and allow us to learn what our purpose is. To the extent we are willing to balance both parents so that we are in equal love and harmony with both of them, we allow ourself to integrate the psychological poles that they represent for us. Forgiving our parents and balancing our love for them allows us to have a balance with relationships (mother) and work (father). As we integrate our parents, we find the treasure that each of them is for us, and we become more and more creative. To the extent we integrate our parents, we naturally extend ourself to them. Remember that what we complain our parents did not give to us is, typically, what we came to give to them.

Exercise

Today, be willing to live your purpose more fully and allow a new you to emerge. Feel what it is you want but haven't received from your parents. Now, imagine yourself as a child giving these very things to them. After you give them these gifts, see yourself throwing your arms around each parent. As you hold them, imagine and feel them melting together with you into pure energy. From this energy emerges the new you.

Tonight, with your partner, let down all of the walls that stand between the two of you. Invite them into your heart. Invite them fully into you. Let no disagreement stop you. Let no condition stop you. You have been sent by All That Is to invite them home. Home is your heart. As you bring them fully into you, you find a pathway opening up that will take you all the way there. Here, you can see yourself and the path to Heaven that your partner is; you can even see the face of God. It is time to celebrate the gift your partner is in your life. Invite them into you tonight, and each of you will become more.

264. ONLY MY WILLINGNESS TO TAKE THE NEXT STEP ALLOWS ME TO SEE WHAT IT IS

When we run around asking what our next step is, we are not willing to take it; we feel we have to see it before we are willing. To be honest with ourself, if we knew what the next step was, there is a good chance we would not take it – even if we knew it was the best thing we could do. Only when we have total willingness is the next step shown to us. Then we move forward, and reach a place that is much better than where we are now.

Exercise

Today, be totally willing for the next step to come to you. It moves toward you because of your choice, your willingness to take it. Allow no distraction, temptation, or problem to get in your way. Say Yes to life.

265. WHATEVER THE CONFLICT, I AM ONLY FIGHTING MYSELF

Everything that happens in our relationship reflects a part of our own mind. Whatever the conflict, we are only fighting ourself. If we were to heal the inner fight, the conflict between ourself and our partner would also be healed. As we are willing to stop fighting ourself in the guise of our partner, we accept that part of ourself that our partner is showing us. As we bring acceptance into any conflict, we find a new confidence about moving forward. There is something much greater for our partner and ourself. As we stop fighting ourself and stop fighting our partner, we receive this gift.

Exercise

Today, bring to mind someone with whom you have conflict. Imagine them standing before you wearing a Hallowe'en party mask. Go unmask them and, as you do, see yourself behind the mask. How old are you? However old that part of you is, ask yourself, 'How is it that I may help you?' What is asked for, and what you give to that part of you is the very gift the person you are in conflict with needs also. As you give it to yourself, you naturally give it to this person, which heals the conflict. Both of you are moved forward.

266. IF I AM NOT IN BEAUTY, WONDER, AND JOY, I AM IN JUDGEMENT

We know that when we are having a bad time, we are in judgement. Any time we are not enjoying ourself and experiencing the beauty within and around us, we are also in judgement. When we have lost our sense of wonder, we are judging something or someone. By our judgement, we are robbing ourself of a really good, creative time, but we always have choice. We can choose to have enjoyment. Our willingness to let go of judgement allows us to experience the beauty, wonder and joy in life.

Exercise

Today, allow to come to your mind what or who you are judging. You may find a long parade of people coming toward you. Be willing at this point just to forgive them. Bless each person who comes to you, and you will begin experiencing life's riches to the fullest.

267. HEAVEN CAN ONLY BE
ENTERED TWO-BY-TWO

Heaven is a state of consciousness full of joy, love and ecstasy. Only through forgiveness, surrender and creativity do we give ourself fully and enter that state of love that opens Heaven. All these things – forgiveness, surrender, creativity – involve togetherness. Heaven can only be entered two-by-two.

While every grievance holds us both back and locks us in hell, our forgiveness frees both ourself and the other to enter Heaven. Whereas hell is a state in consciousness of feeling utterly alone and tortured, Heaven is a state of sharing and oneness with others.

Exercise

Today, let come into your mind the person who can best lead you into Heaven. It could be someone you are having the hardest time with, or it could be the person that you are loving the most. Feel yourself bridging the gap between that person and you. Feel yourself forgiving them, reaching out for them, accepting them, and drawing them into you. Feel the light within you joining and, as you do, feel that sense of joy within you grow.

268. I CELEBRATE WHAT IS GIVEN TO ME

Celebration is one of the highest forms of consciousness and the true state of the Universe. When we bring celebration into whatever is given to us, we allow one of the highest forms of consciousness to begin the process of making joy and healing. When we are given something that appears negative or dark, to bring celebration into it, at first, might seem like an act of courage, but bringing celebration into the darkness allows for every element that is highest in the human race to show itself. When things are lowest, it can be a springboard to take us to that highest place of love and joy. Celebrating what seems to be dark allows for the dawning of the light; it allows for any solution in the situation to begin to show itself.

Celebration lets the love in the situation be shared among everyone, and with love, people can bear up under anything that they have to go through. Love allows us to transcend whatever physical, emotional or mental lesson there is for us to learn. As we celebrate what is given to us, without getting caught in the illusion we turn whatever we are given into a gift. If what we are given is already a gift, celebration lets us experience it fully.

Exercise

Today is a day for dancing the great dance of life. Whatever is given to you, make the most of it. Whatever is given to you, dance and celebrate, find the joy in it. To not be caught by the disguises and illusions of the world is to find that, at the heart of everything, it all has to do with joy, love, and celebration.

269. IF FEELING IS SHUT DOWN,
I CREATE DRAMA AND PAIN
IN ORDER TO FEEL ALIVE

When we cannot feel the energy within us, or the natural excitement of our emotions as they run through us, we create drama or pain to make ourself feel something. If feeling is shut down we create more drama and more pain in order to feel alive. People who have not been able to feel often go to greater and greater lengths to feel something; sometimes even to the extent of creating violence.

When we are fully aware of any emotion, even if it is negative we feel excitement because we know we are healing; we are aware of all the nuances of the sensations as we feel them. What we call emotion and pain is really just how energy expresses itself in certain situations. Our willingness to feel, to open ourself up, brings us back to feeling alive without having to create drama, negativity, or pain.

Exercise

Today, allow yourself to take the time simply to feel things. Take a situation that is dramatic, painful, or unpleasant, and concentrate on the strongest sensation. Then allow yourself to feel fully how it changes as you focus on it. Now pay attention to exactly how the energy of the next sensation manifests itself. Experiencing and embracing every sensation allows both physical and emotional pain to release and unfold. As you apply yourself to this, you find a method of self-healing that you can use in any situation. Healing through experiencing yourself feels good. Moving forward feels good.

270. ANY AREA THAT IS NOT SUCCESSFUL IN MY PRESENT RELATIONSHIP IS A RESULT OF COMPETITION

In subtle and, sometimes, not so subtle ways, every person fights for themselves rather than working for the partnership to succeed. Competition is a lower form of consciousness that leads to power struggle and deadness. It wrecks our relationship because each of us will be trying to take care of our own needs, rather than working together and finding a common purpose. Competition has us believe that we are either superior or inferior to our partner, which does not support our relationship. Our willingness to heal competition allows for intimacy, contact and communication; all of which spell success.

Exercise

Today, take a look at where you are not succeeding in your relationship. What are you competing about? When you have found some answers, share these with your partner. Apologise to your partner for making them less or better than you, whichever is the case for each answer. As you begin to acknowledge these things about yourself, you find yourself moving through the competition and your relationship leaps forward. Your openness and willingness to heal all the hidden aspects in your relationship move you and your partner forward together.

271.   A RELATIONSHIP IS ABOUT STRETCHING NOT STRETCH MARKS

A relationship is about growth and taking risks into whole new areas, extending ourself beyond our comfort zone. Stretch marks are all the scars of the past, the dark lessons that have not yet been transformed. Our relationship is not about scars, past or present, but about the gifts we find in ourself as a result of reaching beyond our own indulgence, and beyond the sacrifice of roles and duties to find the truth.

A relationship is about extending ourself to others. As we are willing to recognise the truth of relationships, we see what we have learned and how much we have grown in each one. Relationships are about letting go of mistaken self-concepts while discovering and embracing more and more of who we truly are.

Exercise

Today, spend some time reflecting on your relationship. Allow yourself to remember who you were before the relationship began, what was missing in your life and what was present in it that you didn't like. Now, look at how both you and your partner have grown since your relationship began, how much more mature, understanding and patient you are. How many hidden feelings have come to the surface to be healed? Recognise the courage that it took to heal these, and to deal with some of the conflict areas within your own mind — feelings about yourself that were hidden away under roles, under things that looked good, but smelled bad. Realise how much you have accomplished with and because of your partner. As you do, you find a natural gratitude comes to you, for you, your partner, and your relationship.

272.   I CAN BE IN HEAVEN
WITH EVERY PERSON I MEET

We could be in Heaven with every person we meet if we allow ourself to feel that good! We could by simply making the choice to give them our love. It is always our choice as to whether we give someone our judgement, or whether we give them our love.

The decision we make shows what we think of ourself. To be in Heaven is just to give everyone we meet that much of ourself. Giving this much of ourself knocks the hell out of the other person and allows them to be in Heaven with us.

Exercise

Today, choose to be in Heaven with everyone you meet. Give them that much. Have that good a time. Dance! The Universe is dancing, so allow yourself to dance with joy. With every person you meet today, tomorrow, from now on, the moment you wake up, begin the dance.

273. THE GREATEST ART IS
THE ART OF BEING MYSELF

Being ourself naturally proceeds from living our purpose rather than living for approval. Our purpose is what we, of all the people in the world, can do the best. If we do not do it, if we are not true to ourself, who will be? Who can be? If we do not do what it is we have come to do, no one can do it. It is left undone until we are willing to give our part, until we are willing to be ourself. Most people are frightened of their own purpose and the greatness that it seems to call from them. In being frightened of our purpose, we are frightened of our own love, passion, and happiness. Most of us feel unworthy, or we try to control our good feelings so as not to be overwhelmed. These are just symptoms of fear that lead us away from our truth, our vision and our greatness. The greatest art, the greatest gift, is to be ourself. Being ourself in all of our grandeur shows how much we love the world. As we unwrap our presence, we give ourself as the best gift that we can give to life.

Exercise

Today, imagine that you are painting a beautiful masterpiece. This masterpiece is you, the picture of your life. Being you is being the artist with an inspired hand, the paintbrush with true colours, and the painting all at once. The greatest art is to be yourself, so give this masterpiece of yourself as your gift to life.

274.   I CANNOT MEET
PAST NEEDS IN THE PRESENT

Many of us choose partners to make up for the needs that were not met in the past, so we keep choosing present situations to make up for what was missing. The problem with this is that we begin to hold our partner hostage for what our past did to us. We try to control them, and make them give to us in certain ways to take care of us, to meet the needs of the past in the present situation. The needs of the past can never fully be fulfilled in the present situation, so as we are willing to let go of the past, we can really enjoy our partner as they are. Trying to live the past now limits our relationship and limits our partner from giving us all they wish to give us. When we let the past go, healing occurs, and we get to receive now what we were trying to get then. In trying to remake the past, we always stay unfulfilled, because, paradoxically, when we let go of the past, past needs are satisfied.

Exercise

Today, look at unsuccessful situations as places where you are trying to get old needs met. Who did not take care of these needs? As you see the past begin to come up, be willing to let it go. Be willing to put it in the hands of God so you can go forward and enjoy everything that wants to be given to you now. Stop complaining about the flower that died. You are walking in the garden. Just raise your perspective, and see how much beauty and fragrance is all around you.

275.   GUILT REINFORCES
WHAT I AM TRYING TO ESCAPE

The simplest fact of psychology is that what we reinforce, we make happen. Guilt is a great reinforcer. Guilt reinforces the very thing that we are trying to get away from. When we have guilt, the thing we are trying to get away from is always on our mind, we are obsessed with it. With obsession there are two modes of behaviour. One is where we totally withdraw from ourself and from life so as not to make that mistake again. The other is where we do that which we would not like to do. For instance, if a person murdered someone, the guilt from that would either have them begin to kill themselves on the inside; or they would, once again, have a certain violent desire to kill someone to defend against the guilt, which then creates a vicious circle.

Guilt does not work because it is a self-destructive form of avoiding lessons. We have all made mistakes. Our willingness to let go of our guilt allows us to know that mistakes can be corrected and the lessons learned.

Exercise

Today, forgive yourself. Put your guilt in the hands of God, who knows better. God only sees your perfection and knows that there is nothing to be forgiven. Guilt holds us back from God. Do not let your guilt stop you from living life. Let your guilt go so you do not let it come between you and anyone that you love. Let your guilt go, learn the lesson, and move forward because your innocence heals the world.

276. EVERY SWAMP GETS ITS ROCK

'Every swamp gets its rock' speaks of two completely different styles of communication in any given relationship. Basically, one person becomes swamp-like and one person becomes rock-like. Swamps are emotional, and tend to personalise communication, whereas rocks tend to generalise, dissociate, and be abstract. Rocks tend to be stoic, while swamps tend to be hysterical. Rocks deny themselves and go into sacrifice, whereas swamps are selfish, and tend to indulge themselves. Swamps are natural talkers, and rocks natural listeners. Rocks always find themselves falling in love with swamps because they love the fluidity and the freedom in sexuality they seem to exude. Swamps, of course, always feel attracted to the confidence of the rock. They feel attraction toward the one in control, at least for the first few minutes. After that, competition sets in. Swamps have natural sexual energy and fluidity, where rocks have lots of rules. Sometimes, they purify the pond to the point where the water lilies die. Rocks are natural givers, swamps are natural receivers. Swamps can be super-sensitive, while rocks seem to be impervious.

It is important to understand these styles of communication, because they form areas of power struggle and competition that carry over into the Dead Zone. The lesson of rock and swamp, actually, must be learned for a couple to get past the Dead Zone. Once we realise that each person is playing a role, the swamp can begin to firm up, and the rock to loosen up. When the competition is let go of, the swamp moves its emotions into its natural waterways, and springs gush forth out of the rock creating a fertile land where water flows.

Exercise

Today, take a look at who is the swamp and who is the rock in your relationship. Begin to create a bridge toward your partner. As you move forward together, both of you naturally win.

277.   I WILL LOSE MY PARTNER'S
WILLINGNESS TO COMMUNICATE
IF I MAKE IT ALL ABOUT ME

One of the most important secrets of relationships is recognising that making every communication about ourself, rather than about both our partner and ourself, will destroy a relationship. Our relationship is not here just for ourself; it is here for both our partner and ourself. There is a problem that rocks and swamps typically get into around communication. Swamps are natural communicators. They tend to personalise things so they speak about themselves and their own feelings. Rocks are out of touch with their feelings. They tend to dissociate themselves and to be stoic, so they are not very good with feelings.

A rock will share their personal feelings about three major times in a relationship and typically only a total of seven times before giving up. On these rare occasions, they open up their heart and talk about what they are experiencing, what their personal feelings are. Sometimes at that point, a swamp will indulge themselves and turn that personal sharing into an attack on themselves, which is just a way of stealing centre stage, again. If the swamp takes the communication and uses it to bring the storyline back to themselves, they have lost a major opportunity. It is important for swamps to recognise those rare times when a rock will take a risk and let down the drawbridge to show their deep, inner feelings. If the swamp succeeds in listening and supporting the rock's communication, the rock will take other risks.

Exercise

Today is a day for supporting and opening communication with your partner. If you are a rock, take a risk to share what is really going on for you. As you do, support your swamp by letting them know that your communication is not intended to make them feel wrong. If you are a swamp, go out to support your rock so that they feel safe enough to lower the drawbridge. Be aware though that, sometimes, swamps encourage their partners to share, but when they really share, the swamp runs. Be sure that when you are asking for your partner to share, you are not also pushing them away because you are afraid of what they might say. Swamps, do not let what your partner shares be just one more excuse to prove that you are unloveable. Rocks are just saying what they are feeling, and they need to get that out before they can move on; all they need is a little support and compassion. This is the time to borrow the rock's natural inclination and ability to abstract, to impersonalise what your partner is saying.

Note: 'Rock' and 'swamp' are terms used by Dr Spezzano to describe two completely different styles of communication in a relationship. Refer to Lesson 276.

278. HYSTERIA AND STOICISM ARE SIMPLY DIFFERENT FORMS OF COMMUNICATION DESIGNED TO AVOID REJECTION

A swamp is a natural hysteric. A rock is naturally stoic. When rocks have unpleasant feelings, they try to suppress them and not let it bother them. They bury the feelings inside just to get through it. Swamps tend to cry about everything except the real feeling that is bothering them. Hysteria and stoicism are forms of communication designed to avoid rejection, but are actually where both the swamp and the rock are seeking approval. Of course, both forms only lead to power struggle and misunderstanding.

Exercise

Today, have the courage to take a risk and share with your partner. If you are the swamp, look at how you are avoiding what you are really feeling, what the true risk would be. Being willing to feel this would move your relationship forward. If you are the rock, get more in touch with yourself, and find what sharing you are avoiding. Taking the risk to share what your major issues are makes the relationship better.

Note: 'Rock' and 'swamp' are terms used by Dr Spezzano to describe two completely different styles of communication in a relationship. Refer to Lesson 276.

279.   SWAMPS FEEL UNLOVED,
ROCKS FEEL MISUNDERSTOOD

No matter how much love swamps receive, they feel it is never enough. A rock feels that no one cares enough about them to really understand what they are feeling. Rocks are really clams because they have swamps inside them. Both sides, however, feel a lack of support and understanding. A rock feels that a swamp just cannot support them, whereas a swamp feels they are just water off a rock's back. The swamp feels all the things that they were missing in childhood, so they make everything about themselves. Rocks feel that in their childhood there was not enough love to go around so they had to give themselves up and sacrifice themselves.

In any kind of misunderstanding, rocks want to get to the bottom line and solve the problem. Swamps have no bottom line; they just want to be touched, felt, loved, understood, and appreciated. In problem-solving, swamps want to be touched first, then everything will turn out fine; rocks typically do not want to be touched until the problem is solved. Rocks tend to be visual and see the world first, whereas swamps tend to be kinaesthetic and feel the world first. Basically, rocks cannot see what swamps are feeling, and swamps cannot feel what rocks are seeing.

Rocks tend to be heroes, even tragic heroes or martyrs; at some level, they are trying to save others or the world because they believe deep down that they themselves are lost. Swamps are just trying to save themselves, so they resent the time that rocks spend on others and not on them. In this way a swamp is correct; if a rock were truly to give them their time and energy, the joining that occurred would create the perfect balance and foundation for much greater success.

Exercise

Today, whether you are a swamp or a rock, talk about these concepts. Share the places where you are different. Communicate with each other about how you might find a common goal and, through that, a greater understanding.

Note: 'Rock' and 'swamp' are terms used by Dr Spezzano to describe two completely different styles of communication in a relationship. Refer to Lesson 276.

280.   ROCKS HAVE AMNESIA
AND SWAMPS NEVER FORGET

Rocks have amnesia because they tend to be thinking about what they consider to be bigger things. To a swamp, nothing is bigger than thinking about themselves. Rocks tend to forget important things like anniversaries and birthdays. They also tend to forget what happened in the past, but swamps never forget an anniversary, and they will certainly never forget something that happened in the past that the rock has not yet apologised for.

Swamps need to share their feelings about the past. Rocks need to let swamps know that in spite of what was said or done, they really love them. Swamps have to be told time and time again that they are loved. They have all of this history in their minds to prove they are not loved, so now they ask to be reassured that they are loved. The rocks, of course, have long since forgotten all about what they said, or did not say. If they told their swamps that they loved them once, that should be enough. The rock's willingness to reach out to the swamp to reassure them, and the swamp's willingness to let go of the past allows for both to move forward together.

Rocks are natural givers, and swamps are natural receivers. Rocks are natural romantics. If they remember to keep the romance in the relationship, and to keep giving to their swamp in thousands of creative ways, they will constantly move the relationship forward. When rocks show their feelings, it can blow a swamp out of the water. Swamps have a natural ability to receive what the rocks give them. If they really want to move the relationship forward, they can give to their rock, and blow the rock's mind.

311

Exercise

Today, whichever style you are, commit to your partner in spite of their being a rock or a swamp. Really choose them because this commitment brings you to the next stage, to a higher level of understanding and mutuality. Rocks, remember your swamps. Move toward them and give to them. Remember all the important things, and relate to them in a very personal way. Swamps, it is time to think about your partner for a change. Be willing to give to them to move your relationship forward.

Note: 'Rock' and 'swamp' are terms used by Dr Spezzano to describe two completely different styles of communication in a relationship. Refer to Lesson 276.

281. BEING A ROCK MEANS
NEVER HAVING TO SAY I AM SORRY

Rocks hate guilt. They hate guilt because they feel so guilty. They believe that somewhere in their lives they have totally blown it and they have not really forgiven themselves for it. This is why they are out to save the world – to make up for their guilt. They feel as if they have made such a big mistake that they need to sacrifice themselves, but because of the inner guilt, whatever sacrifice they make is never enough. Rocks hate apologising because it feels as if they are admitting how incredibly guilty they feel inside.

Swamps are always apologising and abasing themselves. They do not feel that they have done something wrong, but that something is wrong with them. This is why they could not receive all of the love and attention they felt they needed as a child, and why they feel that they never get enough love now. No matter how much the rock sacrifices or gives to them, it is never quite enough to reassure them.

Swamps are also really good at communicating what is not working, so they are good at complaining or criticising. Rocks hate criticism, however, and will tend to overwork or learn things overmuch just so they will not be criticised. For swamps, however, nothing is ever quite good enough. Rocks are always playing 'rock-man-enough', trying to prove to the world how they survived in spite of how tough it was, sometimes doing stupid thing in testing their limits because they are trying to prove themselves to get over the basic guilt. Their motto is, 'No matter how hard it is, I can take it.' Swamps can't take anything. If they get complaints or criticism, they tend to fold, disappear, run away or go into even more swamp-like behaviour. As we begin to understand the differing communication styles, we can see how it is a perfect situation for mutual misunderstanding. In recognising that we have found our natural partner, we can embrace what we are missing, embrace our partner and move ourself, our partner, and our relationship forward.

Exercise

Today, spend time appreciating your partner. They have to act out what you are missing. The swamp's super-sensitivity makes up for the rock's lack of sensitivity. To the extent the rock is out of touch, the swamp will complain about everything. Together, you can really balance and move forward. You can bring humour into the situation as you understand each other and the role that each of you has played. Now it is time to move out of these roles, and find a communication style that works much better for both of you.

Note: 'Rock' and 'swamp' are terms used by Dr Spezzano to describe two completely different styles of communication in a relationship. Refer to Lesson 276.

282. YOU CAN'T GET BLOOD
FROM A ROCK

When rocks and swamps get into a power struggle, it is not a pretty sight. Rocks get even more rocklike and pretend it does not matter. They stonewall their partner, holding all of their feelings inside them, except when threatening to explode like a volcano. Swamps get more swampy, more needy.

If things polarise into a huge power struggle, swamps will become vampires, turning every little thing into an issue about themselves. They try to suck any emotion, attention, love, or any kind of energy at all out of the rock. The rock, of course, counters by becoming even more rocklike, developing a 'you can't get blood from a rock' attitude toward the vampire. Typically, as children, rocks were sucked dry by one of their parents, so now they have a natural defence against vampires. When the power struggle in a relationship has really got out of hand, when swamps become vampires, rocks tend to withdraw, hide, and disappear.

Exercise

Today, ask for Heaven's help to heal this power struggle. Imagine yourself as a child, and forgive the parent who was rocklike and did not seem to care for your needs, or the parent who was a vampire and tried to suck you dry. As a rock, ask for Heaven's help to have all the energy of Heaven pour through you to fill your partner. As the swamp, ask for Heaven's help to truly give to your partner. The acid test of true giving is to notice whether the rock moves away from you or closes down. If they do, somehow you have been giving to take. Just ask for Heaven's help so that you can find within you the energy necessary to truly give to your partner.

Note: 'Rock' and 'swamp' are terms used by Dr Spezzano to describe two completely different styles of communication in a relationship. Refer to Lesson 276.

283.   SWAMPS WANT WHAT
ROCKS GET, BUT CANNOT RECEIVE

When situations in a relationship polarise, rocks tend to give to everybody else what a swamp needs the most. Swamps have natural compassion because of their sensitivity. Rocks receive a certain acclaim or acknowledgement from the world around them because of their natural generosity. This acclaim, however, rolls off their back, because rocks do not want to put their faith in something that might change. As children, rocks were happy, then all of a sudden something happened, and their whole world came crashing down; they do not tend to trust all the nice things that are said to them, all the compliments they are given. Swamps, of course, would love to receive this kind of acknowledgement and recognition, but they are afraid of moving out to others because they fear being overwhelmed with everyone else's feelings. Swamps do not seem to have natural boundaries; they not only feel their own feelings, which are almost too much, but they can also feel and resonate with what everybody else is feeling.

While swamps are supersensitive, rocks have become impervious because at some early date they felt intruded upon, and emotionally raped. Rocks tend to be as impervious as possible to both the joy of giving and to someone trying to take, to whether they are receiving compliments or criticism. Swamps on the other hand are supersensitive. They revel in a good compliment, and love to be appreciated. A little appreciation goes a long way with a swamp, whereas criticism hits them hard. They have no ability to distance themselves from criticism; they do not know what belongs to the criticiser and what would be really helpful for them, as swamps, to acknowledge. There is then a tendency to attack back or abase themselves. It gets truly overwhelming, so swamps tend to limit themselves in their giving to other people.

Exercise

Today, if you are a swamp, give what you want for yourself. If you want recognition, give it. This will help you feel satisfied. If you are a rock, do not distrust what is being given. Rather than believing it is merely a way of trapping you, instead, be willing to let it come deep inside you. You can be aware when others move from a mode of giving to one of giving-to-take. Then, at that moment, you can communicate your own natural boundaries, rather than feel like the clam is being shucked out of you.

Note: 'Rock' and 'swamp' are terms used by Dr Spezzano to describe two completely different styles of communication in a relationship. Refer to Lesson 276.

284. ROCKS HATE HAPPINESS
BECAUSE THEY ARE AFRAID

Rocks hate happiness because they are afraid of what might come next. They do not trust a good time or a compliment, because rocks know that Palm Sunday is followed by Good Friday. Rocks are unwilling to give up the control to enjoy something, even for a short time; they know that when happiness occurs, a conflict is sure to follow. Rocks never want to let themselves get soft, so they are always in a state of readiness for war. They are good to have around in bad times because when the shit hits the fan, it is no surprise to a rock.

Exercise

Today, whether you are a swamp or a rock, realise that after you have reached a new level of intimacy in your relationship, or a new height in your life, typically, you move from the mountain top down into the next valley. Yes, the next conflict does occur, but it occurs only because you have reached a level at which you can now handle the next problem. With true understanding, you can move through it easily. Remember that answers come in at the same time as the problem; you do not have to linger in a conflict. The best and most successful way to move through conflicts is to be willing to give at such a level that you step from mountain top to mountain top.

Note: 'Rock' and 'swamp' are terms used by Dr Spezzano to describe two completely different styles of communication in a relationship. Refer to Lesson 276.

285. MY RELATIONSHIP IS A REFLECTION OF ME

Rocks look at a relationship through rock eyes. In other words, they experience a relationship as, somehow, not nurturing them, and not giving them the understanding they need. The relationship seems controlling and hard. Rocks experience their relationship as a heavy rock – a burden to carry and a place of sacrifice.

To swamps, the experience in their relationship will seem swampy. It will not give them the support that they need, and it will not be personal enough for them. The relationship takes energy from them, energy that they feel should naturally be theirs. A swamp looks at a relationship through muddy glasses so it seems to have lots of unfocused emotions and no clear direction for them.

Exercise

Today, begin looking at your relationship from a larger perspective. Sit down, close your eyes, and imagine that you are, somehow, melted down to your pure energy. Now, imagine that your partner, whether rock or swamp, is melted down to their pure energy. Let all of this energy come together and, as it does, observe what is born out of it. You may feel the difference, or you may see the difference, but either way, it is a giant move forward. It is a whole new form for the relationship.

Note: 'Rock' and 'swamp' are terms used by Dr Spezzano to describe two completely different styles of communication in a relationship. Refer to Lesson 276.

286.   WHAT I HOLD AGAINST
ANYONE KEEPS ME FROM FEELING LOVED

When we have a judgement or grievance against anyone, we distance ourself and close the door to receiving. What we hold against them blocks the way for us to feel loved. The people around us may love us a great deal, but we are unable to feel it because we have closed the door and pulled away. Our willingness to let go of judgement opens the door so that we can receive.

Exercise

Today, let go of any grievances that you have toward anyone. Bless them, and feel yourself opening the door to receive, once again. Feel all of the love that comes through this doorway, feel all of the abundance that is coming toward you.

287. VISION IS LEAPING THE ABYSS TO LOVE AND LEAVING A BRIDGE FOR OTHERS TO FOLLOW

Vision means giving ourself so much that we turn ourself inside out. This kind of love, this kind of giving, leads us to see far into the future for a way that works for everyone. It allows us to leap the abyss of the unconscious mind and to transcend nothingness. Vision allows us to move into a much greater area of love where we see new answers. We are then able to make a bridge for others to follow, to find the language to speak the unspeakable. When we are in vision, we are living our purpose – giving the gift of ourself in such a truly creative way that the path is made safe for those who follow behind us.

Exercise

Today, know that what is before you is an opportunity for vision. Whether the situation is difficult or easy, love can be born at a much higher level. Your willingness to totally, thoroughly give yourself is the willingness to let this kind of love be born again on the earth.

288. WHEN I FEEL I DID NOT LIVE UP TO MY PARENTS' EXPECTATIONS, I REALLY BELIEVE THEY DID NOT LIVE UP TO MINE

Many of us believe that we did not live up to our parents' expectations, and so we always feel inadequate, as if we are never enough. Some of us moved into perfectionism, while others moved further into that feeling of inadequacy, or even neurosis, where nothing is ever good enough for them. There is an interesting phenomenon going on here: if we believe that we did not live up to our parents' expectations, we actually believe it was they that did not live up to ours. We believe that they weren't good enough for us, that they did not live up to what we felt they should have done as parents. No matter how our parents acted, this attitude keeps us feeling as if we did not live up to their expectations. Our willingness to let go of our expectations will free both ourself and our parents, so we all move forward.

Exercise

Today, be willing to change your attitude toward your parents. The following exercise is in four parts, as an experiment to help you make this change.

For part one, close your eyes. Imagine how your parents were when you were a child, and how you believed they were total failures as parents. Notice how you feel as a result of that attitude.

In part two, imagine your parents at this time. Pity them, feel sorry for them, 'Oh, my poor Mum. Oh, my poor Dad.' They did not quite make it, but now you feel both above them and sad for them.

323

Look at what you are feeling now in the situation, and also how you feel about yourself.

And now the third part is to imagine that your parents are still the way they were when you were a kid. Take the attitude that they are doing the very best they can, given their inner and outer circumstances, their childhood and what happened to them. Given what they know, this is the very best they can do. When you look at them with this attitude, notice how you feel about them and yourself.

With part four, imagine that you chose your parents for a specific purpose – that they reflect the most important, yet projected, areas of your mind that you came to heal, bridge and integrate. You chose them as the best people to help you learn what you have come to learn. Now, how do you feel? How do you feel about yourself?

If you have done this experiment truly, you begin to see that it is only your attitude toward your parents that dictates your experience of them. If your attitude did not produce the highest results, you can choose again.

289. ALL ACCUSATIONS ARE SELF-ACCUSATIONS

Anything we accuse anyone else of is something that we are accusing ourself of; every time we attack other people we are attacking ourself. We judge others for how they are behaving, but judgement hides guilt. Every place where we accuse another person is a place where we are punishing ourself, a place where we feel guilty. If we remember that these people are only acting the way they are because they need something, rather than accuse them, we could give to them. Giving to, supporting, and forgiving them would allow them to blossom forth, and release us from the situation.

Exercise

Today, learn true freedom. Take a look at your world. Where do you feel grievances or judgements? Let go of your accusations against other people. Be willing to give to and support them. To release yourself from situations you feel stuck in, forgive the other person, because the accusation you let go of allows you to experience the freedom and innocence within.

290.
MY RELATIONSHIP
WILL CHANGE AS I CHANGE

The answer for creating quick change for ourself and our relationship is to stop complaining, stop blaming our partner, and give up our grievances. Our willingness to change ourself is what will make the relationship better. As we step forward, the attractiveness of that step forward naturally brings our partner along with us, and they begin to change. Any area where our partner is stuck, is an area where we are unwilling to step forward and change. Any stuck place in our relationship can be changed by our willingness to step forward.

Exercise

Today, look at what seems to be stuck in your partner and your relationship. How would you like to have it? Be willing to ask the Universe to make those changes for you. Ask your Higher Mind to move you forward where those changes could be made. Your willingness naturally and easily moves you forward so that your relationship, your partner and you will all feel like the new improved model. Let go of any grievances that hold you back from moving forward.

291. MY WILLINGNESS TO FIND
WHAT FEELING THE CONFLICT HIDES
CREATES A MAJOR GROWTH OPPORTUNITY

There are hidden feelings in each person on both sides of every conflict. If we are willing to find what we have hidden away, what we have not wanted to feel, we create a major growth opportunity for ourself. As we burn through these feelings, we naturally move forward, and the conflict begins to change. We move up to a whole new level of healing and *connectedness*, where communication begins.

Exercise

Today, look at a situation where you are in conflict. What is the feeling inside that you have hidden away? Do not be afraid of this feeling. Be willing to feel it all the way through until it is completely gone. As you burn it away, everything changes for the better.

292.   IF I REALLY WANT IT,
THERE IS A WAY

With the power of our mind and the power of choice, it is true that if we really want it, there is a way. Our desire and willingness always open the door for the solution to come in. There is a way, the miracle will occur, if necessary, for us to succeed, if we really want it. That is, of course, unless we are in a situation where what we want would hurt us. At that level, we always feel some ambivalence, so we do not fully want it.

Some people who are at the point of death ask for healing, and it occurs. They rise up to a higher level of understanding and life. Other people at the point of death ask for a miracle, but are really afraid to receive one because a miracle would be counter to their belief system. They would rather die, and be right, than have to change their beliefs. If we are willing to change our beliefs and to change anything that is locked away inside us, there is a way, even if we do not have the vision to see it at this point. All it takes is for us to want it wholly.

Exercise

Today, some situation in your life could come to a total success. All it takes is a few seconds of focusing on that thing and wanting it, totally. At that point, everything begins to work out for you.

293.   THE GREATEST FEAR
IS THE FEAR OF HAPPINESS

It is easy to see that people are less afraid of death than they are of happiness. As we look around, we know of many people who are dead or dying, considerably fewer people who are happy and, even more rare, people in happy relationships. Our greatest fear is of happiness, which it can also be said is the fear of Love, or the fear of God. To find God means we would be totally obedient, we would have all the answers to our life, and we would be totally happy. The fear of happiness is our fear of surrendering this much, of having to let go of our way of doing things, and of having to melt down all the blocks, controls, and rules we set up to live our life the way we are.

Exercise

Today, let go of your thoughts about what brings you happiness. It is time to resign as your own teacher. Ask Heaven to specifically show you what would make you happy, and to give you the strength to enjoy it.

294.

I AM ALWAYS IN
THE PERFECT PLACE TO LEARN
THE LESSON I MOST NEED TO LEARN

Everything is connected and nothing really happens by accident. We are always in the place that is perfect for us to learn what we most need to learn. 'When the student is ready, the teacher appears.' When we are ready, the situation is presented to show us exactly what we are to learn and grow with at this point in our life. The people are there to help us move forward, to teach us, and to support us.

Exercise

Today, take time to realise that you are in a perfect place for the lessons that you are learning, for the healing that you are doing, and for the growth that you are ready to make at this point in your life.

295. MY RELATIONSHIP TO HAPPINESS IS REALLY MY RELATIONSHIP TO MYSELF

It is easy to see how happy we are because our happiness is what we give to ourself, and what we are willing to allow for ourself. Often, we do not recognise how much we are loved, and that we are given everything we are willing to receive. So many blessings, gifts, happy experiences, and joyful, loving situations pass us by just because we are not open to them. Our choice to allow more happiness into our relationship to ourself actually increases the happiness in every relationship we have, especially with our love partner.

Exercise

Today, take a good look at how much happiness you are experiencing. No matter how much it is, you could be experiencing so much more. The key to increasing your happiness is in your relationship to yourself. How have you been treating yourself? Do not be so hard on yourself. Be willing to relax and enjoy yourself. Be willing to give to yourself.

296.
WHAT I RECEIVE IS
WHAT I THINK I DESERVE

We can measure what we think of ourself, and what we think we deserve, just from what we are receiving. If we feel we do not deserve anything, because we are unworthy and have no value, we will not let ourself receive. We are worthy, and we have value because of who we intrinsically are, not because of what we do. We are a child of God, we deserve it all.

Exercise

Today, acknowledge that you are worthy and have value. You are worthy because you are a child of God, who is loved and forever remembered in the Mind of God. You have intrinsic value because you have the ability to create and give life. You, with your love, can bring the world to a new birth.

297. MY PURPOSE BRINGS FULFILMENT

Living our purpose is one of the keys to finding happiness. Many of us wonder what our purpose is, but our purpose is not really something we do, it is something we are. The more we unfold ourself, the more we develop ourself, the more we hear the call to what we truly want to do, the more we find our happiness. Doing what we truly want to do, with integrity, brings us happiness and fulfilment.

Exercise

Today, be willing to listen to what it is you really want to do, and to follow it. It is the path leading home. Living your purpose brings you fulfilment, an incredible gift that you can share in your relationship.

298.   THOSE AROUND ME ARE
IN SERVICE TO MY MIND

Everyone around us is in service to us. God comes at us in a thousand disguises to show us the ways that we keep ourself from God. Each person wants to help us re-member ourself; they are God calling to us. If we do not love the people we can see, how can we love God, whom we cannot see? Our willingness to move through all of the disguises allows us to recognise God in everyone. As we do not allow ourself to be stopped by our judgements, which are actually just how we limit the people around us, we are willing to see God in them. The situation explodes forward in joy and success, and we feel how much we are loved. To see God in everyone allows us to feel the joy that is present at every single moment.

Exercise

Today, practise seeing God in anyone who is close to you. Look into their eyes throughout the day, look beyond their bodies, and see God smiling at you. As you recognise yourself seeing God in everyone, enjoy the love and all the gifts God has for you.

299. I CANNOT LOSE ANYTHING
I FULLY VALUE

All of us have felt victimised by loss, abandonment, and situations changing so fast that we feel left out, but anything we fully value, anything we are fully committed to is ours. The only way we could have suffered a loss is that, at some point, we stopped valuing this person or thing. Anywhere we experience loss is a place of attachment, which is valuing something outside ourself in order to compensate for feeling valueless. Attachment is never true, and even makes what is true, untrue. The extent to which we are attached is the extent to which we are off our centre. This brings delusion, sacrifice and even self-destructiveness. Our attachment becomes a repository of our happiness, so we must be in control to keep the source of our happiness safe. The happiness that comes from outside can never fully sustain us. Valuing others and ourself is much easier.

Exercise

Today, ask the Universe to carry you back to your centre. Be willing to claim back your happiness and value, rather than rely on something outside you. Feel them fully inside you. As you do, remember the power of your choice and commitment, and give your happiness and value to the situation where you thought you lost someone or some thing. As you fully give to something, what you give becomes yours. Notice that as the situation opens to you, you once again feel the natural connection between you and that person or thing in the situation.

300. MY RELATIONSHIP IS THE REFLECTION OF MY BELIEF SYSTEM

If we do not believe that we can have it all in our relationship, we get to be right. If we believe something about the opposite sex, we get to be right. Anything we believe is what our partner and ourself are acting out in our relationship. Our relationship shows us our own belief system, so if we do not like what we have, then changing our mind will change it.

Exercise

Today, take a look at what your relationship shows. What does it show about men? About women? What does it show about sex? What does it show about love? What does it show about support? What does it show about communication? If it would be helpful, use a pen and paper. Write down the categories such as sex, money, love, men, women, etc., and next to each write what is happening with it in your relationship. In a third column, write what the belief must be to have the situation be as it is. Examine each of your beliefs. If you do not like any of them, or could have them be better, change them. Take a moment for each and say, 'This was a mistake. What I now choose is _____.' Use the power of your mind to move yourself forward.

301. GUILT CREATES WITHDRAWAL OR AGGRESSION

When we are feeling guilty, we withdraw because we are afraid of doing the same thing over again. We either remove ourself from the path of life, or attack those around us to get away from feeling guilty. In the same way, if we lay guilt on those around us, they will respond either by withdrawing from us, or by becoming aggressive back at us. Everyone hates guilt. It is the hot potato we always try to pass on to the people around us. We never want to take responsibility for our guilt because it just feels bad. It is the destructive illusion that creates, either within or outside us, exactly what it is trying to stop. Our willingness to let go of our guilt allows us to remember our own and everyone's innocence.

Exercise

Today, look at areas in your life that seem to express either withdrawal or aggression. These are areas that are not working for you. Ask yourself what you must be feeling bad about to act in such a way, and let it go. As you remember your innocence, support yourself and the people around you, which moves everyone to a new level of success.

302. MY INNOCENCE IS ONE OF THE
BEST GIFTS I CAN GIVE TO MY PARTNER

Our innocence allows our partner to unfold before us. It allows them to give all of the gifts and love they have ever wanted to give to us. With innocence, we feel totally loved, we feel creative, we feel that everything is working out for us in every area of our life. This naturally makes our partner's life a lot easier, too. Our innocence is the extent to which we can freely love our partner and everyone around us. It is the extent to which we can freely give the gift of our creativity to the world. Our innocence brings back wonder, and a state of beauty to the relationship; it brings enchantment back. Our innocence blesses our partner, because it allows them to feel loved and cherished, and to experience the treasure life is. For ourself, it allows the love we have always dreamed of.

Exercise

Today, choose innocence. Feel as innocent as possible in every situation. Any bad feeling that surfaces is just coming up to be gotten rid of, to be let go. Welcome it, even when it seems to come from outside you, and let your innocence be the truth that accelerates all of this bad feeling out of you. Let your innocence open you to receive all the gifts that you are being given, and you can then give all the gifts to your partner. Innocence is a state of being without guilt. It is your true worth, knowing that you are valuable, not for what you are or what you do, but for who you are.

303.   MY WORRY IS A
FORM OF ATTACK

Our worry is a form of fear, and all fear comes from our attack thoughts. When we worry about someone, we have no confidence in them or the situation. Our worry says that negative things could happen, so we are using the power of our mind to create a lack of confidence for them, and to allow fearful elements in the situation. Worry attacks the situation; choosing to bless it would help build the situation and those in it.

Exercise

Today, every time you feel tempted to worry about someone or something, give your blessing. Your blessing is your trust and your positive choice for the best thing to happen for everyone in the situation.

304. WHAT I LOVE, I BECOME

We naturally gravitate toward what we love. The more we move toward what we love, the more we enjoy ourself, and we begin to resonate with it. We find that what we love is also within us. This allows a giving and receiving, a sharing and joining in love, which lets us know it as ourself. What we love, we then plant in our heart and help it grow like a garden. We want to give it to everyone, so they, too, can receive and enjoy what we are receiving and enjoying. Enjoyment always wants to be shared.

Exercise

Today, look at who it is you love. What are you really enjoying in your love for them? Allow yourself to feel your natural gratitude toward this person or situation. Gratitude allows you even stronger resonance with the very gift you are experiencing. Your gratitude not only opens the door to love, it increases love.

305. NOT TRUSTING OTHERS
IS REALLY NOT TRUSTING MYSELF

When we do not trust others, we actually do not trust ourself with them. We do not trust that we will not be used, or taken advantage of, because we do not have confidence in the situation. If we trusted ourself, we could be with the most seemingly untrustworthy of characters, and we would have the natural confidence to be with them and to create a successful situation. If we do not have trust, we could be with the most trustworthy people, and we would feel betrayed, because we lack the confidence to communicate what is vital to move the situation forward.

Exercise

Today, look and see where you are not trusting people, and give confidence to yourself in this area. Trust yourself enough to communicate what you need to make the situation a greater success.

306. THE EXTENT OF SCARCITY
IN MY RELATIONSHIP IS THE
EXTENT OF MY COMPETITION

Any area in our relationship that is not fully abundant – whether communication, money, sex, free time, happiness, or whatever else – is an area where, somehow, we feel that we are right, or that we are a little bit better than our partner. It is an area in which we are fighting to get certain needs met by them, or from the situation before they do. The extent of scarcity is the extent to which we are not yet in partnership.

Exercise

Today, look at the areas where you would like to have more in your relationship. Begin building partnership in these areas, and begin supporting your partner. Where you support your partner, the scarcity begins to fall away.

307.   NEVER QUIT DATING

If we want to keep life in our relationship, we keep giving life to it. As we keep creating time for ourself and our partner to focus on the relationship itself, we get to know each other better by just enjoying ourself and having a good time together. When we think we know our partner, we are deluding ourself unless we know their true greatness; anything else is our self-judgement projected onto them. Never quit dating, because the more we get to know our partner, the more we truly love them, and the more enjoyment we will naturally have.

Exercise

Today, take time for yourself. Take time for your partner. Renew yourself and your relationship, and keep moving forward. Make a date, and do something different, something creative, something that you would really enjoy.

308. UNHAPPINESS IS A FORM
OF REVENGE ON MY PARENTS

If we are unhappy, what we are saying to the world is, 'My parents did not raise me right.' One of the great ways we get revenge on our parents is just to fail, or not be happy. We go around in life with our sad face saying, 'Look at what you did to me, Mom and Dad. Because you failed, I am screwed up.' We are cutting off our nose to spite our face. If they failed, it can only be because we have also failed. To let our happiness rely on the behaviour of others only brings suffering. As we stop living in the past, and forgive our parents, it frees both ourself and them.

Exercise

Today, it is time to choose a more mature and self-empowering attitude, one that moves you forward. It is time to give your parents your happiness, which would move their life forward as well as yours. The best gift you can give yourself is also the best gift you can give to them. Happiness is the best policy for all concerned.

309. TRUE ABUNDANCE IS HAVING ONLY WINNERS

When we have winners and losers in any situation, the communication has not come to full fruition. There are still areas of hurt and fear, a fight is still going on at some level. When there are losers, our belief in scarcity is reinforced, so do not stop communicating until there are only winners.

Exercise

Today, do not adjust to pain. Continue any communication until both sides feel as if they have won, and there are only winners.

310. TO BE MYSELF IS TO BE A STAR

A star is a person who shines so brightly, who gives their gifts so fully, who loves so completely that everyone is drawn by the light of this star to find the way home. For us to truly know ourself is to know that we are a star. For us to truly be ourself is to recognise the genius in us, and to know what a gift we are to everyone around us. Stars may do very quiet things, but they shine an intense love-light that burns through the darkness.

Exercise

Today, recognise yourself as a star, and allow anything that stops you from shining to fall away. Choose to forgive, or let go of any grievance or judgement that allows you control over yourself, others, or the situation. Choose not to use anyone or anything to hold yourself back. Choose to utterly and completely love. Nothing else will satisfy you. Nothing else is worthy of you.

311.   ALL PAIN IS THE
RESULT OF MISUNDERSTANDING

Suffering means there is something we do not understand. A full understanding heals all of the needs that result in pain, and allows us to move through the resistance that pain is. It helps us realise the love and bonding that is present. Wherever we have stopped and refused to go on is an area of pain, fear, and unmet needs. Understanding allows the process to unfold, the fear to be overcome by willingness, connection and love, and the needs met so that we are naturally in rapport with the people around us.

Exercise

Today, go into rapport with the people around you. Join them. Joining them allows the understanding that heals. Bonding brings insight as love brings compassionate wisdom.

312. I JOIN WITH SOMEONE WHO IS ATTACKING ME

Defence creates attack, because the defence is a kind of chip on our shoulder that just begs to be knocked off. Any pain inside us calls to other pain. Violence on the inside calls for violence on the outside to come toward us. As someone is attacking, move toward them, because when there is no resistance, there is nothing to attack. When we have joined with the person attacking us, the attack in them deflates. Any attack is a call for help. Somewhere, deep inside themself, the person attacking us believes we are the person who could help them. Of course, they have resistance to that, too, and fight against it. They feel almost angry at their attraction to us and, sometimes, that ambivalence creates the attack. If we respond with closeness, awareness, and nurturing, the fight ends and both of us move forward to a new level.

Exercise

Today, move toward someone who is attacking you. Call them. Write to them. Send them love. If no one is attacking you now, go back to the past where you have been attacked. In your mind recreate the scene; this time though, move out to support them. Move toward and join them. Give them the help that the attack was calling for.

313. HAVING IT ALL IS
THE PROMISE OF A RELATIONSHIP

It is important to know that we can have it all. Adjusting to limitations and giving up on having true abundance or having everything work in your life is not the highest maturity. A relationship can create the inspiration for us to keep moving past our limitations. The love within a relationship can move us past the deadness and conflicts to higher and higher levels. Each problem we transcend, and each temptation we pass by, brings us to a new level where ourself, our relationship, and our whole life becomes more abundant. The promise of the relationship is that as it keeps unfolding, we keep unfolding, and more and more grace comes to us and fills our life.

Exercise

Today, take time to relax, and imagine that you are standing on the surface of your relationship with your partner. All of a sudden, together, you begin sinking down into the ground past all the conflicts, and all the deadness. Imagine that the two of you keep sinking through the ground until you get to a more essential place. Whether this place is a meadow, an open space, or a place of light, just know the true essence of the relationship. Feel all its possibility, and know that this movement through all of the misunderstandings is leading you toward having it all.

314. THE COMPETITION IN MY PRESENT RELATIONSHIP BEGAN IN THE FAMILY I GREW UP IN

All families, no matter how healthy, contain subtle, or not-so-subtle aspects of competition. This shows especially if there was any kind of scarcity – not enough money or love to go around, or not enough of a balance so that everyone got to enjoy each other fully. The competition that we now face in our present relationship is something that began a long time ago with the taking on of our personalities.

Our personalities are all built on a sense of comparison and specialness: 'Don't I deserve love? Don't I deserve love a little bit more than my brother or sister, or anybody else?' These aspects are now so much a part of us that they are like a body stocking. Every personality marks a place where we gave up a gift in ourself to gain everybody else's approval, and to feel included. Personality is like a cellophane wrapper between other people and ourself, because it keeps us from receiving. Personality keeps us self-conscious which prevents us from reaching out to people, and being expanded, spontaneous, outrageous and fun.

Exercise

Today, look at the competition in your life, and at where it began a long time ago. Realise that there is enough for everyone in your present relationship. As you realise that, you can re-balance the past. Every time competition is brought to your awareness, say to yourself, 'The enemies that seem to have sprung up in my family I will now see as my allies, because the more they succeed, the more I succeed. The more my partner succeeds, the more I succeed. I will reach beyond this competition, and support my partner. I will see their true self. When I feel self-conscious, self-tortured, or caught by the voice of distraction in my head, I will reach out to someone else, creating freedom and flow for both of us.'

315. WHAT I EXPECT OF ANOTHER IS WHAT I AM NOT GIVING TO THEM

All expectations come out of demands, which come out of fear that we might not have what we need. That is why we demand it rather than ask for it. When we are expecting something from another, the reason we are afraid they might not give it to us is because we are not giving it to them. We could turn our expectation into an invitation. This, and just being willing to give the very thing that we are expecting from our partner or those around us, creates success. An invitation is much more naturally responded to, and when we give what we need, we feel satisfied, healed of the need, and we are open to receive.

Exercise

Today, look at the expectation you may have of someone, whether it is your partner, your parent, your child, your boss – whomever it is. Where do you feel unrequited? Rather than expecting anything of them, feel yourself giving them the very thing you would like to have from them. You will soon find a natural giving and receiving between the two of you.

316. THE HELPER ROLE ALLOWS ME TO FEEL SUPERIOR WHILE BEING AFRAID OF AN EQUAL PARTNER

The helper role is all about feeling a little bit better than those we are taking care of. That is why it is a role. The role covers up a feeling of inferiority, of not being good enough or worthy enough; it is a compensation. We tend to choose someone who can be co-dependent with us, someone who is also really afraid of moving on. We move into collusion in a relationship to hold ourself back, with one person being the identified problem person.

Another way we take on the helper role is to help someone improve until, finally, they get to the point of being equal with us. At the point just where we could really go on to an equal-level relationship, we push them away, and they move on, leaving us empty-handed. We are afraid to stand as an equal partner, because we are afraid of really getting hurt. We feel we are not worthy to have the relationship succeed, or that we do not have enough power or confidence to handle an equal partner.

Exercise

Today, look at all the times in your life when you have chosen someone in order to be the helper. Was it so that you both would not move forward, or did you see the potential in them, and when they got to a place of healing and equality, you pushed them away? Whatever your situation, be willing to be equal, to share your feelings, and even to share your experiences of not feeling quite adequate. Step forward in your life, not by playing a role, but by allowing for your happiness, allowing yourself to receive, and allowing your partner to become your equal. Bless yourself as much as you are blessing them.

317. THE TRUTH CREATES ABUNDANCE

What is experienced, but not said, holds us back. When there is no communication, there is no joining, and we cannot move forward. When we are afraid to tell something to our partner, not telling it creates deadness. What we are withholding, whether it is our feelings, something that needs to be handled, or something that has happened, creates a certain blockage between our partner and ourself. When there is no connection, abundance will not be generated. The truth creates a line of connection. Our level of connection with our partner generates true abundance – not just money, but joy, happiness, creativity, and all of the good things of life.

Exercise

Today, find out where you are withholding yourself. What you are withholding may not be true, but it is the truth of your experience at this point. Once you finish sharing it, you can integrate it into the relationship, and you can both move forward. Your truth creates abundance.

318. IF I DON'T HAVE SOMETHING IN MY LIFE, I AM IN CONTROL

Our control stands in the way of success. The highest level of success is something we flow with, not something that is planned. We do not control the wave when we are surfing or conquer the mountain we are skiing. We go with the flow of it, and to the extent we do, we become successful. Our control says that we think we have a better answer, not only for ourself, but for anyone else who would care to listen. Control hides our fear of loss, getting hurt, or having it be so good that we would be overwhelmed. We control ourself because we would rather not have it be good than be overwhelmed, or have to deal with old pain that might not even be there. Willingness to give up our control allows us to see what answer life wants to show us.

Exercise

Today, let go of control and trust that everything is coming your way. Recognise that you do not have to make the dawn to have the sun come up every morning. Recognise that you do not have to push the river to make it flow. Recognise that the Universe is running just perfectly, and everything is moving toward success, if you would just get out of the way. Imagine that you are putting your future in the hands of Heaven, relax, and know everything is on its way to you.

319. NO MATTER WHAT MY PAIN, GIVING CREATES HEALING

When we choose to totally give ourself through any negative feelings, or to be in service, we create a breakthrough. Whether we are feeling ashamed, embarrassed, hurt, jealous, afraid, in despair, empty, useless, futile or lost, where we give ourself, we create our birth. Where we give, we move out of deadness and into flow; we move out of self-consciousness and self-torture into grace. True giving brings receiving; it is one of the greatest healing agents in the world.

Exercise

Today, move through your pain by giving. Are you feeling numb? Are you feeling deadness? Whatever the pain, choose to give. Look around you. Where would your giving improve the situation? Now, reach out to other people and support them. As you give to them, things get better for them and for you.

320. A POWER STRUGGLE IS MY DEMAND ON OTHERS TO MEET MY NEEDS

Our needs can be fulfilled by both people simply taking the next step, rather than engaging in a power struggle. In a power struggle, somehow, we think the other person is the source of our receiving, that they are the ones who should make us happy. We fight with them to do it our way to meet our needs, but fighting with our partner is just a way of delaying ourself from moving forward in life. Our willingness, simply to take the next step, would create the fulfilment of our needs and those of our partner also.

Exercise

Today, stop fighting. Close your eyes, relax, and ask that the next step come to you. Say Yes to whatever is coming in your life, knowing that it will contain the answers to what is plaguing you now. Just say yes. Be willing to be open to whatever it is that is to be taught about the situation, and how it could become the very best. Be willing to move off your position to have it be different for you and your partner.

321.   WHEN I WANT TO HAVE
A NEED FULFILLED, I LET GO

Needs are demands whether spoken or unspoken. Whether we are aware of them or not, they create resistance to our receiving. No need is fulfilled from outside ourself, because at the deepest level, needs are illusions. They are things we think we need when we do not recognise our wholeness, which is the most essential part of us. In our everyday life, where we rush around trying to get all of the things we think we need, we forget this place where we have everything.

Exercise

Today, let go of your needs. Close your eyes. Now, imagine sinking down within yourself until you come to a place of total wholeness for yourself, a place of no needs. Another way, if this is better for you, is to imagine yourself moving forward in time, even beyond this life, to a place of great creativity where you are totally whole. Recognise that your needs are naturally released as you reach this place of wholeness – the essential reality of your mind where you have it all.

322. EVERY BLESSING
I GIVE BLESSES ME

Whenever we wish someone the best or give someone love, we feel good. Every blessing we give is a blessing that we give to ourself. Every time we help someone, the help we give them and the healing they reach gets added to our life.

Exercise

Today, close your eyes and allow to come to your mind people who need your blessing, who need your love sent to them, who need the power of your mind added to their life. As you give to them, feel how good you feel. Know that your giving multiplies the power of your blessing. Throughout the day, any time you meet someone – people on the street, people you pass by, people at work – just bless them.

323. THE MORE I GIVE OF MYSELF
TO ANOTHER, THE MORE I
SEE WHO THEY ARE

When we criticise, we limit our ability to see another person, and to understand them. The German poet, Rainer Maria Rilke, said that we can only approach a work of art through love. How much truer this is when we approach a human being. If we bring the love that allows us to understand, the worlds upon worlds, and the mystery that they are, open to us. The more love we bring to someone, the more we see and know them as they truly are. The more love we bring to the person we are with, the more we naturally feel inspired to support and enjoy who they are.

We are in sacrifice when we are with people and we are not enjoying them or ourself, so it is easy to see that counterfeit giving is occurring. If we are not enjoying someone, it is because we are not giving to them. The more we give to anyone, the more we get to enjoy ourself.

Exercise

Today, look at some of the significant people in your life that you are not enjoying. Now is the time to reach out to them, to extend yourself until you get to the point of enjoying them. You will find how much you have removed yourself from some of them. Just give and give and give until you only see their beauty, and how much fun it is to be with them.

324.   IF I SEE A PROBLEM,
IT IS MY PROBLEM

Whether we accept it or not, if there is a problem, it is our problem. Denying it does not help us change this fact. Just because we do not see the snake in the grass does not mean that it will not affect us if we step on it. If we see a problem, it is our problem, and we are called upon to do something about it. If we see a job that needs to be done, it is our job, and we need to respond in order to make it better. Recognise that what we see is what we are called upon to take care of. As we expand our awareness, we expand our flow. People who want to help will see and hear the calls for help all around them. Our willingness to respond to these calls will move us forward. We will find our natural place as the focal point for healing, and our natural place as the leader in the situation to make everything better. We can do this and still live our own life. If we see a problem, it is our problem; ignoring it will not help, responding will.

Exercise

Today, look out at your world and see who really needs help. What is the problem that you could respond to or make better? Respond now.

325. MY SELF-CONCEPTS
ARE KILLING ME

Every self-concept is something that we are trying to prove. It is a goal, actually, that we are trying to head toward. We are trying to prove certain things so as not to get in touch with the negative things we believe about ourself. The amount of energy that every single self-concept demands wears us out. The energy we use, whether consciously or subconsciously, is robbing us of what would naturally build our happiness. We have thousands of self-concepts; all of them are sucking us dry. They are demanding energy from us, demanding that, for each self-concept, we go on another useless crusade to prove something that does not need to be proved.

We all want to have a good concept about ourself because we think that a good self-concept naturally makes us feel better. Every thought we have about ourself, however, is not the truth because it is just a thought. Unless it is meditative or creative, thinking is always one step after the event and is, in effect, a form of resistance and control. Our essence is some-thing much more whole that never really needs questioning. When we have doubts about ourself, and think of ourself as negative and bad, we create positive self-concepts; we now have a whole layer of all these good things we think about ourself, which are merely compensations. If we were to pierce this layer, we would find a garbage bin full of negative self-concepts deep in the subconscious and, even, the unconscious mind. If we really knew what we thought about ourself, we would probably not be able to stand it. The good news is that these negative self-concepts are not true either. When we pass by these self-concepts, we reach a new depth where we find positive beliefs about ourself, beliefs that are not merely compensations. This is the realm just before we hit bliss and ecstasy, the area just before enlightenment. It is the doorway to seeing things as they really are.

Exercise

Today, be willing to move through any self-concept, positive or negative, that you get in touch with. Each self-concept you let go of moves you closer to reaching the knowledge of your essence and wholeness. You know when you are getting close because you feel joyful and good about yourself. You feel how much you are loved, and how much you love. You feel your natural creativity. Let go of all your self-concepts because they are robbing you of you.

326. EVERYTHING THAT HAPPENS IN MY LIFE IS A COMMUNICATION TO A SIGNIFICANT OTHER

Everything in life is a communication, so everything that happens to us, everything that we have done, or that has been done to us, is a communication to a significant other. As we look at the mishaps in our life, if we really want to see what is going on, we will see that we are always giving a message. This message is to ourself, God, our parents, our significant other, even ex-significant others, and to anyone else who truly happened to be in the situation. The mishap occurred in the first place because we were so frightened of communication; we would rather have something happen to us to try and communicate it for us, than to be in touch with ourself and communicate directly to the other person. Subconscious communication has much less of a chance for success. Sometimes, having negative things happen to us is a way of getting back at others and, sometimes, it is a call for help on our part. Sometimes, we actually have negative things happen to us as a way of telling someone we love them, but this is pure sacrifice, and it is really harmful to our own life. There is some major misunderstanding between ourself and the other person if we sacrifice ourself to get their love or approval.

Exercise

Today, choose three major experiences in your life. With each experience, ask yourself what you are or were communicating to each significant person there. As you understand what messages you were giving, you begin to understand what was going on with you that you

364

created such an event in your life. *Learning to turn your subconscious communication into conscious communication allows you much greater success in your life. Bringing what is in the darkness into the light creates healing.*

327. IF I DON'T TRUST, I DON'T LOVE

If we do not trust someone, we are not feeling love for them. There is something else going on, which is probably some form of control. We might be feeling our need that makes them attractive to us, or we might be feeling our desire for this person in some way, but what we are feeling is not love. If we are not trusting them, we are not even trusting ourself, because to the extent we trust ourself, we trust another. When we are not giving ourself in trust, there is no way that we can receive with confidence.

Trust is the power of our mind being given to another person to support them toward integrity and truth. Trust is not being naive, but an investment of the power of our mind into a situation to make it more positive. As we give trust, a most vital factor in any relationship, we are giving love to our partner. Trust goes hand in hand with love.

Exercise

Today, give trust to your partner, and to anyone around you who really deserves it. It is the best gift that you can give, because there is no problem that trust cannot heal. You have the confidence. As much as you trust yourself and your own personal power, you can trust anyone. Remember, trust is not naivety. Trust yourself as to what your instincts tell you is going on, then use trust as a transformational tool, which makes the situation safe, and empowers you.

328.   IT IS ONLY THROUGH
COMMITMENT THAT I RECEIVE

This is the good news: only through commitment do we receive. Many people, especially many independent people, feel there is no life after commitment. What they are talking about is not commitment, but some form of contraction, sacrifice, or holding themselves back. They are remembering a time when they were love-slaves and did things to win approval. To the extent a person is independent is the extent to which they are afraid about going into sacrifice again. Neither our independence, nor our sacrifice has anything to do with commitment. Our commitment is our choice to give ourself fully in every way we know how. As we give more of ourself, we naturally receive more. Commitment means 'to send with' – *com* means 'with' and *mittere* 'to send'. Our willingness to send ourself to someone, to commit ourself, allows us to receive from them.

Exercise

Today, acknowledge where you have a fear of commitment because you have misunderstood it as a form of sacrifice. Be willing to let all of that sacrifice go, and to know that you can make truer choices, that now you can give yourself truly, and that you do not have to be afraid of being captured. You can speak the truth so as not to be used. Allow yourself to make the choice to give yourself so you can succeed.

329.   LOVE COMES TOWARDS ME
ALL THE TIME

Love is always coming toward us, but our lack of vision, awareness, and openness does not allow us to receive it. Our judgements and grievances create a bad feeling about ourself, which does not allow us to see that all good things are moving toward us. Our willingness to let go of our bad feelings and just open our eyes would allow us to see all the love and good things coming toward us, and receive them.

Exercise

Today is a great day for feeling how much you are loved at every moment. Imagine that you are in your very favourite place. Now, imagine that all the love your family has ever had for you is coming toward you, as well as all the love of anyone who has ever believed in you – teachers, friends, co-workers, mentors, and creative colleagues. See the love of your spiritual teacher coming to you. Now, see all the love of God coming to you, it is always coming to you. As you see all this love coming toward you, open yourself and receive it, feel it. Feel how much you are loved.

330.   IF ANYONE IS THE BAD GUY, EVERYONE LOSES

Whenever we judge someone to be the bad guy, we go into power struggle with them; we avoid them or attack them, even if only in our mind. We set up a struggle in which we are trying not to be affected by them, or we are trying to beat them. Anywhere someone loses, whether they lose or we lose, we have all lost. We have created a situation where somebody has to pay the bill. Guess who it is going to be? This judgement is actually just a way of hiding things that need to be handled or communicated. It is a projection of our own self-judgement. As we are willing to look beyond 'good guys – bad guys', and move beyond our competition to understand, there is a place, paradoxically enough, where both of us could be satisfied – now and in the future.

Exercise

Today, choose for everyone to win. Close your eyes, relax, and think of the person you are judging. Who is it that you believe is wrong? Who is it that you believe is the bad guy? Ask the part of your mind that has all the answers to take care of this problem, and to show you that paradoxical way that everyone can win, not only now, but also throughout eternity. Do not stop until everyone can win.

331. COMMITMENT CAN COME
ONLY OUT OF SELF-VALUING

The reason we have such a hard time with commitment and do not think we could last for the long haul is that we do not think anyone, including ourself, is worth that kind of continuous giving. We do not value ourself, so we do not value other people. To the extent we do not value ourself, we find ourself locked up in roles, duties and rules – doing the right things for the wrong reasons. Commitment allows us to do the right thing for the right reason. With commitment, we live from a place of greater responsiveness, truer choice, and higher ethics. As we commit and, thus, give value to others, we correspondingly give it to ourself.

Exercise

Today, value yourself, and really give to yourself. As you learn to value yourself, you are able to see a constant unfolding that is happening with you and with others.

332. LETTING SOMEONE ABUSE YOU IS NOT A SERVICE TO ANYONE

It is important to give ourself basic respect, and to ask for self-respect from those around us. Letting someone abuse us is not a service to anyone. Respecting ourself is to not allow ourself to be abused. It is important to prevent people from harming us, not only for us, but because, later, their guilt will create a vicious cycle of either withdrawal or recurrent attacks. Sometimes, the ego puts us in situations where we get abused, and we let it happen because of our concepts of non-violence or feelings of weakness. We put ourself in abusive situations because, in some way, we feel guilty and feel we need to sacrifice ourself. Every form of abuse is a place where we get others to punish us for subconscious guilt. As they punish us, it increases their guilt and, therefore, their self-abuse also.

In any situation where we are feeling emotionally or, even, physically abused, doing whatever it takes to prevent the other person from abusing us is crucial, for it will not help anyone. Sometimes, we need to communicate very strongly with them or, sometimes, we might need to remove ourself from the situation because of the nature of the event. In either case, but especially if we remove ourself, if we keep pouring love and support toward the person, the situation will begin unfolding for us.

Exercise

Today, be willing to explore the guilt you are feeling that is creating the situation, because you can change it instantly. Ask yourself, 'If I were to know, at what age did this guilt spring up?' Then ask, 'With whom did it come about?' Now ask, 'What was happening that I felt guilty about?' Remember, guilt is a mistake. Resolve to heal it. In whatever situation you were in, you left your centre. Ask the Universe to carry you back to your centre, and from there, to help you extend the light within you to assist everyone back to their centre, and even to deeper centres within you as needed for a feeling of peace and innocence. Notice how good all of you feel at this point. Bring all of this good feeling into your present situation and see how this affects it.

333.   EVERYONE IS DOING
THE BEST THEY CAN,
GIVEN INNER AND OUTER CIRCUMSTANCES

When we do not understand why someone is acting in a certain way, we simply need to ask ourself what we would have to be feeling to act that way. We all behave according to what we feel, which comes from what we believe, value, or think about ourself. These are the products of the different experiences and choices we have made in our life. As we realise that, given what is going on with us, we are doing the very best we can, we have understanding and compassion for ourself and other people in the human condition.

Exercise

Today, take time to sit, relax, and close your eyes. Allow yourself to go back to a situation where you made a major decision against yourself and your life. Who was in that situation with you? What were they doing? What must they have been feeling to act the way they did? In any kind of traumatic situation, everybody is acting differently, 'but feeling the same way'. You know how painful that situation has been for you. Everyone in it was feeling the same way underneath, or it could not have sprung up with you. When you reach that feeling, you have a sense of compassion for them and for yourself. Now, make another decision about yourself and your life. In that situation, realise their behaviour was a call for love. Feel your light reaching out and connecting with everyone in the situation. As the connection occurs, notice how the pain and conflict seem to fall away for everyone.

334. EMOTIONAL PAIN
CAN BE AN EXCELLENT TEACHER

If we do not avoid emotional pain or do not try to run away from it, we use it as our teacher. When we avoid emotional pain, we are avoiding certain lessons for our growth. Our willingness to have the courage to feel the emotional pain, to feel through it, allows us to see what it wants to teach us, and what it wants to give us. As we feel it all the way through, it disappears. To take this new attitude toward emotional pain allows us to move into certain situations that we would otherwise avoid, and to see the resolution of situations where we would otherwise create attack or avoidance.

Exercise

Today, take a new attitude toward pain. Be willing to face the feelings that are inside you, and those coming toward you. Know that your willingness gives you a certain responsiveness and strength that, somehow, have felt missing. Use emotional pain as your teacher; it will be a kind teacher, if you do not resist it.

335. EGO IS EVERYTHING
THIS SIDE OF ONENESS

Oneness works through co-operation, connection, and mutual support. The ego, however, is out for itself, hoarding its little bit to feed its own needs, and insisting on separateness. The extent of our separateness is the extent to which we feel pain or fear, look for specialness, experience problems, get competitive, or feel needs. Our ego has us doing many useless tasks to create security for ourself and to build up our self-concepts. All of these are a waste of time, because who we truly are does not need to be built up. Who we are is more essential than that. Who we are is more whole than that. Our ego is a form of separation that is evading oneness.

Exercise

Today, allow yourself to move toward people, and to join them. See the areas where you are keeping yourself separate, and realise that separation is totally unnecessary, and unsuccessful. Your communication, and your willingness to join and co-operate create a new level of partnership, where you get to experience the joys of oneness, abundance, love, happiness, and creativity.

336.   IF I DO NOT ACCEPT WHERE
I AM, I CANNOT EXPECT TO MOVE AHEAD

When we are in a very difficult situation, and we resist and reject it, we get stuck. As soon as we accept what we are experiencing, we are able to move to the next step. If we were caught in a rip-tide, and we fought against it, swimming to try to get out of it, we would wear ourself out until we drowned. If we just relaxed and let the rip-tide carry us, however, it would swing us in a greater and greater arc until, finally, we were carried beyond it. At that point, we could swim away freely. Where we refuse to accept the situation, we wear ourself out. By resisting certain situations, we get stuck there.

If we find that we are trying to accept a situation so that we can be released from it, but we are not moving forward, it is because we have adjusted or adapted ourself to the situation. We have adapted to something that is not true. Adjustment and adaptation are just forms of sacrifice and compromise where we feel we have lost. Acceptance moves us forward.

Exercise

Today, instead of judgement, use acceptance in any situation you encounter. Be willing to accept any difficult situation you are in, and feel yourself moving through it. Do not compromise, communicate. Do not adjust, resolve. Do not resist, accept.

337. GUILT INSISTS ON PUNISHMENT, MISTAKES CALL ONLY FOR CORRECTION

When we feel bad or guilty, we create punishment for ourself to get rid of the feeling. After we have punished ourself, we feel okay about ourself for a while, but the punishment reinforces a self-concept of guilt about us that is untrue. Sometimes we see this in a child's behaviour where they are a 'spanking looking for a place to happen'. They feel so bad about themself that they have to act in such a way to call down some form of retribution. Once that happens, they feel settled and calm. Of course, if we spank them, we may win the battle, but lose the war, because this type of behaviour towards a child will beat into them the very thing that we are trying to prevent.

Similarly with adults, we call in all kinds of things to punish ourself, physical illnesses, accidents, mishaps, failures, lack of money, any kind of penalty we can use to get over this feeling of guilt. The situations that punish us, however, make us feel bad, too, which just increases the guilt. When we feel badly, we act badly. With guilt, we use withdrawal or aggression and, of course, these are defences that generate more attack, which keeps the vicious cycle of guilt going. If we realised that the things we have done are simply mistakes, we could learn the lesson and correct the mistakes, and let go of all this guilt. When we have guilt, we beat ourself up, but then we are much less responsive to the lesson at hand. When we feel we have sinned, and beat ourself up, we attach sin to guilt instead of just correcting the mistake. The word *sin* actually comes from an old Greek archery term meaning, 'to miss the mark'. Sin, then, is just a mistake, and it can be corrected.

Exercise

Today, let go of all the things you are feeling bad about so that you can learn the lesson. Your willingness to learn is the easiest way to release the bad feeling of self-punishment. What is the lesson life is trying to teach you? Guilt refuses to learn the lesson, so the problem keeps getting repeated. It is an idea about yourself you have made up, and it is ego-generated to keep you locked into certain self-concepts. Since guilt is untrue, simply let it go, now, and whenever it arises.

338.   EVERY RELATIONSHIP
HAS A CHRONIC PROBLEM

Every relationship has an area that is a catch-all for all of the misunderstandings, grievances, and missed connections. Anything that needs to be taken care of will show up in a particular aspect of our relationship as a chronic problem. It could be communication, money, sex, lack of success, health problems; whatever the chronic problem is, and it could be anything, it is the aspect that will promote the greatest growth for our relationship, for ourself and our partner. Chronic problems are common because every relationship chooses one area to be the closet for unfinished business. We can attend to this area, but, at the same time, it is necessary for us to recognise that a chronic problem is just a symptom of the many areas of disconnection in our relationship. As we connect to our partner, we will find even this chronic area gradually improving.

Exercise

Today, do not despair. Every relationship has a chronic problem. What is your chronic problem area? As you realise what the chronic problem in your relationship is, imagine it standing between you and your partner. Coming from your heart, imagine a beam of light and love passing through that chronic problem and connecting with your partner's heart. This beam of light and love then links you, and draws you closer together. Now, imagine that a light from your forehead beams out and passes through the problem to connect with your partner's forehead. Continue to imagine beams of light passing through the problem and connecting you with your partner. Imagine beams shining from your throat to your partner's throat, from your stomach to your partner's stomach, from your abdomen to your partner's abdomen, from your genitals to your partner's genitals, and finally, from the base of your spine to the base of your partner's spine. As those lights shine through the problem, you are able to step through it, toward each other and into each other's arms. Hold each other and, as you do, imagine beams of light shining from both of your crowns, connected together and shining toward Heaven, reaching for the answer. Now feel you and your partner melting into each other and know that what will emerge from this is the next step.

339. PERMISSION BLESSES MY PARTNER AND THOSE AROUND ME

Permission is an act of Leadership. It is a natural place of authority we have reached by transcending our personality, by shifting from a place of self-restriction to finding our spontaneity and responsiveness. When we come into a relationship, we have certain areas of giftedness where we have already given permission to ourself. Where we have these places we can naturally give our partner permission to receive in the same areas where they are in conflict. Through the authority vested in us by truth and our own growth, we can give them permission to no longer be caught in the conflict; we can support and invite them to a new place of understanding and consciousness. Giving permission is one of the easiest ways to free someone who has locked themself up, because as we give permission to those around us, it frees them. Our permission blesses our partner and those around us, just as we have been blessed by them in those areas where they have reached Leadership.

Exercise

Today, bless everyone. What permission would you like to give to your partner? What permission would you like to give to those who associate with you? The more you give this permission, the more you free them, and the more you feel a sense of gratitude and support moving toward you and your life.

340. I DO NOT HAVE TO DO ANYTHING FOR GOD EXCEPT REMEMBER HEAVEN

The best gift we could give to God is to remember our home. Heaven is a place of happiness, no matter what experience is occurring here. When we are in a very difficult situation, and we begin to remember Heaven, to use another metaphor, we begin to remember total happiness, we make the choice to experience it. Remembering Heaven at the point of difficulty begins to move the situation forward. Our remembrance of Heaven sets up a resonance in all our brothers and sisters, and in everyone we love, so that, at some point, everything that is not happiness, that is not Heaven, that is just an illusion will fall away. The more we remember Heaven, the more we bring Heaven to earth. We do not necessarily have to do anything for God. We do not have to lead crusades, or accomplish major projects, necessarily; all we have to do is remember the love and happiness that Heaven is. As we remember this in each situation, everyone is freed, beginning with ourself.

If God loves us so much, why would God ask us to suffer? When we think God is asking us to suffer, this is our projection on God, our way of making God small. In the Bible where it says, 'Vengeance is Mine, sayeth the Lord,' it does not mean that God is going to be vengeful against us. It means that God wants us to give up our vengeance to Him. Our projection says that God is going to get us. That is why we punish ourself and go into sacrifice so many times, out of our guilt. We are saying, 'God, don't bother to punish me – I'm already doing it myself. Don't send the lightning. I'm taking care of it down here. Look at how bad I'm hurting.

Aren't I a good person?' All we really need to do for this love from God is just to receive the love and be happy. This is remembering Heaven, our home.

Exercise

Today, remember Heaven. Write it on your refrigerator, your bathroom wall. Write it at your place of work, so there is something that catches your attention to remind you to be happy, to remember Heaven, to remember that no matter what is going on, you can choose to change it by your choice for Heaven. You do not have to be a martyr for God. Why would the highest force in the Universe need your blood or your suffering? Somebody can be really helped by your joy. Spread Heaven by remembering it.

341. EVERY RELATIONSHIP HAS A PURPOSE

Just as each person has a personal purpose, so does each relationship. Basically, the purpose of every relationship is to create and experience happiness. Where there is unhappiness, the purpose is healing. This always has to do with some form of forgiveness, which is a form of giving where we have withdrawn. Every relationship has the purpose of happiness and healing, but more specifically, each relationship, as it reaches its true partnership and creativity, will have a personal function that allows more creativity to come into the world. Sometimes, this will be in the form of children, creative projects, or a level of consciousness that each person attains as a result of the relationship. Sometimes, the purpose will be the inspiration our relationship provides as a healing factor to all the people around us, letting them know that there is hope for relationships, and that we can be ourself and still have love.

Exercise

Today, explore your relationship. What is the purpose of your relationship? By you and your partner coming together, what has your relationship come to give the world? Out of the love of the two of you, there will be a gift to the world.

342. WHATEVER ABUNDANCE I ALLOW MYSELF TO RECEIVE, I NATURALLY GIVE TO MY PARTNER

In any relationship we will have areas of accomplishment that our partner has not yet achieved, areas where we fully give ourself. As a result of this giving and creativity, a natural abundance comes back to us. As we receive this, we naturally have a gift for our partner. Whatever particular talent or gift resonates in us will begin to resonate in them by our closeness and intimacy. They discover that they have certain talents that they did not know they had in particular areas. The extent of our joining is the extent to which our partner will naturally begin to act out this particular gift or talent, and receive it on their own. The area in which we have already succeeded contains the gifts we are bringing into the relationship; both ourself and our partner bring gifts to the relationship. This abundance that we bring is what we give to make the relationship grow.

Exercise

Today, see what you have that is a gift for your partner. If you have been complaining that they are not giving you a certain thing, this is exactly what you have enough of, for both of you. Out of your richness, you can provide this gift until it is in both you and your partner. From this new level of partnership, there will be new gifts and talents for both of you.

343.   IF I DON'T FEEL, I DIE

Without feeling, we cannot feel alive, we cannot feel joy, we cannot feel enough to know that we are in pain, and need to change what we are doing. Most of all, our feelings help us to find what is meaningful. Meaning goes along with feeling. It gives us direction and purpose. When we are fulfilling our purpose, when we are living out of true meaning, we are living Heaven's meaning, not all of the useless little jobs we make for ourself. In this, we find a state of joy, love, and creativity. It is important to feel as much as we can so we can expand ourself, because if we do not feel, we die. What feels painful is there as our barometer, indicating the need to change some choice we made in our life. What is negative can be felt and let go of.

Exercise

Today is a day to give up being one of God's frozen people. Allow yourself to really feel. Allow your feelings to direct you to all the states of love, joy, fun, and happiness. If there is a bad feeling, feel it until it is gone, or make the change necessary. Really allow yourself to feel good today. Learn how to say, 'Aaaaaah!'

344. FEAR IS THE BASIC EMOTION
UNDER ANY NEGATIVE EXPERIENCE

Under every negative experience, the painful emotions involved can be traced back to fear as the core dynamic. What is
going on in any negative situation is that we are afraid of
something, or we are afraid we will lose something. The ways
to end this fear come from responses, such as loving, forgiving,
supporting, giving, trusting, and asking for Heaven's help. All
of these create confidence in letting go, accepting, understanding; they all have a way of moving us out of our fear, and
moving us forward.

Exercise

*Today, write down three negative experiences, or three situations that
are less than great in your life. Feel into the situation to discover what
it is you are afraid of, and put that next to each experience. What form
of responsiveness would heal this fear? Next to the fear, write down the
antidote that pops into your mind. Whatever answer comes in, apply
it to the situation. Even in the most difficult situations, see and feel
yourself responding with the antidote so you can move out of your fear,
and move forward.*

345. ESSENCE IS ALWAYS ATTRACTIVE

Our essence is the part of us that is not looking for anyone else's approval. Essence does not create a personality for itself; it does not go into sacrifice to be included. Our essence is something that is so attractive that it shines out from us. It is spontaneous, intuitive, fun, and rascally; it is so attractive. People love this energy when it flows. It doesn't matter how young or old we are, if we weigh too much or too little, or what our build or IQ are; it just matters that we let this essence out. It creates an aura around us, charisma, and a field of influence, and everyone loves it. Essence shines out and creates our beauty. It creates the excitement, the stimulation, and the electricity around us.

Being in our essence is a natural form of Leadership. When we have integrity, and are acting from our essence, we are able to move in creative ways toward that sense of true joining that does not ask people to give up their gifts to be part of the crowd; it allows people to come to us. Essence is always attractive and confirming. It makes people feel good.

Exercise

Today, stop doing all the things that you think people demand of you. Stop acting in all those nice little ways that personality asks you to act. Just come from your essence and shine. Let out your essence, and have a really good time. Essence brings both attractiveness and outrageousness, with a sacred reverence that is both more ethical and authentic.

346. A LACK OF MONEY MEANS A LACK OF GIVING AND RECEIVING IN MY RELATIONSHIP

Relationships can generate abundance, but that has to do with the amount of giving and receiving within them. Where there is a money problem, a lack of warm, soft cash, there is an energy problem in our relationship. This energy problem could be that we are caught up in a power struggle, or in a form of revenge. It could also mean that we are coming from a place of roles and duties, which is not real giving and receiving. Our willingness to let go, and move beyond these energy blocks allows us to generate abundance in our relationship.

Exercise

Today, shift out of your money problem. Tell the truth, and move into true giving and receiving. Make true contact with your partner. You will love it, not only for the intimacy, joy and good feelings, but because there will be a lot more money to support the creativity in your relationship.

347. SEEING GOD IN EVERYTHING, AND ALL SITUATIONS ALLOWS LOVE TO TAKE ME HOME

If we see God in everything, we know that life is being taken care of for us, and we can relax. Our vision allows us to see the love in everything, and how much we are loved. When we see this, we do not have to work so hard; we just allow ourself to receive. Seeing God in everything and all situations draws us towards Heaven, a state of ecstasy and bliss. We feel the joyful understanding that God, who loves us a million times more than we know, is in everything, totally surrounding us. As we are willing to know this, we get out of our own way, and release our pain and our mistaken self-concepts. We feel ourself being drawn toward all that love. We are willing to bring Heaven to earth.

Exercise

Today, see God in everything, and in all situations. See God in the eyes of your children, in the eyes of your co-workers, and in the eyes of your partner. Let the love take you all the way home.

348. APPRECIATION MOVES ME
OUT OF COMPARISON AND ENVY

Comparison is always a way of feeling pain, now or in the future. Sometimes, we feel better than someone else, but it is only a matter of time before we meet someone ahead of us, and feel the pain caused by comparison. We compare because we are hoping we will find ourself a little bit better and, therefore, a little bit more deserving of love. Instead, we could know that we are deserving of love now.

Envy is a feeling that gets us completely stuck. We see someone as better than we are, and we envy what they have, not recognising that what we see in them is also within us, at least as potential; otherwise we could not perceive it. Our appreciation allows us to heal envy and move forward, because it allows us to enjoy others' gifts. As we enjoy their gifts, we receive them, and as the energy within us resonates with those gifts, they begin to unfold in us. Our willingness to be in service to the people we envy, which is a form of giving to them out of deep appreciation, allows us to develop those gifts that we see in them, in the quickest possible way. Our appreciation is the beginning of enjoyment of these gifts.

Exercise

Today, give appreciation as a gift to yourself and to everyone around you. Appreciation creates a flow that moves you forward. It allows you to feel blessed by the people and gifts around you, because what they have, you can enjoy, too. As you enjoy it, you feel the gift emerging in you.

349. WHEN I DO NOT FEEL UNDERSTOOD, IT IS BECAUSE I DO NOT UNDERSTAND

Many of us come out of childhood feeling as if we are not understood. Many of us also feel that in our present relationship, we are not understood. If we were to look deeper at our childhood, or at our present relationship, we would realise that we can only be feeling this way if we do not understand what was happening with our parents, or what is happening now with our present partner. People act a certain way because of how they are feeling. Sometimes, they are so caught up in their own pain that they do not have the power, energy, or time to be able to focus on us and see what we need. Our understanding of the situation creates the healing of our own needs. Understanding releases the fear in the situation, and it releases us.

Exercise

Today, look at situations in which you feel misunderstood in your life. Ask yourself, 'What is it that I don't understand about them?' As you raise your understanding of what is or was going on in those situations, you find yourself being understood.

350. WHEN THE RECEIVER IS READY, THE GIFT APPEARS

This is just one more secret to help remind us that we are in charge of our world, that we are not stuck with not having what we want. When we are ready to receive, the gift appears. To prepare ourself to receive the gifts that we would like in our life would certainly mean getting over fear. It would also mean having a sense of worthiness about ourself. We could open ourself to receiving all of the things we think we want by knowing ourself as worthy, and asking for the grace to transcend our fear.

Exercise

Today, get ready to receive. Do what you intuitively do on the inside to allow yourself to be ready to receive the gifts you wish. What holds you back from receiving? What could you allow yourself to choose or to do that would assist you to open your heart for the gifts that are coming to you now! Receive them!

351. COMPLAINING IS INFERIORITY IN THE FORM OF ARROGANCE

Our complaining comes out of a sense of inferiority, a sense that we do not have much power in the situation. Complaining takes the form of arrogance. We feel above the situation, as if this should not be happening to us. Our complaint is a verbal or mental attack on the situation that is happening. In our arrogance, we expect things to change, and for others to change to meet our needs, but we are the one being asked to change. One of the ways in which we could easily change, and feel better about ourself, is to give ourself some recognition, value, and respect. As we change in this inner way, the outside situation begins to reflect the change.

Exercise

Today, take a close look at yourself. What are you complaining about? Where are you complaining to yourself? These are just areas where you are reinforcing a sense of inferiority. Take a step forward, or choose to value yourself more, because as you do, the situation that you feel stuck in will change.

352. UNLESS I BECOME LIKE A LITTLE CHILD, I CANNOT ENTER THE KINGDOM OF HEAVEN

Only by becoming like a little child can we enter Heaven. The key here is not to become childish, but to become childlike. This is not a state of immaturity; it is, actually, the only true reality about our connection with the Universe and God. A child lives a simple life, which allows the mind to focus. A child is open to all that comes toward them. A child lives a life of wonder, and feels the joy of discovering everything. A child is innocent, and feels worthy. A child looks to its parents knowing that they will give it all good things. In the same way, with our innocence, we could look to God. We could look to the Universe and the world around us with expectancy, knowing that all good things are coming our way. As we open ourself, and let go of the thought that we have to carry and do everything, that it is our job to make it all better, we let God do it, or let God do it through us. We then take a natural delight and humour in the situation that surrounds us.

Exercise

Today, let go of all the cares and worries you have, all your sense of duty, and everything you feel you have to do. Imagine yourself living a very simple life. It is a life of love, a life of enjoyment. This is the life of the child, the life of a master. Ask yourself, 'What will come to me today? What will happen? What gifts will I receive?'

'It's summertime, and the livin' is easy. The fish are jumpin' and the cotton is high. Your daddy's rich and your mama's good lookin', so hush little baby, and don't you cry.'

353.　　LOVE ALLOWS ME TO
GET OUT OF MY OWN WAY

Our ego is the calcified belief in our separation. Our ego is our fear, guilt, and insecurity. The more our fear, guilt and insecurity are present in us, the more they set up barriers to our success which, at some level, is what the ego wishes. It wishes us to be delayed, because it wants us to think that we need it. The ego, however, is a very small aspect of our mind trying to act as if it is totally needed. It is that which is always exaggerating or shrinking us.

Love allows us to get out of our own way. It allows us to transcend this fear and these calcified ways of reacting. Love allows us to freely receive. Love raises us above the worries and cares, and creates the responsiveness that brings contact and joy.

Exercise

Today, go out there and love. Get out of your own way. Love everyone you meet, and let the love that wants to come to you from God through others reach you.

354. SACRIFICE IS BASED ON A VICIOUS CIRCLE OF SUPERIORITY AND INFERIORITY

When we are sacrificing, when we are taking care of others in the untrue helper role, we feel above them. We feel as if we are just a little bit better so, of course, we will take care of them. In truth, the reason we feel above people is because we actually feel inferior, and we do not feel up to going to meet them without protection. We feel that we need a role that raises us above the situation, which is how sacrifice got started. We were in a situation where we were experiencing loss, and rather than experience it, we backed away. We felt like it was too much for us, so we took on the role of helping people around us to avoid our loss and, ironically, we got stuck in the loss. We have not completed the mourning, nor have we gotten over the loss. As a result of defending ourself against feeling this old loss, and against present losses, we have thrown ourself into a situation where we can feel superior to other people, but it is only to hide our feeling of inferiority. This inferiority, this old pain, creates a situation that blocks us from receiving, and wears us down.

Exercise

Today, examine any area where you are feeling yourself a little bit above, where you are condescending to help, or any situation where you feel below, where you feel other people need to be helping or taking care of you. These are situations where you are in sacrifice or failure, because either way, you do not feel good enough to be their partner. You just do anything you think they want.

Allow yourself to drift back to that original unmourned situation, and ask for Heaven's help. Give to everyone in the situation, allowing love and grace to pour through you, filling everyone there. This releases the present situation of sacrifice, and allows you to move forward to more equal partnerships in your life.

355. DEADNESS IN MY RELATIONSHIP AND IN SEX CAN BE HEALED BY HAVING BALANCED RELATEDNESS TO MY FAMILY

The root of deadness in our present relationship is related to fusion in our relationship with someone in the family we grew up in. Fusion, a place of muddled boundaries, is where there has been some form of competition, or a lack of closeness and love, where we lost our bonding with that family member. Sometimes, it can be with more than one family member and we can be fused with our parent of the same sex or even with a sibling, but most of the time, we are fused with our parent of the opposite sex.

When we are fused, at some point we come to a place of burn-out because we feel as if we have sacrificed too much. At other times, we come to a place of repulsion or even revulsion because we feel as if we are too close to them and do not have our own life with our own boundaries. If this fusion from our childhood is not healed, we become fused with our partner, and eventually there is deadness in some area of our relationship. Fusion is counterfeit bonding and counterfeit closeness. It is counterfeit intimacy, which is not a place of higher consciousness, but rather a place of avoidance. It sets up situations in our relationship where we repeat the pattern from childhood, and go into burn-out or repulsion or revulsion. We then have a sense of anger or rage toward our partner because we blame them for our exhaustion, or because we do not have an understanding of the natural boundaries of our life, and theirs.

Our willingness to forgive that parent and give forth to them sets up our natural boundaries and allows us to live our life, rather than the life we think they wanted for us, a life of sacrifice. Our willingness to give to our parents, or to the siblings with whom we are fused allows that natural balance to occur that gives life and breath to our present relationship.

Exercise

Today, take a deep look at your life. Ask for Heaven's help in forgiving and creating balance in the earlier situation with your parents and siblings, so that new life can be brought to your present relationship. Close your eyes, imagine the family you grew up in, and ask your Higher Mind to set up a natural balance and centredness within you, one that ends all competition and fusion.

356. FUN IS ONE OF THE TRUE FORMS OF RESPONSIVENESS

Fun comes from one of the higher states of consciousness. It is an inspired state through which we bring humour and flow into the situation. To bring fun into any situation is to generate more energy of expectancy. Fun has the same dynamics as luck, so when we are having fun, we naturally create more luck. Fun and humour go hand in hand. Fun, appreciation, inspiration, spontaneity, naughtiness, and rascality are all forms of Leadership. Fun is true responsiveness to the situation which, paradoxically, becomes more productive where fun is present.

Exercise

Today, remember fun, no matter how difficult things are. When things are difficult or serious, they get stuck because seriousness and heaviness come out of roles and duties. Be a leader and bring fun and humour into any situation. Your naughtiness, irresistibility, and fun are great gifts to your partner, and to any work situation. Dance in fun continuously, because after all, you are not going to take this reality seriously, are you?

357. IF I THINK SOMEONE IS
USING ME, I AM USING THEM
TO HOLD MYSELF BACK

Whenever we think someone is using us, we are actually using them to hold ourself back. When we do not feel that we are someone's natural or equal partner, we give ourself up to be used, which then has us feel hurt, or in sacrifice. In truth, we are using this person. If we were to look fully at the dynamics of the situation in our subconscious mind, we would see that we are using the situation because we are afraid of moving forward, or facing intimacy and ourself. Our willingness to move forward totally transforms the situation.

Exercise

Today, when you think someone is using you, realise that you are actually using them to hold you back. Do not use anyone or anything to hold you back. Be willing to move forward, and say Yes to that next big step in your life.

358.   ALL PROBLEMS ARE
A RESULT OF FEELING SEPARATE

According to *A Course In Miracles*, there is only one problem, and this problem creates all problems. It is the experience of separateness. There is a feeling of lack of connection beneath every single problem we experience. Out of this lack of connection, a feeling of fear arises because, for various reasons, we create little attack thoughts or grievances that result in the illusion of separation. In reality, we are connected with everyone and everything that is.

Exercise

Today, look at the problems you have. These are places where you feel disconnected. Who do you feel disconnected from? Close your eyes, and imagine that you are connected with all of these people, because the truth is that you are. Just allow yourself to feel your natural connection because it will resolve the problem right now.

359. WHAT I TAKE IS WHAT I LOSE

An interesting, paradoxical dynamic is set up with taking, because the more we take, the emptier we feel, the more we try to get, the more insecure we feel. The more we take, the less we are satisfied. Taking sets up a dynamic in which we cannot receive and where we reinforce our own fear, so where we take, we lose. We lose in terms of our own self-image, and in any feelings of satisfaction that we could have ultimately attained. Basically, taking has the same dynamics as indulgence, which also does not allow us to feel satisfied because we feel guilty instead. It does not refresh or renew us. It does not allow us to make contact. Taking is what we do because we do not feel worthy enough just to receive. When we become independent, we try to hide our taking and pretend that we do not need anything. In a state of independence, we live like ascetics inside, pretending that we need very little, but there is a surreptitious taking. What we take is what we lose, whereas what we give is what we receive. We always have choice.

Exercise

Today, know you are worthy of receiving. Look at areas where you may be taking, because the subtle guilt that comes from taking does not allow you to enjoy, and it keeps you feeling less than yourself. In any situation where you catch yourself taking, do what it takes to catch yourself giving.

360. DOUBT IS A TRAP
I USE TO STOP MYSELF

Doubt is one of the best traps of the personality to keep ourself from moving forward and taking the next step. Just at a point where we are ready to move into a higher level of flow or consciousness, doubt assails us. We then tend to get trapped in the doubt rather than explore the doubt itself to find the truth.

Many of us in a relationship come to a place of doubt. We doubt whether our partner is our true partner, so we go into drought. With the awareness that doubt is a trap, we do not have to be stopped from taking the next step. When in doubt, we can easily attain a new level of commitment by asking ourself, 'Who needs my help?' When we respond to that person, our doubt begins to move because doubt is designed to block responsiveness, stop and contract us, and make us smaller. If we are unable to move through all of the doubt at the moment, by reaching out to help someone we can, at least, move through a layer of the doubt. When we reach out to someone, we naturally set a flow in motion.

Exercise

Today, let go of the doubt and, once again, move into the flow. If you are doubting of your partner, now is the best time to choose them. By your choice, you allow the relationship to unfold. This is the time your commitment and faith is most needed to move the relationship to a higher level. To know the truth about your partner, you need to see it from this progressed viewpoint. This naturally allows you to research the area in which you have doubt, the area that has stopped you. Begin your exploration to find the truth.

361. WHEN MY HEART IS BREAKING, GIVING CREATES NEW BIRTH

Heartbreak contracts us and shuts us down. At the point of heartbreak, we can take all that feeling moving through us, and if we choose to give, our heart and consciousness begin expanding. As we give through the heartbreak, all the ancillary feelings of despair, futility, uselessness, loneliness, emptiness, and jealously begin to heal, just through the giving. Giving through heartbreak creates a high stage of consciousness and a great deal of love. Our willingness to keep giving transforms us. Instead of having to go through all the pain of heartbreak, we create an easy birth. When our heart is breaking, to totally give as much as we can, saves our life, transforms the pain, wins back the part of our broken heart from the past, and saves us a great deal of time.

Exercise

Today, in any situation where there is any kind of hurt, just be in service or give through it, and find yourself easily moving to a new birth.

362. HAPPINESS TAKES NO PRISONERS

When we feel happy, we naturally feel trust. There is no reason to control, or to use emotional blackmail to tie people to us. When we feel happy, we feel love and creativity. When we feel creative, there is no need to control others, or to take prisoners. When we have prisoners, we lose a lot of time, because we have to be a prison keeper. We are just as much in prison as our prisoner is. Happiness takes no prisoners.

Exercise

Today, in any situation where you find that you are taking prisoners, just allow yourself to choose happiness. Allow yourself to generate the happiness, and as you do, you will move to a level of consciousness where you would not hold yourself back by taking prisoners.

363. LOVE IS GIVING EVERYTHING, WHILE HOLDING ON TO NOTHING

Love does not ask for security, love just asks to be able to love. Nothing can stop our love. No matter if the person rejects us, or if they run away from us, they cannot stop us from loving them. Love asks for no guarantees. Love asks for no insurance. Love just wants to love, to give everything. In that love is a birthing, a fire that purifies. In that love is the greatness of being. In that love is all vision and purpose in life. The love that we give opens us to a new level of feeling, and a new level of joy.

Exercise

Today, give by letting go. Be willing to let go in any areas where you have looked for insurance, or for some formal way of holding on. Imagine giving yourself totally, one hundred percent, all of you, for when you do, there is no need for control.

364. EVERY FAILURE HIDES REVENGE

When we fail, we are getting back at significant people around us, especially our partner. Every failure in life is also a form of revenge on our parents. As we are willing to look at all the places where we feel we have failed in our life, and especially where we are failing now, we can begin letting all of this go, which opens a way for us to succeed.

Revenge and hurt go hand in hand. Where we are getting revenge, we will still feel hurt. All hurt contracts us. Every time we have been hurt, we made our heart smaller. When we get hurt, we go into contraction because we somehow feel insulted by what has happened; we somehow feel as if we have been belittled. When we feel hurt or resistant, we are using the situation to make ourself feel even smaller than we are.

Revenge and failure can continue long after we have forgotten or repressed an old hurt. It is important to pull ourself out of the contraction when we are aware of it. Any kind of responsiveness will do this, any kind of forgiveness or giving. Many other things create flow, such as appreciation, understanding, trust, integration, letting go, and commitment. They move us out of this stuckness and contraction where our heart freezes, where we lock ourself into a certain mode of acting – a defensiveness – until we can deal with the pain.

Exercise

Today, ask yourself, 'Who am I getting revenge on? What am I getting revenge for?' Once you have made a little list of these particular things, ask yourself, 'Am I willing to keep failing in my life just so I can get back at these people?' As you are willing to move forward, your playfulness is a way of moving beyond any kind of contraction. Play creates flow. Be willing to share anything that needs to be shared, but be playful about that sharing. See how much you can play today, and how much you can get yourself into the flow. Play is the little sister of creativity, so treat it well. It will release old feelings of hurt and revenge, if you allow it to do so.

365. EVERYBODY WANTS TO GET TO HEAVEN, BUT NOBODY WANTS TO DIE

'Everybody Wants To Get To Heaven, But Nobody Wants To Die' is the title of a song from a number of years ago. The point was that, whatever Heaven is, it is different from what we are experiencing right now. Thus, to get to Heaven, we would have to die to our present self. We would have to change. We would have to forgive and let this go in order to move to a state of consciousness, joy, and love.

Exercise

Today, get busy right now. Get moving on toward Heaven. What are you waiting for? Allow to come into your mind the one person that you could forgive, and in forgiving, take a giant leap toward Heaven. As that person comes into your mind, see what you have not forgiven them for. Ask yourself, 'Would I use this to stop myself, or hold this particular thing against myself?' If you would not hold it against yourself, you are free. Ask for Heaven's help to accomplish the forgiveness so it can be taken care of for you. Your willingness to have it occur gives forth to the situation, and it moves you forward.

366. GOD SAYS TO ME THROUGH OTHERS, 'IF YOU CAN LOVE ME IN THIS FORM, YOU CAN GO ALL THE WAY TO HEAVEN.'

The beauty of relationships is that, if we can forgive one person about one particular thing, we can forgive all people about this particular thing. Every time we forgive anyone, we forgive everyone. Sometimes, we feel much closer to people outside our families than we do our own partner. This is because the person closest to us naturally brings up more of our hidden conflicts. If this same person were further away, we would not get into conflict with them either. Our conflicts help us see what, within us, needs healing. If we could go all the way to total forgiveness and love with one person, we would find Heaven.

Exercise

Today, take a moment to close your eyes, and see your partner standing in front of you. As you look at your partner, look inside them and see God laughing, smiling, and pouring love through your partner to you. Look at your partner and see total love coming to you, wanting to give all of the gifts of the Universe. Just receive this bounty, and feel how much you are loved. You are loved more than you will ever know.